LUMBERING STATE, RESTLESS SOCIETY

COLUMBIA STUDIES IN MIDDLE EAST POLITICS

COLUMBIA STUDIES IN MIDDLE EAST POLITICS
Marc Lynch, Series Editor

Columbia Studies in Middle East Politics presents academically rigorous, well-written, relevant, and accessible books on the rapidly transforming politics of the Middle East for an interested academic and policy audience.

The Arab Uprisings Explained: New Contentious Politics in the Middle East, edited by Marc Lynch

Sectarian Politics in the Gulf: From the Iraq War to the Arab Uprisings, Frederic M. Wehrey

From Resilience to Revolution: How Foreign Interventions Destabilize the Middle East, Sean L. Yom

Protection Amid Chaos: The Creation of Property Rights in Palestinian Refugee Camps, Nadya Hajj

Religious Statecraft: The Politics of Islam in Iran, Mohammad Ayatollahi Tabaar

Local Politics in Jordan and Morocco: Strategies of Centralization and Decentralization, Janine A. Clark

Jordan and the Arab Uprisings: Regime Survival and Politics Beyond the State, Curtis Ryan

Friend or Foe: Militia Intelligence and Ethnic Violence in the Lebanese Civil War, Nils Hägerdal

Lumbering State, Restless Society

EGYPT IN THE MODERN ERA

Nathan J. Brown, Shimaa Hatab, and Amr Adly

Columbia University Press
New York

Columbia University Press
Publishers Since 1893
New York   Chichester, West Sussex
cup.columbia.edu
Copyright © 2021 Columbia University Press
All rights reserved

Library of Congress Cataloging-in-Publication Data

Names: Brown, Nathan J., author. | Hatab, Shimaa, author. | Adly, Amr, author.
Title: Lumbering state, restless society : Egypt in the modern era / Nathan J. Brown, Shimaa Hatab, and Amr Adly.
Other titles: Columbia studies in Middle East politics.
Description: New York : Columbia University Press, [2021] | Series: Columbia studies in Middle East politics | Includes bibliographical references and index.
Identifiers: LCCN 2021007833 (print) | LCCN 2021007834 (ebook) | ISBN 9780231201704 (hardback) | ISBN 9780231201711 (trade paperback) | ISBN 9780231554220 (ebook)
Subjects: LCSH: Egypt—Politics and government—20th century. | Egypt—Politics and government—21st century. | Egypt—Social conditions—20th century. | Egypt—Social conditions—21st century. | Egypt—Economic conditions—1952-
Classification: LCC DT107.825 .B76 2021 (print) | LCC DT107.825 (ebook) | DDC 962.05—dc23
LC record available at https://lccn.loc.gov/2021007833
LC ebook record available at https://lccn.loc.gov/2021007834

Columbia University Press books are printed on permanent and durable acid-free paper.
Printed in the United States of America

Cover design: Milenda Nan Ok Lee
Cover photo: © ChameleonsEye / Shutterstock

To the memory of
Samer Soliman
and to subsequent generations of Egyptians following his path
or forging their own to understand, analyze,
and better Egyptian society and politics.

CONTENTS

PREFACE ix

Chapter One
Multivocal yet Authoritarian Egypt   1

Part I. The Egyptian State   21

Chapter Two
Governing Egypt: The Construction of the Modern Egyptian State   25

Chapter Three
Between State and Regime: The Evolution of Egyptian Authoritarianism   44

Part II. Egyptian Society   63

Chapter Four
The Rise and Decay of Social Control—and the Perpetuation of Authoritarianism   65

Chapter Five
Civil Society Organizations: Limited Political Agenda
and Mounting Resistance   92

Chapter Six
Islam and Religion in Egyptian State, Society, and Economy   111

Part III. The Egyptian Economy   145

Chapter Seven
Market Making without Development   147

Chapter Eight
The Military's Civilian Economy   179

Chapter Nine
The Uprising of 2011 and the New Regime   204

NOTES   235

A SELECTIVE GUIDE TO SCHOLARLY WRITING ON EGYPT   249

BIBLIOGRAPHY   259

INDEX   269

PREFACE

We aim in this book to introduce Egyptian politics to different, if sometimes overlapping, groups: those who know little about Egypt (but want to learn); those who have little background in the academic study of politics (and might find an overly scholarly approach full of off-putting jargon); those who have been trained as political scientists but know little about Egypt; and finally, those who know Egypt and its politics well (but are ready for fresh perspectives).

Addressing these different audiences has led us to be careful in our choice of terminology (explaining those terms we feel we need, such as "corporatism"), judicious in our introduction of new concepts (such as "habitus economy"), and still bold in some of our interpretations—so that we do not write incomprehensibly to those with no background but offer insights to those with deep prior understanding. We have adopted a comparative approach in framing much of our analysis without the formality of a comparative research design; that is, we draw on examples and comparisons from other cases in order to frame our presentation of Egypt and highlight its broader implications but do not present this as following any explicitly comparative methodology. And we have marked off areas in which our interpretation leads us a bit off the beaten path without positioning ourselves explicitly in every scholarly debate that has taken place.

While writing for such different audiences can be challenging, the task has emphatically not been complicated by an attempt to bring together three different scholarly voices. Our expertise and understandings have been complementary rather than contradictory. One of us (Nathan J. Brown) has worked on a variety of subjects (most recently on religion, law, and judicial structures). He took the lead on most of those sections that focus on formal political structures (mainly in part 1), as well as in editing the entire manuscript for consistency of style and usage. Shimaa Hatab was the primary drafter for most of part 2, drawing on her expertise in political mobilization and social movements in Egypt and in comparative perspectives. Amr Adly brought his expertise in political economy and development, leading our efforts in most of part 3. We all commented on each other's drafts, adding material where we had special expertise, and all pitched in on topics, such as religion or the 2011 uprising, where our expertise overlapped. The argument presented in this volume is the result of discussion among the authors and reflects our consensus view. Our individual views on some issues varied; we put this forward as a collegial project but not as a sum of individual contributions. The result is thus an integrated work rather than an anthology. All three of us have conducted primary research in Egypt, observed the society over time, and participated in international scholarly discussions about Egyptian politics in comparative perspective.

The purpose of the book is in part to draw on rich bodies of social science scholarship and political analysis produced in the Arab world, the United States, and Europe. In that way, the book incorporates recent scholarship on Egypt but also addresses broader questions in political science involving regime type, social movements, and economic development. But the book is not merely a summary. We have worked to develop and advance a persuasive and coherent presentation of modern Egyptian politics, society, and economy—and to do so not by walling Egypt off from comparative analysis, but by treating Egypt in terms of concepts and debates that have proven useful for understanding politics in terms of global trends and broader phenomena.

That broader perspective does not lead us to expect to locate Egypt as moving along a single path. Indeed, global politics seems to be moving in different directions at the same time: toward a more liberal direction and away from it. Politics is growing more participatory but not always more stable or democratic. Authoritarian regimes have tumbled in Latin

America, Europe, Africa, and Asia, where they have been succeeded by a wide variety of both authoritarian and democratic regimes, as well as several kinds of hybrids. States have grappled with a desire to control and manage societies characterized by growing complexity in the creative ways that people organize, mobilize, and spread information—and state control has sometimes withered but other times grown stronger. Socialism and communism have decayed or collapsed so thoroughly that for a long time there was talk of a "Washington consensus" among international actors who argued that free market economic reform would raise any floundering economy. But that consensus has now crumbled without a return to the past. Alternatives to political democracy, social pluralism, and economic liberalism have arisen—but democracy, pluralism, and liberal economics have not disappeared.

This ferment spans continents, but we will focus on how the trends have operated in Egypt. The strong authoritarian, state corporatist, and socialist regime that appeared so strong a half century ago gradually loosened and gave way to one that sometimes promised democracy, free association, and economic reform—but delivered none of these things.

While we will focus on Egypt, our understanding is necessarily comparative. A number of countries have sparked scholarly interest in the way they have confronted a similar array of problems, and we seek to present our analysis in a manner that draws on—and contributes to—more general ideas about regimes, development, social movements, and state structures. Brazil, Hungary, the Philippines, Poland, Argentina, and Korea have all diverged from the paths of democracy, pluralism, and liberal economic development (or if they have generally followed some of these paths, they have experienced unexpected bumps and detours). But the divergences have been very different in degree and kind. Understandings of the changes have sometimes been all too teleological—asking how democracy, pluralism, and prosperity can be realized instead of asking what trends are actually operating—with the result that scholars are sometimes better able to explain what did not happen than what did.

If we understand that global trends show divergences as well as commonalities, we are similarly alert to the different ways that Egyptians experience, view, and act in politics. Our openness to diversity leads us to insist that Egypt cannot be seen as speaking with a single voice or as an embodiment of a single will.

After an introduction that will give the necessary background on Egyptian society and politics, our book presents its analysis in three sections: one on the state and regime type; one on society; and one on the economy. In each section, we structure our inquiry around a pressing debate among social scientists that will frame our understanding of Egypt. And we select non-Egyptian cases in each section for comparative purposes, to shed light on the Egyptian case but also on the general phenomenon. For regime type, we do not ask why Egypt is not democratic. Instead, we ask what regime it has and how that regime sustains itself (when it does). We compare Egypt primarily to cases in Europe to understand what factors shape a particular country's trajectory. For society, we examine what happens when state corporatism breaks down, and we seek to understand how social movements operate in an environment that is far from pluralistic. We compare Egypt primarily to Latin America and other regions to gain a more general understanding of these questions. Finally, we consider the evolution of Egypt's economy away from socialism but absent any particular alternative direction. Concepts like "crony capitalism" and the "East Asian model" animate many discussions of economic development. However, they do not always provide the most helpful way to understand economic policy making and performance. In the economic section, we compare Egypt primarily to the East Asian cases.

We hope that our efforts in analyzing and explaining Egyptian politics will meet the interests of the diverse audiences for whom we write. Our task is a large one, but it is not boundless, since there is one audience we do not mention. By writing in English, and by assuming little prior knowledge of Egypt on the part of the reader, we are not writing for an Egyptian audience. Or rather, we are not doing so in this edition of the book. But we also plan to contribute to Arabic-language discussion about Egypt. Our intention is to modify the present text in order to develop an analysis that is appropriate for an Egyptian (and broader Arabic-speaking) audience—those who will need a bit less historical background but who may still find some insights into the politics of their homeland.

In writing this book, we have benefited from much moral and even a bit of material encouragement. The three of us were initially brought together through overlapping experiences with the nascent Arab Political Science Network (APSN); Ahmed Morsy of the APSN has quietly cheered us along. We were also hosted at workshops run by the Project on Middle East

PREFACE

Political Science (POMEPS) and the Department of Political Science at the American University in Cairo. Marc Lynch, the director of POMEPS, has been encouraging of this project from its inception, carefully reading two drafts of the manuscript—for which readers should thank him as much as the authors! POMEPS sponsored a session in which we discussed the project outline; Tarek Masoud and Lisa Anderson provided some valuable early guidance at that session. When we had a full manuscript, we held a workshop at the American University in Cairo at which we subjected Mustapha Kamel al-Sayyid, Cherine Shams, Samer Shehata, Ayman Ismail, Mohamed Fahmy Menza, Nadine Sika, and Omar Ghannam to a daylong discussion of our draft. Rosalie Rubio, Mark Berlin, and Aparna Ravi helped us polish our prose, iron out wrinkles in our argument, and communicate our ideas more clearly; Caelyn Cobb led a supportive team at Columbia University Press that included copyeditor Ryan Perks and production editor Kathryn Jorge. The Institute for Middle East Studies at George Washington University funded some critical editorial support as we worked to fashion our ideas into presentable prose. Sultan Alamer helped us enormously with the index.

The dedication to this book speaks largely for itself, but we cannot resist a final word: Samer is deeply missed, but we hope those who knew him find this book a fitting tribute to his legacy.

Chapter One

MULTIVOCAL YET AUTHORITARIAN EGYPT

A reader who perused different scholarly tomes on modern Egypt might wonder if each book actually described the same place. Is Egypt a country where economics drives all politics, or one where all economic questions are answered based on a shifting political foundation? Or does religion come first? Is it a place where a strong state and stable regime, controlled by a succession of canny authoritarian rulers, has entrenched itself so deeply in power that it cannot be dislodged? If it is, then was the uprising of 2011—which led the country into a protracted period of uncertainty—a complete anomaly? An exceptional interlude? A harbinger of a new era? Or a struggle on the surface that never actually challenged the "deep state"? Was the 2013 overthrow of the post-2011 system a return to normal or something altogether new? Is Egypt a place where the state can be equated with a single ruler (as in "Nasser's Egypt"), or one with a complex web of institutions that each have to be taken seriously as political actors? Or, more radically, is it actually a place where one should start by analyzing not the state but the society—Islamist groups, social movements, new and old media, or the different components of the country's private sector? Does Egypt's foray into socialism in the years after 1950, and its retreat from that system in the 1970s, represent a series of stark reversals or a camouflage for continuity? Is it a mark of the state's strength or its weakness?

2
MULTIVOCAL YET AUTHORITARIAN EGYPT

Our answer to every single one of these questions is a qualified yes. We are not contradicting ourselves: Egyptian politics exhibits many diverse features, many of which are in tension with each other and all of which vary considerably over time. This book is an effort to guide readers through Egyptian politics in a manner that is clear and fair to the distinctive features of Egypt but also alert to the ways in which Egypt resembles other societies. In the process, we will be using many of the insights gathered by political scientists to understand the sorts of questions we are asking about state formation, regime type, social movements, and political economy. We will try to understand how strong states emerge; how different regime types arise and evolve; when and how various kinds of social organizations emerge and advocate political agendas; and how wealth and power interact.

Indeed, using such comparative and conceptual tools will allow us to present a consistent answer to the questions with which we open this chapter. Egypt's modern state has built strong institutions; it has also been led by regimes that tried to master, control, and lead those institutions with some sustained but no permanent success. So the image of a strong state has validity. But that state is also unwieldy. We will thus tell the story of the state's emergence and of the attempts of different regimes to steer and manage it.

The state has been built while members of Egypt's society have periodically developed strong formal and informal ways to organize themselves. So the image of a state struggling to control a restive society holds as well, though more at some times than at others. Egypt's rulers have tried to regulate, constrain, and even combat many of those efforts, reaching a peak in what we will describe as "state corporatism" (a system in which the state establishes specific organizations to represent various parts of society and then coordinates among these groups)—again, with some sustained but no permanent success. At its height, the Egyptian state controlled most of the economy directly, backing off in recent decades while avoiding full liberalization.

These trends—the attempt by rulers to exert control over various forces that escape, steer, resist, and cope with that control—have been more pronounced since 2011, when a national uprising led to a tumultuous period of upheaval followed by a reassertion of tight central control.

The story of Egypt as we tell it does not begin with one actor (ruler, regime, or state), nor is it shaped by one factor (religion or economics).

Instead, it is a story of shifting interaction among them: a series of rulers who have built or remolded regimes that struggle to control a sprawling state apparatus; a state apparatus that has grown into new areas of society and economy but has been forced in recent decades into a partial retreat; and Egyptian social actors who have organized with varying success and across a variety of fields (politics, economics, and religion) in different ways to shape the state and its policies. We tell of an Egypt that speaks with many voices but in which one voice—that of an authoritarian leadership—strives to be louder than all others.

And it is a story that describes a slow arc of change: of growing state control followed by uneven retreat, and of growing authoritarianism that has to run hard to stay in place in the face of a sometimes restive society.

In presenting our analysis, we strive to deliver a comprehensive view of Egypt today, drawing from and contributing to broader debates in political science. We work to show how authoritarianism, corporatism, and socialism came to shape Egyptian politics, society, and economy—and how they have decayed without resulting in a liberal democratic order. And we will show that Egyptian politics is less the product of a single force than of the interplay among many leading forces.

Egypt is not the only country that presents political analysts with a confusing array of choices about where to start and which forces to listen to. We seek to explore politics by exploring Egypt, and vice versa. And in this we are aided by the fact that many of the trends we see in Egypt manifest themselves globally in a variety of societies, allowing us to develop a strong comparative focus.

Our comparative gaze will shift depending on the topic. When we consider the emergence of the modern Egyptian state, we will look to early modern Europe, as well as to states formed under imperial rule, to anchor our understanding. When we turn to Egyptian society, we will draw on Latin American societies that have experienced similar struggles over how society interacts with state structures. And when we focus on political economy, will offer comparisons with other liberalizing countries, as well as those in East Asia often cited as models of market- and export-led development. Our task will not be to show how Egypt is exactly like these other countries, but to use these comparisons to point out both commonalities and puzzles. In economics, for instance, Egypt has adopted many of the liberalizing policies employed by countries in Latin America, Eastern

Europe, and East Asia, but without resulting in a liberal economy. We will probe these divergent outcomes.

MODERN EGYPT: STATE, SOCIETY, AND ECONOMY

In one fundamental sense, the Egyptian state, society, and economy are as old as can be: these entities have existed over all the millennia for which written records exist. We begin our story, however, not with pharaohs, Nile floods, and pyramids, but in the modern era, which is to say the past two centuries. In this book, we will focus almost all of our attention (with only a few exceptions) on the past seven decades, beginning in the middle of the twentieth century.

The reason for this focus on the modern period is that some fundamental transformations that took place since the early nineteenth century have shaped how we should approach understanding Egypt. That dividing line is arbitrary in some ways, because important political, social, and economic trends developed slowly over time; the Egyptian state of the nineteenth century was built on the foundation of what came before. But the year 1800 can be used as a convenient marking point (and most, but not all, accounts of modern Egyptian history begin with the French occupation of the country in 1798 or the rise of the dynasty of Muhammad Ali in the early nineteenth century).

Prior to that point, Egypt was governed as a partially autonomous province of the Ottoman Empire, a multinational power covering much of the Middle East and southwestern Europe with its capital in Istanbul, in present-day Turkey. Egypt was primarily an agrarian society before 1800, with most agricultural production consumed locally (that is, most was designed to meet subsistence needs), though there was some national trade in surplus production as well as some involvement in long-distance trade. The state's role in most Egyptians' lives—especially the vast majority, who lived outside Cairo—was limited. Basic services such as education, health care, and housing were not state affairs. Even taxation operated inefficiently and unevenly.

It was Egypt's position in world trade routes that led France to invade in 1798, as a way to curb the sway of its rival (the British Empire) over global commerce and especially traffic between Europe and India. While the French were evicted after three years under combined British, Ottoman, and Egyptian pressure, Egypt did not revert to direct Ottoman control. While the Ottoman Empire claimed to still govern Egypt, a new autonomous dynasty arose in Cairo in the wake of the French occupation, led by Muhammad Ali, the leader of a military force the Ottomans had brought in (ironically, to shore up their own control) from Albania. Quickly establishing his control over Egypt, Muhammad Ali began an ambitious program of economic and military expansion to neighboring territories; building more effective taxation, harnessing Egyptian labor more centrally (and even conscripting Egyptians into the army) to support expansion; encouraging the cultivation of crops that could be marketed internationally; making attempts to foster Egyptian manufacturing under state command; and launching expeditions into neighboring areas.

We will examine this program and its repercussions more fully in the following chapter. For now, we will note that Muhammad Ali's efforts ultimately brought him into conflict with various countervailing forces: the Ottoman Empire, intense European pressure, and fiscal limitations. In the face of these combined pressures, the new regime was forced to scale back its ambitions. The dynasty was restricted to Egyptian territory and some of its economic and military projects were dismantled.

Muhammad Ali's descendants still made an effort to use their political control in support of political strengthening and economic development within Egypt. In the second half of the nineteenth century, they pursued a series of reforms and projects (such as deepening irrigation canals so that Egyptian land could be farmed in the summer, when the Nile River was low; encouraging the cultivation of cotton for export; and building a transportation system of railroads and ports so that Egypt could send that crop to Europe). Those Egyptians able to amass land grew quite wealthy, as did those involved in trade (some of whom were foreign).

This program—which included ambitious urban construction and the digging of the Suez Canal—was quite expensive, ultimately resulting (as we will see in chapter 2) in bankruptcy and European financial control. That was followed in 1882 by military occupation by Great Britain. The British claimed to be restoring the ruling dynasty in Egypt, accepting that Egypt, while autonomous, was still part of the Ottoman Empire. So the British occupation worked through existing arrangements rather than replacing them. But British authorities forced Egypt's rulers to cut back much of their ambitious program of public works (especially those unconnected with irrigation and agriculture) and resisted calls to invest in new areas (such as education). When Britain found itself at war with the Ottoman Empire in World War I, it declared a protectorate over Egypt and mobilized Egyptian supplies and even people to support its war effort. The resulting burdens, and Britain's clear plans to increase its domination over Egypt, led to a popular uprising at the end of the war, forcing the British to grant the country partial independence in 1922.

In 1923, Fuad (the descendant of Muhammad Ali then governing Egypt) proclaimed himself king and promulgated a constitution that allowed for competitive parliamentary elections. Subsequent decades saw tussling between nationalist political parties (the largest one, the Wafd, emerging from leadership of the postwar popular uprising against the British occupation), with the monarchy and the British still playing strong roles in Egyptian politics. In the 1930s, increasing education and urbanization attracted a growing middle class to politics. The 1940s witnessed the rise of ideological movements of various stripes (the religious Muslim Brotherhood, nationalist Young Egypt, and some leftist groups), who saw organizations and demonstrations outside of the electoral process as the most effective way to realize their vision for Egypt. Yet even as this agitation was growing, the Egyptian state was becoming more powerful. Its rulers finally negotiated a treaty with Britain in 1936 that removed many (but not all) of the vestiges of the British occupation. They also threw off the "capitulations"—a set of agreements allowing foreigners in Egypt to be governed by the laws of their home countries instead of Egyptian law (and thus making taxation or the passing of laws protecting Egyptian industry from foreign imports quite difficult). World War II (which Egypt did not enter directly, though it served as the site of some battles and hosted British troops) led to some additional emergency measures (such as price controls and arbitration of relations between workers and owners in Egypt's emerging industrial sector) that rendered the state much more of an active presence in the Egyptian economy. Likewise, by the mid-twentieth century, the Egyptian state was a far more intrusive presence in Egyptian society than it had been during the British occupation.

But the story of these decades is not simply one of state growth. New social actors were forming, some organizing formally through syndicates, unions, and other bodies (and some remaining informal) and asserting themselves into the political arena more forcefully. Large landowners, for instance, played powerful roles individually (in the parliament or through access to top officials) as well as through their own syndicates. They pressed for policies that maximized their profits, especially from the international trade of cotton crops. The new groups that focused on the middle class, such as the Muslim Brotherhood, stepped up their activities and even formed paramilitary groups that led volunteers in support of the Palestinian cause in the 1948 war over the establishment of the State of Israel on Egypt's eastern border. State investment in public works and a growing private industrial sector created a working class (especially in the textile, construction, and transportation sectors) that became increasingly disillusioned with the institutionalized political parties, forged alliances with radical social forces, and organized strikes against foreign employers and financiers. Rising education encouraged the formation of vibrant cultural societies that laid the groundwork for a series of new civil society groups, including feminist organizations. Alongside older women's organizations anchored in the narrow elite, the newer groups focused on rights to universal suffrage and socioeconomic issues that produced women's subordinate position in society. Many of these new groups shared a strong nationalist orientation, as Egyptians feeling constrained by international colonial capitalism led calls for an "Egyptianization" of the economy and the construction of national industries. Others focused on the political struggle, demanding that British troops (still occupying the Suez Canal) leave the country—and some even launching raids against British bases.

This growing activity, while it led to increasing political contention, nonetheless left the regime itself untouched, even as it struggled to respond to (or contain) popular demands. This changed in 1952, when the army, one part of the growing state apparatus, proved able to reconfigure the system. A group of officers overthrew the monarchy and, after some hesitation, declared the event a "revolution," deciding to reconstruct the political system. Their leader, Gamal 'Abd al-Nasser (whom we will call "Nasser" for short, following general English usage), became president as the officers' project gradually widened from political reform to a much larger set of economic, social, and foreign policy goals. Insisting on a global role for an independent Egypt (which evolved into a claim to leadership of the entire Arab world), the emerging regime was highly nationalistic. Economically, it pursued the further Egyptianization of the economy through nationalization of foreign-owned capital while extending support to Egyptian private enterprises. But while Nasserism began with state support for industrialization, it evolved into socialism, with most large economic enterprises nationalized and many social services provided by the state; it also resulted in a single political party, the Arab Socialist Union, which sought to organize the entire society in support of the regime's revolutionary program. Harsh authoritarian measures were deployed to enforce the new system and autonomous movements (such as the Muslim Brotherhood and the communists) were suppressed.

While that effort produced great changes in Egyptian politics, society, and economy, it began to run into trouble after a decade and a half. Egypt's defeat in the 1967 war with Israel, coupled with Nasser's death in 1970, marked a crisis of Nasserism. But more was at stake than military defeat and the death of a single leader. The economic achievements of Nasserism seemed to be stalling; the welfare services it promised were proving burdensome, and social groups (workers and students, for instance) who had been organized by the regime were rediscovering an independent and critical voice.

The 1970s thus saw the beginning of a retrenchment and diminution—but not a repudiation—of the Nasserist experiment. The sole political party gave way to a multiparty system dominated by Nasser's successors (Anwar al-Sadat and Hosni Mubarak), and some authoritarian measures were relaxed. Socialism gradually gave way to a relaxation of restrictions on the private sector and the rules governing foreign investment. And some social movements were able to form or revive themselves (like the Muslim Brotherhood). But every step seemed uncertain and ambivalent, leading to a loosening of the system rather than an abandonment of it.

Indeed, it is this pattern of change—whereby construction of a strong state, authoritarian system, socialist economy, and close control over all aspects of social activity gave way to a series of ambiguous arrangements—that draws our attention in this book. In 2011, those ambiguous arrangements drew the attention of the millions of Egyptians who participated in a national uprising under the slogan "The People Want the Fall of the Regime." The slogan made clear what so many wished to abandon while ensuring that there was no consensus about what should replace it. We seek in this book to explore not only the evolution of Egyptian politics from Nasserism to a semi-authoritarian system, but why that system came under such severe attack in 2011 and what has happened since.

CACOPHONOUS EGYPT

As should be clear from this brief account, Egyptians have often disagreed and struggled over how their country should be governed. Egypt can be confusing—and much analysis misses the mark—because there are many who claim to speak for the country. Analysts are often inclined to listen to a single source. We seek to remedy that by understanding Egypt as a complex state and society.

Many times when Egypt is discussed, an analyst will refer to the country by the name of the leader. It is as if Egypt speaks with one voice and is a product of one will. "Al-Sisi's Egypt" is authoritarian, "Sadat's Egypt" made peace with Israel, and so on. It is not surprising that such shorthand is used. Egypt's presidents are powerful figures, and they certainly claim to speak and act for all of Egyptian society. If one does a bit of historical digging—say, by looking back at Egyptian newspapers from the 1960s or 1970s—one would get the impression from the public record that the president's word was uncontested and final. But we wish to present a far broader sample of Egyptian political voices.

And we run into another problem as well: basic terminology is often controversial. Those who argue about the best political direction for the country disagree about which terms should be used and what they mean. Words are connected to politics.

When scholars use words like "authoritarian" or "revolution," they often disagree on what they mean, but they generally justify their choices by the clarity offered by their favored definition. A clear definition of "revolution," for instance, should serve the purpose of telling us what a revolution is and what it is not, so that we can explain why or when such events happen. But when the arguments are not just among scholars but among contending political forces, the choice of terms is connected not just to analytical clarity but to political values (of course, such values are a part of many scholarly writings as well).

So many of the terms we need to use are loaded, and some are especially loaded in the case of political debates among Egyptians. In Egypt today, the term "revolution" is generally applied by those who want to emphasize the strongly popular nature of a radical change. Was the 1919 revolt against the British a revolution? What about the 1952 overthrow of the monarchy? In Egypt, to refer to the events of 1919 as an "uprising" rather than "revolution" can be taken as a dismissal of the nationalist struggle against British imperialism; to refer to 1952 as a "coup" is to cast doubt on its claim to legitimacy. Likewise, if one refers to the events of 2013 as a "coup" rather than a "revolution" against the Muslim Brotherhood, which had won the previous year's presidential elections, it is taken as a sharp declaration of one's political inclinations. What is at issue is not simply a dictionary definition, but one's political positions vis-à-vis these events.

In this book, we will write as scholars and try to follow definitions that are precise—but we will note the political power and emotional meaning of certain words among those who study Egypt, and the even deeper disagreements in political discussions among rival camps in Egypt.

And we will try to avoid the tendency to view Egyptian politics as something that is projected from a single strong leader. In this we are not denying the centrality of the presidency to Egyptian political life. But neither are we starting exclusively there. Instead, our analysis incorporates Egyptian society by looking at politics from a variety of vantage points, not simply from the top down. Our leading characters, then, are not merely presidents but also bureaucrats, officers, judges, feminists, trade unionists, activists, investors, and farmers. We will ask not merely what the leader thinks and does but also how Egyptian state institutions have been built and now operate; how Egyptian society is organized and how social actors behave; and how the economy functions and economic policy is made.

As we address these questions, we will be alert to some larger themes, ones far broader than the Egyptian political experience. We will be mindful of the fact that Egyptian politics has almost always been authoritarian, that its leaders are not fully accountable to any kind of democratic mechanism. In that way, the Egyptian political system resembles that of most other societies in world history, where authoritarianism (broadly defined) has been the rule and democracy the exception. But authoritarian systems, while they lack fully democratic checks on their rulers, still show great variety, and they evolve considerably over time.

Egypt, for instance, has some very strong institutions—the military, various internal security and intelligence services, the judiciary, and even the official Islamic religious establishment. Egyptians have shown varying signs of social activism and powerful groups have tried to affect official policy. Egypt also has had a series of elections—ones in which the opposition can often run (but generally is not allowed to win). It shares some of these features with certain systems but not others. We will compare Egypt to other authoritarian systems to see what is distinctive about Egypt and what it tells us about the varieties of authoritarianism.

Similarly, Egyptian society has been organized in ways that have been heavily regulated by the state. At its height in the 1960s, state regulation became sufficiently rigorous and intense that it can be called "state corporatism" (a term we explore in more depth in chapter 4), a system in which almost all forms of organization, ranging from agricultural cooperatives to student unions, were controlled by the state or the sole political party at the time. But Egypt has also seen state controls that operate far more loosely, and even a recent mass uprising that brought the political order to its knees and left an indelible imprint on the society. We will compare the way that state and society interact in Egypt, keeping an eye on similar systems elsewhere.

And the Egyptian economy has also gone through phases of socialism and attempted liberalization. Yet even when Egypt's rulers have used the language of economic liberalization, the state's role has remained quite strong, formally as well as informally. Still, non-state structures, informal mechanisms of coordination, and networks of families, friends, and kin shaped much of Egypt's variegated private sector. We will trace the role of important economic actors, both state and non-state. Some, like businessmen, will be familiar to anyone trying to understand economic policy making. But others, such as the military, will be a bit more unusual.

THE STRUCTURE OF THE BOOK

We proceed first, in part 1, to understand the Egyptian state and the regime. In part 2, we focus on Egyptian society. And in part 3, we turn to the Egyptian economy. Our purpose is not to examine these topics in isolation but to add progressively to our analysis, so that we see how state, society, and economy have interacted. And in the final chapter we will use the understanding we gain to explore the tumultuous period since 2011.

With the purpose of understanding Egypt in comparative perspective, each chapter begins with a question posed in general terms and amenable to comparative analysis while also allowing the authors to advance an integrated understanding of Egyptian politics, society, and economy. We will begin with a focus on politics and the regime. In chapter 2, we will ask where strong states come from. While Egypt is an old society with a governing apparatus that goes back millennia, the modern Egyptian state—with its strong presence in all aspects of social and economic life; its extensive bureaucracy; and its complex structures for educating Egyptians, preaching to them, housing them, adjudicating their disputes, and so on—was built in the nineteenth and twentieth centuries.

Scholars have often assumed that state building is the result of two related processes. In the first, Europeans built the first modern states on their home continent, and in the second, Europeans and their imitators spread the model throughout the world. It is therefore quite common in comparative scholarship to assume that most non-European states are weak.

This process helps us understand certain general aspects of state formation, but Egypt fits neither of these situations well—or rather, the process as it has played out in Egypt partakes of a distinctive combination of these two paths. This chapter will show that the Egyptian state was not born in a single moment or created in an act of intentional design. Instead, it is a set of effects, many of them unintended, that stem from long-term social and political trends, a history of imperialism and of independent state building, the creation over an extended period of an extensive and intrusive set of state apparatuses, and a series of regime strategies, many of them ad hoc in nature. Chapter 2 will show state formation as an outcome of struggles over sovereignty and state control at the national and international levels; the evolution of major state structures (the presidency, political parties, the military); and the effects (often unintended) of various Egyptian rulers and regimes and the sequence of regime type. In these ways, Egyptian state formation will be shown to more closely resemble the European example in some of its evolutionary and competitive dimensions while still having some distinctive aspects, especially with regard to the deep impact of imperialism on the timing and the contours of institutional development.

In chapter 3, we will ask how authoritarian systems operate. This is a question that scholars often ask in different ways, but we will argue that we cannot focus only on long-term processes (since they cannot explain much change over time), nor only on the short-term question of why rulers build regimes as they do (since doing so comes close to assuming that the system is whatever any particular ruler wants). We will instead combine long-term and short-term analysis, viewing authoritarian systems as the products of evolution over time.

An earlier generation of scholars often focused on the socioeconomic conditions under which authoritarian rule arose, showing much less interest in how these systems formally operated. When they turned their attention to institutions, they often focused on obvious ruling structures, such as the military and ruling parties, and treated other institutions as weak or uninteresting. This is reflected in popular discussions as well, with talk of a "deep state" in which a small group of senior leaders wield power behind the scenes. Chapter 3 offers the idea of a "wide state" by looking at the Egyptian system as a product, not of a single will or conscious design, but of an accretion of actions by various actors—rulers, but also institutions and social and political forces. In one sense, there is a deep state in Egypt. But it is not all-powerful—its various components are sometimes at odds with each other and its centerpiece, the presidency, has played a shifting role. Not only should its ability to act coherently not be exaggerated; its mastery of the levers of the vast state apparatus is clumsy at best. And, at critical moments (most notably but not exclusively 2011), its ability to control Egyptian society and politics has been challenged.

And beyond the collection of entities that comprise the deep state lies a vast array of state structures that extends far into Egyptian society. Almost all can be shaped or steered by the mechanisms of the deep state but most also possess varying levels of autonomy. Judicial bodies have struggled to attain some level of fiscal independence as well as some control of appointments within their own ranks. The state religious establishment now selects its own senior leadership.

Of course, the presidency is still in a central position, and when push comes to shove, it has ways to override any law or procedure to impose its will. But push rarely comes to shove, and critical state institutions have realized a degree of internal autonomy and social and political forces can sometimes hem in the presidency's options or act independently of its will. The presidency manages the state apparatus by appointing individuals to key positions (such as the prosecutor general or the chief editors of state-owned press outlets), practicing co-optation (doling out higher salaries, plum appointments, or other benefits to key individuals or institutions), and fostering institutional duplication (with an array of courts to use if one proves unreliable, overlapping security services, and so on).

The analysis in part 1 will thus explain the origin of Egypt's state and describe something of its structure and the regimes that have led it. We will move outside the state in part 2 to examine Egyptian society. But we will not leave the state and the regime behind.

The Egyptian state has exerted tremendous energies in organizing Egyptian society, but we will show in part 2 that those efforts have shifted over the years and with varying degrees of success. One chapter will probe how much the state can mold society from the perspective of the state and regime; one will examine these efforts from the perspective of society; and a third chapter will focus specifically on religion as an important field for political, social, and even economic activity.

Specifically, chapter 4 will focus on the periods in the third quarter of the twentieth century when what we call a "state corporatist" system was built by the regime but then began to decay. Under state corporatism, the regime used a shifting blend of repression and inducements to fold all social organization and activity into state-controlled bodies or into the sole political party. This system was imposed upon society at the same time as much private property was nationalized and extensive welfare benefits were promised by the state. In short, authoritarianism, state corporatism, and socialism all marched together. Beginning in the 1970s, however, all three begin to loosen a little. The regime became more tolerant of opposition—within certain limits. Exclusive corporatist structures began to decay. And there was a retreat from socialism. But these trends reflected more the evolution of the authoritarian regime rather than a sudden change in the regime's nature or structure. The Egyptian experience will be analyzed in comparative perspective, especially as it relates to corporatist arrangements in Latin America, as almost every regime that came to power in Latin America in the 1930s and 1940s developed corporatist ties with different social groups.

Chapter 5 will shift the balance to the period after the regime's control loosened—to some extent—and social organization became more active and various, though still within sharp limits. What happens in societies when state corporatism falters and decays? Most understandings of the end of authoritarianism are drawn from what scholars (and policy makers) have come to call "the transition paradigm," in which authoritarian regimes decay, collapse, and are replaced by democratic ones, often by various actors coming together to agree on democratic rules. The end of state corporatism is often equated with regime change. But what if state corporatism does not end but slowly and only partially decays? And what if the regime stays in place? This pattern is actually quite common. And it fits Egypt, where post-corporatist liberalization politics did not lead to fully-fledged democratization or trigger mere repression. What happened and why? In chapter 5, we will shift the analytical focus away from regime strategies, placing more attention on social response and the agency of civil society actors. We will examine how political liberalization throughout the 1990s and 2000s led to the proliferation of civil society organizations and the emergence of grassroots activities that challenged the regime's policies. The significant increase in civil society organizations and advocacy groups, however, did not bring unalloyed success. The regime continued to restrict social activists and pit different groups against each other (most notably Islamists and non-Islamists), undermining any common political agenda. We will investigate the interactions that took place in the realm of civil society, elucidating how religion has been woven into Egyptian society (a point considered more fully in the chapter 6), and probe whose interests civil society organizations represent and what strategies they adopt to serve these interests. Although the regime curtailed independent popular mobilization during the 1990s and 2000s, there was some ephemeral and tactical coordination among ideologically different social groups that helped politicize some issues and put claims on authority in the years leading up to the uprisings of January 2011, thus setting the stage for our consideration of post-2011 politics in chapter 9.

In chapter 6 we will turn our attention to religion, first by asking what religion is doing in a book about politics. We will show that Egypt is not unusual in having religion and politics intertwined but it is unusual in *how* they are intertwined. We will show how religion is woven into the fabric of the state and governance but also how it underlies a considerable portion of social and economic organization. We additionally explore religious movements, those that are less directly political and those that are intensely political. We will show variation over time as well through the rise of religiosity, the rise of religious movements, and the resulting political and social changes.

Armed with an understanding of how the Egyptian state and society are organized, and how that organization has evolved over time, we will move in part 3 to integrate the economy into our analysis. Chapter 7 asks why economic liberalization does not always create a liberal economy, one in which the state acts to guarantee contracts and property rights and facilitate private economic exchanges that take place on the free market.

The Egyptian state's economic policies changed greatly in ways that dismantled important parts of the socialist experiment and allowed others to wither. But for all its apparently liberalizing steps, it did not wind up with a liberal economy. The early *infitah* (the policy of economic opening) of the 1970s was followed by successive rounds of trade liberalization, private-sector development, attraction of foreign investment, and privatization of state-owned enterprises through the 1990s and 2000s. Almost four decades out from the beginning of the transformation, Egypt no longer had a state-controlled economy. Even though the state remained a relevant actor in certain sectors, such as public utilities, infrastructure, and extractive industries, private-sector enterprises came to control most output, employment, and investment. Private-sector domination did not necessarily mean, however, the triumph of the free market. Private property rights and contract enforcement remained weakly enforced amid rampant corruption and poorly upheld rule of law. It became difficult to locate Egypt's economy in the 1990s and 2000s on the spectrum between state-controlled and market-based systems.

The underlying argument is that the Egyptian state has ceded its dominance over resource allocation to a large and very diversified private sector. Just as the social realm saw the state confronting some limits without building a democratic system, in the economic realm state control confronted problems without giving way to a fully liberal market economy. The privately controlled economic space expanded greatly but in a manner that did not lead in the direction the (neo)classical conceptions of a free market—i.e., an understanding of the economy as a sphere in which anonymous profit maximizers interact at an arm's length in the presence of state institutions that serve the task of upholding the market (by enforcing contracts, for instance).

We will show how the nature of change was often missed because the state's ability to direct and shape the outcomes of the liberalization process was often overstated. As authoritarian and unchecked as state power has been, there were large areas beyond state control, some of them populated by various private activities that analysts (and rulers) had trouble understanding. Neither scholars nor rulers had a clear understanding of what an increasingly privately controlled economy looked like. Political economists simply overlooked private businesses that managed to enter the market without enjoying strong political connections. Many also ignored the hundreds of thousands of self-employed individuals, informal workshops, household businesses, and small firms and microenterprises that were pulled by, or pushed into, the market with the retreat of the public sector.

Chapter 8 will turn to the complicated question of the military's role in the economy, widely acknowledged to be critical but seemingly impervious to analysis and even the collection of some basic information.

As the public sector was ceding more space to the private sector, the Egyptian military built an economic empire of its own. Did this economic empire enable the military after the 2011 revolution to claim political power, or restrain it from doing so? And how did the existence of such activities shape its interests and self-perception as a corporate actor? In answering these questions, we will place Egypt in comparison with other countries marked by similar experiences. The Egyptian military expanded its economic activities without necessarily impeding private-sector growth. This has occurred not only in Egypt but also in Turkey, Indonesia, and China. We will argue that it was not (as might be assumed) simply the push of economic interests or ambitions for business that led to the military's growing and imposing economic role. More significant was the pull of a civilian economy that provided resources for the re-politicization of the military.

Thus, the best way to understand Egypt's military-civilian economy is through politics rather than economics. We will show that the military economy has never been dominant in any sector in Egypt. The evidence thus far does not support the view that the military economy is a revival of Nasserist state-led development. Moreover, it could have grown—and it actually did—side by side with a bigger private sector since the 1980s and 1990s. A military-civilian economy is less a challenge to economic growth than a hindrance to any political transformation. Access to economic resources generated autonomously of any other sector and unaccountable to any actor within the state or civil society proved essential in enabling the military to ascend to power after 2011 and to abort any meaningful political transformation. Money is being used for politics rather than vice versa.

Finally, we will conclude the book in chapter 9 with a consideration of Egyptian politics since 2011. We will use the analysis of the previous chapters to make the fast-paced events, the rapid reversals, and the confusing tumult of recent years a bit more comprehensible. We will tie the trends we have identified in previous chapters to the dramatic uprising of 2011, the complicated aftermath, and the new system that established itself after 2013.

We will examine the period as a whole in order to present a holistic understanding of events. The authoritarian regime, decayed corporatism, and partly liberalized economy analyzed in earlier chapters appeared to be stable in 2010. But in January 2011, an unexpected uprising led many Egyptians—and many scholars—to conclude not only that a regime had collapsed but that new forms of politics and economics were emerging. After 2013, however, a new authoritarian order emerged—one that restored some of what had appeared overthrown while evolving into more than a mere reconfiguration of past patterns. The regime came to new terms of "political settlement" without entertaining the idea of a corporatization of society. The regime issued new regulations that ensured depoliticization of the society and its exclusion from the decision-making process. The regime has relied heavily on an assemblage of coercive institutions without offering any policy concessions, developing pork-barreling networks, or revamping the institutional frameworks that encapsulated diverse elements of the popular classes under the previous regimes.

How do we understand this puzzling series of events? What explains the failure of the regime's containment strategy and the remarkable burst of societal forces on January 25, 2011 that led to the ousting of Mubarak? How did emerging opposition groups manage to overcome their historical divide and coordination dilemma? How did the fleetingly triumphant political and social forces of opposition fail to lay the groundwork for legitimate democratic rule? And what is the nature of the regime that has established itself in the wake of the post-2011 upheaval?

To answer these questions, chapter 9 will examine a series of events that started with the failure of the regime's coping strategies amid the remarkable burst of popular mobilization on and after January 25, 2011. Then it will investigate how emerging opposition groups, which could adopt unifying demands to remove the head of the regime, still lacked a common democratic version to replace the old system. Lastly, it will investigate how state institutions—initially thrown into disunity and disarray in the national uprising—banded together to dislodge Egypt's first elected president. The chapter will integrate an understanding of events based on long-term trends and structures with one that is based on short-term maneuvering and the actions of specific groups. This integrative approach incorporates historical and institutional legacies without sidestepping the issue of what causes the rupture, how historical and institutional legacies condition the transitional period, and how historical processes shape regime outcomes.

PART I
The Egyptian State

In this section, we will begin our examination of Egyptian politics by focusing on the Egyptian state and how Egypt has been ruled. Our comparative focus will also be broad—we will present the emergence of Egypt's modern state in terms of global patterns of state formation; we will similarly explore Egypt's regimes in terms of global patterns of authoritarianism.

Our inquiry will address two basic questions. First, where do strong states come from? Second, why are authoritarian regimes built the way they are?

The first question will draw our attention in chapter 2 to a long historical sweep (the past two centuries) and to the Egyptian state apparatus as a whole. The state today has an enormous presence in Egyptian politics, society, and economy; in order to understand that looming presence, we will ask where strong states come from. We will answer that question partly in comparative terms, observing that the two historical models that scholars often fall back on to explain state formation do not fit the state-building process in Egypt. The first view is that state building took place when ambitious rulers worked to amass revenues and build armies in a harsh and competitive security environment in early modern Europe; a second, alternative view is that state formation occurred when Europe molded much of the rest of the world—much of which we now refer to as "the global South"—in its image through imperialism.

That distinction has some merit but often results in too stark a delineation between Europe and the rest of the world—as Egypt shows. In the Egyptian case, which is actually not unusual in the global South, the expansion of the state did, as in the European experience, have a strong domestic basis in attempts to mobilize Egyptian resources, but it lacked some (though not all) of the competitive security environment of constant warfare that took place in Europe. The second process, based on imperialism, also helps explain patterns in the Egyptian case, as European countries made demands on, steered, and placed limits on what the Egyptian state could do. However, imperialism worked through other trends; it did not impose a state but instead shaped one. Especially after the middle of the twentieth century, there was a great expansion in the scope of the state that had its own domestic logic—though it was also one that may have led to an overreach and a retraction. We will trace that overreach and retraction in the realm of the state in part 1, but we come back to society in part 2 and the economy in part 3.

In chapter 3 we will shorten our historical focus and narrow our analytical gaze by asking why authoritarian systems are built the way they are. In other words, we will redirect our attention from the state as a whole to a narrower group of rulers. We generally use the term "regime" to refer to the system and set of rules by which a state is run. But the term is also used a bit loosely for the rulers and the systems they create (so we speak of "Nasser's regime"), and when we do so, we thus move among the state, the system by which the state is run ("regime" in the more specific sense), and the ruler without always being clear we are doing so. And we also sometimes edge into treating all aspects of the system as if they are the creation of a specific ruler—as if Nasser, the regime he led, and the Egyptian state are difficult to disentangle. And indeed, they sometimes are, but we will still try. In this chapter we will attempt to explore these implicit assumptions by focusing on the last half century or so, the period during which the state reached its most dominant presence, but also the period when there was some slow and uneven decline in that domination. We will explore this not only in general terms but also by examining specific state institutions (the judiciary and the military) that provide critical vantage points for understanding the evolving relationship among state, regime, and ruler.

Overall, we will be telling a single story: of the emergence of a strong state, the emergence of authoritarian regimes that lead that state, and the slippage that took place in those regimes' ability to control the state.

We will follow this story historically—that is, we will trace how it operated over time, encompassing a couple of centuries, but getting into more detail the closer we get to the present. Egyptians who discuss politics often do so in historical terms because shared historical memory makes it easier to express ideas and arguments. So, for instance, Egyptians might refer to "Nasserism" to recall a period of socialism, authoritarianism, and ambitious foreign policy that reached its height in the 1960s, and they continue to use that term as a way of describing controversies today. A critic might say that the regime has forgotten the Nasserist promises of social welfare. Another might use the term negatively to charge that the regime has a Nasserist mindset, meaning it wishes to control everything. But for our book, we work historically for a different reason: we wish to understand why certain actors and trends arose. And we seek to do so in a way that is based not on the particularities of Egypt alone, but in ways that allow us to understand how processes (like state formation or the decay of authoritarian regimes) occurred in this particular context.

In parts 2 and 3 we will return to many of these same themes—state control, partial and uneven retreat of the state—but we do so less from the vantage point of key institutions within the state and more from the point of view of the society (part 2) and the economy (part 3).

Chapter Two

GOVERNING EGYPT

The Construction of the Modern Egyptian State

Where do strong states come from? Do they get built, and if so, by whom? Or do they emerge from long-term processes that nobody really controls? In this chapter, we will show long-term forces at work, but we will also show how rulers and others struggle to react to these forces in order to shape the development and structure of a strong state.

In Egypt, the existence of a state has not really been at issue. It is its growth in the modern era—the expansion in spheres of activity that the state governs, regulates, and controls—that needs to be explained.

We have already observed that Egypt is an old society with a governing apparatus that goes back quite literally to the dawn of recorded history. In that sense, the Egyptian state is literally older than the Pyramids. But most of the modern state apparatus that Egyptians encounter in their lives today—with its presence in all aspects of social and economic life, its extensive bureaucracy, and its complex structures for educating, preaching to, housing, and regulating workplace conditions for them; for overseeing their old media and policing their newer social media; and adjudicating their disputes—was built in the nineteenth and twentieth centuries, with some critical structures built on top of older foundations dating back to earlier centuries.

And that means that Egypt does not quite fit, or might make us rethink, what we understand about strong states and where they come from.

Scholars have often understood state building as occurring according to one of two processes, most clearly elaborated by Charles Tilly.[1]

First, in early modern Europe, states emerged through a competitive process in which rulers built bureaucracies, extracted resources, and fought each other in a manner that was mutually reinforcing for the successful states. Unsuccessful rulers who could not keep up the pace or lost on the battlefield often saw their principalities disappear from the political map. The winners built sovereign states, dominating their societies internally and fending off (or even swallowing up) external rivals. In the nineteenth and twentieth centuries, those successful states often built stronger administrative and regulatory capabilities; they worked hard to build a sense of national identity among their citizens through their language policies, educational systems, and other tools; and they also took on greater social welfare functions, providing more education, pensions, and health care to their citizens.

But in a second path to state building, those same successful European states replicated their form throughout the world through colonization and imperialism (carving up much of the globe), and then by decolonizing, turning these former colonial territories into independent states. Some places that were not colonized copied European financial, taxation, and bureaucratic systems. In short, Europeans built the first modern states on their home continent and then spread the model elsewhere, either by imposition or by serving as models to emulate. Since the non-European states often had shallower roots, it is quite common for scholars to assume that most non-European states tend to be weak, and even that they are European creations.

There are some broad ways in which this helps us understand state formation, but Egypt fits neither situation well—or rather, the process as it has played out in Egypt partakes of a combination of the two paths. Egypt may not be all that unusual in this regard.

Egyptian state formation was not simply imposed by Europe. Ambitious rulers based in Egypt worked on their own to build up a strong state; the modern Egyptian state, in other words, is not an external imposition. Its rulers encouraged—and profited from—long-term economic changes, such as the growth of world trade. But this was not simply an Egyptian process. European influence was also deeply felt—not so much in creating the

Egyptian state, but in shaping it, limiting it, and also encouraging it to grow in certain areas.

In short, the idea of two separate paths is too sweeping an explanation to be profitably applied to the particular case of Egypt. It seems to be based on a caricature of non-European politics in which local agency is overlooked and distinctive patterns downplayed.

Those who built the Egyptian state, while they were subject to international and economic forces, had choices, even during periods of strong European control. (Great Britain and France both occupied the country, the former for decades.) So we need to explore both forces at work in order to understand why rulers chose some paths and avoided others. When we explore this question, we can turn to historians for help—those whose writings on Egypt are often particularistic and detailed rather than sweeping. When we take a historical view, we will see some global forces at work—expansion of trade, imperial rivalries, and the like—but we will focus on the motivations of key actors (especially Egypt's ruling family and imperial powers until World War I, and then a series of presidents after the mid-twentieth century).

When we review the modern period, we also see that the Egyptian state was not born in a single moment or created by a single actor. Instead, it is a set of effects, many of them unintended, that stem from a collection of actors reacting to various long-term social and political trends. It was deeply shaped not simply by long-term forces but also by a series of regime strategies, many of them ad hoc in nature.

We need to delve into the details to find out how these local and global forces worked. In this way, we will focus in more detail on the very broad question we posed in the previous chapter: How was the modern Egyptian state built in the nineteenth and twentieth centuries?

State building was an outcome of struggles over sovereignty and state control at the national and international levels; the evolution of major state structures (the presidency, political parties, the military); and the effects (often unintended) of various Egyptian rulers and regimes and the sequence of regime type.

We will proceed by examining the evolution of governance structures, exploring three periods in modern state formation in Egypt. First, we will review the experience of state building in the nineteenth and early twentieth centuries, when many of the basic structures (ministries and other bureaucracies, courts of law, and educational structures) were built.

Second, we will turn to the period after World War II. In the 1950s, a system emerged in which the dominant players were a strong presidency, a single political party, a rubber-stamp parliament, and a powerful set of security bodies. A form of "Arab socialism" placed much of the Egyptian economy under direct state ownership; that which the state did not own, it regulated quite heavily. In the 1950s and 1960s, it used this strong position to support a series of welfare commitments to educate, house, employ, and provide medical care to Egyptians.

Finally, we will see how this system came to face a series of crises by the late 1960s—military defeat, strong pressure on state finances, economic problems, and social discontent—leading to a reconfiguration of how state structures related to each other and their role in society. We will probe the country's economic trajectory more fully in part 3.

After tracing the historical evolution of the *state*, in the following chapter we will focus much more on the *regime* in the present and see how those who lead the Egyptian state do so.

STATE BUILDING AND IMPERIALISM IN THE NINETEENTH CENTURY

Almost all of the institutions that govern Egypt today—the ministries, security services, educational structures, and so on—trace their origins back to the nineteenth or twentieth centuries. A few, such as the religious complex of al-Azhar, the large complex of state-managed religious institutions, have far deeper roots (though it is worth noting that even al-Azhar was an independent institution and was only folded clearly into the state in the modern period).

To be sure, Egypt has been governed—and taxed, regulated, mobilized, and policed—for millennia. But if governance has been long-standing in Egypt, many institutions have not. In the nineteenth century, Egypt's rulers adopted a series of measures in order to strengthen their ability to mobilize the society's resources, develop the country economically, and make it more powerful internationally. In so doing, they built the set of structures that govern the country today. In some cases, they did so on the foundations laid by the Ottoman Empire, which had governed Egypt since the sixteenth century.

The context in which state building took place in the nineteenth century was one of enormous economic and political change at the international level. Economically, rising European hegemony brought with it a great expansion in international trade. Economic development in Europe and improvements in transportation led in turn to a great increase in demand for products (some of which Egypt could produce, like cotton and sugar) in Europe.

Politically, the growth in power of European states—underwritten by improvements in military technology, the strengthening of national states (the "winners," in Tilly's analysis), and their increased ability to mobilize resources through taxation and conscription—allowed them to project their authority and power outwards. But it also fostered severe rivalries among the European powers, leading them to check each other's expansionist ambitions. The Ottoman Empire—which included Egypt within its domain up until World War I—exercised only loose influence in the country. It was both a part of the European state system but also an object of it, as rival European states sought to exert influence over (and sometimes took control of) parts of Ottoman territory.

Countries outside of Europe, like Egypt, could take advantage of increased economic opportunities provided by growing world trade, but in the new environment they also appeared to Europeans as an economic prize (access to raw materials or markets) to be won. They could fall under the sway of one European power or play them off against each other; they could also emulate some of the techniques of state building pioneered in Europe.

Egyptian state building took place in this context.[2] Accounts of modern Egypt often begin by pointing to key events in this story—the French invasion of 1798, the coming to power of Muhammad Ali in 1805, or the British occupation of 1882. While these events were important, the process of state building was a bit more gradual. A ruling dynasty (founded by Muhammad Ali) achieved autonomy in, and control of, Egypt. It took the administrative practices inherited from the era of more direct Ottoman rule and watched Ottoman and European developments closely. We will refer to this period as that of the "khedival state" after a new title, "khedive," that Muhammad Ali's successors eventually assumed. The khedival state grew gradually, encouraging economic development and eventually borrowing in order to finance its ambitions, but also operating under watchful European eyes. This state gave way to one overseen by the British after 1882, but the British occupiers steered the state and made major policy decisions—they did not abolish the governing and administrative structures in the country; the khedive and the structures that had been built in the nineteenth century remained. Thus the story of state building is one of gradual but still dramatic change. We now turn to this story in a bit more detail.

In the seventeenth century, Egypt was part of the Ottoman Empire, but it was effectively ruled by military strongmen based in Cairo. At the end of the eighteenth century, the French (under Napoleon) briefly occupied the country, but popular rebellion and British and Ottoman pressure ultimately forced the French to withdraw. The Ottomans then sent Albanian troops to help them restore their rule, and the commander of these troops (Muhammad Ali) ultimately managed to establish himself as ruler of the country. He worked to mobilize Egyptian resources (imposing taxes, constructing new industries, developing agriculture, and conscripting troops) to build a strong military force that conquered neighboring areas. While nominally an Ottoman governor, he threatened the Ottoman Empire with his conquests, ultimately leading the European powers to step in and compel him to abandon territories outside of Egypt in return for recognizing him and his descendants as autonomous rulers of Egypt. Over much of the next century, Egyptian state formation followed something that looked a bit like the process Tilly described for early modern Europe—though with Egypt falling somewhere in between the status of winner and loser.

It was a winner because Muhammad Ali's dynasty operated within the country without challenge; it was a loser because European powers put strong limits on Egypt (and one eventually occupied the country). As the khedival state was built, the European powers required that the Egyptian military be greatly reduced; they also successfully imposed their understanding of "capitulations"—arrangements in which their citizens would not be subject to Egyptian law but instead the law of their home country. The effect of this latter step was to complicate Egyptian economic policy: foreigners resident in the country could not be taxed or have their activities regulated without the consent of their home governments.

In the second half of the nineteenth century, the khedival state began to take advantage of the expansion in world trade and growing demand for Egyptian crops (especially cotton to supply new textile industries in Europe) to develop the country economically. New ports were constructed; railroad networks built; irrigation canals dredged; and the Suez Canal dug. Some of these projects were financed by new taxes, but the Egyptian state also borrowed heavily from Europe to finance the program.

The program was built on, but also further enabled, a stronger state administrative apparatus. Officials took a more active role in trying to direct agricultural production; a steady stream of regulations and laws were issued; and local officials were made more aware of the watchful eye of the central government in Cairo. The khedival state's development program placed great strains on state finances. As we have seen, the taxing of foreigners was limited by the capitulations. A "Consultative Assembly" of notables—a revival and expansion of assemblies that had been convened earlier in the century—was formed partly by election. The body was induced to approve a law offering future tax forgiveness in return for immediate large payments to the khedival state. In this respect, it appeared that Egypt was still following a European path, one in which states bargained with their societies over matters of taxation and revenues (bargaining that often took the form of rulers negotiating with parliaments).

Finally, overborrowing brought the program into danger: in 1875, Egypt was forced to declare bankruptcy and accept a measure of European financial oversight (including the appointment of European officials to the cabinet) and an onerous program of debt repayment. This sparked resentment and political conflict. The program forced austerity on the khedival state. In the face of this austerity, the assembly of notables attempted to summon European ministers in order to question them (thus, in European eyes, attempting to evade bankruptcy arrangements), and army officers publicly protested after their pay was cut. European powers who suspected that the ruler, Isma`il (the grandson of Muhammad Ali), was encouraging the unrest leaned on the Ottoman Empire (still nominally sovereign in Egypt) to depose him in favor of his son in 1879. But the political crisis continued, with an Egyptian army colonel, Ahmad `Urabi, emerging at the head of a movement of notables, senior officials, and army officers pressing back against European financial oversight and political involvement. In 1882, the British invaded Egypt to put down the movement; they would go on to occupy the country for decades.[3]

The period before the British occupation thus saw significant economic development within Egypt, much of it oriented around the production and export of cotton. Accompanying this was a slow expansion of the administrative capacity of the khedival state. The emergence of new political actors—large landowners and senior officials gathered in an assembly—and the army moved Egypt away from narrowly personalistic rule by the descendants of Muhammad Ali, but steps toward a more inclusive parliamentary system were cut short by the British occupation.

But if British control of Egypt brought fundamental changes at the top, in many areas of administration, state building continued unabated. A new court system, designed in the years before the British occupation, was introduced, based on a hierarchical French model with written codes, judges trained in law schools, courts of appeal, and judicial prosecutors. A nationwide system of policing was strengthened. Local officials—provincial governors, village mayors, tax collectors—were guided by a stream of central directives.

In short, the khedival state survived, and even grew in some areas, though the British imposed cutbacks in other areas. The occupiers also imposed some new priorities: they continued selling off state and ruling family lands to repay Egypt's foreign debts; they resisted Egyptian pressure to increase expenditure on education; they disbanded much of Egypt's military; and they focused much public investment in transportation and irrigation, based on the policy of agricultural development. The British occupied the country, but their ability to direct and implement policies and push new laws and regulations was still limited to some extent by the capitulations, which continued to allow foreigners (and thus many large-scale commercial and even smaller retail enterprises) exemption from new Egyptian law and courts. There was even a special court system (the "Mixed Courts") to adjudicate any dispute in which a foreigner had an interest according to a French-inspired law code negotiated between Egypt and European powers.

Nor did the British occupation bring about a radical formal change in the way that Egypt was governed. It remained nominally part of the Ottoman Empire (though as we have seen, the Ottomans had little say in what happened inside country). Descendants of Muhammad Ali continued to rule as khedives, supported by Egyptian ministers. But the British insisted that its consul general (their chief representative in the country) have his way on all important policy issues, placed British advisers in key ministries to guide their nominal Egyptian superiors, and maintained a small body of troops within the country. While the occupiers allowed consultative assemblies to meet, these bodies were merely advisory.

With the outbreak of World War I in 1914, the British and Ottoman Empires were formal adversaries, and the British officially pronounced the link between Egypt and the Ottoman Empire severed. They declared martial law, effectively suspended the capitulations, and mobilized Egyptian supplies and the labor force to support their military efforts. During the war, British officials developed plans to incorporate Egypt more fully into the British Empire.

But before that could happen, a nationwide rebellion broke out against the British occupation. In 1919, a group of Egyptian leaders—former officials and other prominent individuals—mounted a nationwide petition campaign in support of their claim to represent the country at the postwar Paris Peace Conference, based on the argument that Egypt had contributed heavily to the Allied war effort. British authorities arrested the would-be delegation (which termed itself the Wafd, after the Arabic word for "delegation"), leading to demonstrations in Cairo that spread quickly to other urban centers and then to the countryside.

While the British were able to put down the uprising, it became clear that they would have to find an alternative that was less intrusive than bringing Egypt into their empire. Egyptians refer to the uprising of 1919 as a "revolution" today not only because of the mass mobilization but also to indicate that a demand for independence was asserted—and partially met. The British sought to negotiate with various Egyptian leaders but found that some were too weak and others unwilling to make the concessions they desired. Finally, in 1922, the British simply made a unilateral declaration that Egypt was independent while claiming that they were still responsible for some vital matters: defense, British imperial communications (e.g., the Suez Canal), protecting foreigners and minorities, and Sudan (a region to the south to which both Britain and Egypt laid claim).

INDEPENDENCE AND STATE BUILDING

The effect of Britain's unilateral declaration of Egyptian independence was to give Egypt's state far more autonomy in matters of internal governance and policy than it had before. This autonomy (or independence) was not unlimited: the British government insisted on a say over some critical issues; and the capitulations and the Mixed Courts continued to limit the reach of Egyptian law, with especially strong effects on Egyptian finances (taxes on foreigners—including tariffs to protect Egyptian industries—could only be levied after torturous international negotiations).

And Egyptian political leaders found independence did not lead easily to an ability to act coherently. The descendant of Muhammad Ali, now styling himself "King" of Egypt, appointed a group of leaders to draft a constitution. The Wafd—converting itself into a political party—insisted that only elected representatives could write such a thing, and therefore boycotted the process. The resulting document, issued in 1923, governed Egypt (with two interruptions) until 1952, but it left critical ambiguities. It allowed for a strong monarchy but also an elected parliament. The Wafd, while it criticized the Constitution, did enter parliamentary elections and easily won them. The strong rivalry between the Wafd and the throne continued over three decades, diminishing gradually over time, but still leading the king at various times to rig elections against the Wafd or suspend the Constitution.

As time wore on, the Wafd found that it did not have a monopoly on organizing Egyptian society. Other political parties arose (some of them splitting off from the Wafd) that gradually eroded the Wafd's strength. But more significantly, perhaps, new social movements formed that focused less on parliamentary elections and more on organizing new generations of Egyptians, particularly in urban areas. The Muslim Brotherhood was perhaps the most successful of these movements; founded in the late 1920s, it became a major presence in Egyptian social life over the next two decades. Other movements of various ideological stripes (religious, nationalist, and leftist) arose, some of them taking positions on political issues or pressuring political leaders on public policy.

The Egyptian state was operating not only in a more contentious and complicated domestic context but also one that was still circumscribed internationally through the continuation of certain aspects of British occupation, the presence of British personnel in key positions in the state apparatus, the capitulations, and the Mixed Courts (which, as described previously, protected the special status of foreigners).[4] In the quarter century after Britain's unilateral declaration of independence, however, these gradually lessened. An Egyptian government headed by the Wafd finally negotiated a treaty with Great Britain in 1936 that recognized full Egyptian independence. While the treaty, ostensibly between two sovereign states, preserved a strong role for Britain in Egypt's security affairs and foreign policy, the close involvement of British officials in other areas gradually declined.

The conclusion of the treaty allowed the Egyptian government to ask for an international conference to end the capitulations and the Mixed Courts. With strong British support, the conference was held in 1937 and saw the negotiation of a twelve-year abolition process. This allowed the Egyptian state to exercise fiscal autonomy for the first time. It could now levy taxes, protect its own industries, and police foreigners.

The shift was real but not total. Over the short term, the limitations in the defense realm were quickly felt when Britain entered World War II and asked for Egyptian support under the recently negotiated treaty. Egypt did not formally enter the war, but it did declare martial law to allow it to take measures in support of the British war effort—a state of emergency that has remained in effect (with some short interruptions) up to the present. In 1942, when the British feared that an Egyptian government might use the conflict in North Africa—German troops were then advancing on Egypt—to oust the British, they surrounded the palace and forced the king to appoint the Wafd to head the cabinet. And British troops remained at the Suez Canal. In 1954, the Egyptians and British negotiated a British withdrawal, and just as that was completed, the Egyptian government nationalized the Suez Canal, which had been owned by a British-French company. The British and French invaded and occupied the Canal Zone but were forced to withdraw due to intense international pressure.

In all these ways, Egyptian independence, declared in 1922, took over three decades to be fully realized. But as this independence gradually expanded, it made state building efforts possible in several realms. The educational apparatus was greatly expanded, with schools built first in major cities and then in towns and villages. The legal system was unified, with an end to the Mixed Courts in 1949 and separate courts for "personal status" in 1955. Policing was removed from the restrictions imposed by the capitulations. The 1936 treaty did not merely allow Egypt to assume responsibility for its own defense—it required it to do so; the Egyptian military, which had been kept tiny under the British occupation, began to build a larger force, and it opened an academy to train officers.

But it was not merely institutions that could now be built. Fiscal autonomy made it possible to adopt new economic policies that favored Egyptian development. Egyptian leaders were no longer restricted by foreign powers who saw the country as a producer of cotton and agricultural products, and they could invest in new infrastructure projects, such as electrification. Reform-minded leaders argued successfully to use state revenues to build universities and to abolish tuition.

And wartime measures led to price controls on some basic commodities (authorities wanted no food riots or disturbances to public order, as had happened in previous years, when World War I caused domestic inflation and dislocations that helped fuel the uprising of 1919). When the war ended in 1945, the mechanisms were in place for heavier state regulation of prices and markets.

In 1952, regime change led to an intensification of this state building. Indeed, for this reason, the events of 1952 are often referred to by Egyptians as a "revolution." The regime change itself—consisting of a seizure of power by a group of military officers—was nonviolent and the political restructuring at the top was gradual (the officers first deposed the king, then abolished the monarchy altogether a year later; they then built a new political system in the mid-1950s). And the years after 1952 did indeed see dramatic political change. But once again, there was strong continuity as well, as the new regime built on trends and used tools that were already in place.

The generation of military officers brought into the military academy in the late 1930s had been imbued with a strong nationalist mission; in 1948, when they were sent to fight a war over the creation of the State of Israel, they were defeated in a manner that led many to blame the country's top political leadership. Many of these officers had been politically active in the 1930s (joining movements like the Muslim Brotherhood), and some retained links to leftist, nationalist, or Islamist movements. A secret group was formed within the military, calling itself the "Free Officers," and it was they who moved to take power in July 1952. After some internal power struggles, one of their members, Gamal ʿAbd al-Nasser, emerged as president, a position he held until his death in 1970.[5]

The Free Officers' regime ushered itself in with a pledge to reform the system, but increasingly the new rulers decided—especially after the officers led by Nasser, who favored continued rule, defeated those who wished an earlier return to civilian life—to restructure the political system in some fundamental ways. The new regime abolished all political parties and formed a series of organizations, the most ambitious of which, the Arab Socialist Union, folded into itself many of the existing institutions in the country (such as labor unions, professional associations, and even much of the press). Free Officers and their allies and followers were given key positions, not merely in the military and security apparatus, but throughout the state. Political activity was sharply curtailed into regime-controlled organs and opposition was repressed harshly. When the regime allowed a parliament to be reinstated in 1957, it vetted all candidates for election and allowed the body little authority.

Throughout its first decade, the new regime made use of economic measures as a political tool. Land reform undermined many members of the old political elite (including the royal family and many leading members of the Wafd), whose wealth and influence was grounded in ownership of large estates. The nationalization of economic enterprises was a political tool as well. The regime confiscated the holdings of those it accused of corruption under the pre-1952 regime; it also nationalized the Suez Canal and the private property of British and French citizens as part of the conflict over the canal in 1956. When Israel joined in the attack on Egypt in the fall of that year, Egypt retaliated by nationalizing property owned by Jews (both Egyptian and non-Egyptians) and some other foreigners (many of whom had held on to their foreign citizenship for many years to benefit from the now abolished capitulations). The result of these policies was to make the Egyptian state the owner of some very profitable economic enterprises.

Having edged into this role sometimes for tactical political reasons, by the 1960s, the regime became enthusiastically socialist in ideology, turning the state's leading economic role into a part of its strategic orientation. It coupled its economic program with an ambitious foreign policy, seeking to lead the Arab world (thus developing the term "Arab socialism" to refer to the program).

Almost all large economic enterprises in the country were nationalized, including banks, tourism, industry, and transportation. A series of land redistributions—beginning in the land reform undertaken when the regime took power in 1952 and continuing into the 1960s—broke up Egypt's large estates, dispossessing large landowners and requiring those receiving land to join state-sponsored cooperatives, effectively bringing much of agriculture within the state sector as well.

Official policy provided not merely for the ownership of existing economic enterprises but also for the founding of new ones under state ownership. The policy of import substitution industrialization—pursuing industrialization by encouraging domestic industries to make products that used to be imported—was the foundation for many of these efforts. Pre-1952 regimes had also favored import substitution, but they generally encouraged it through the private sector; the new regime not only stepped up the official commitment to the policy but also placed the new industries under state ownership. Import substitution policies tend to be concentrated initially in industries that require less investment or advanced technology (such as food processing or textiles), but the post-1952 regime tried to encourage Egyptian enterprises to invest in more capital-intensive industries, such as appliances and steel.

But Arab socialism did not merely mean state ownership; it also meant strong welfare commitments. The state subsidized basic commodities and fuel and provided housing, free education through the university level, and health care throughout the entire country. Some of these commitments (such as on education or fixed prices) actually predated the post-1952 regime (some were enacted as wartime measures during World War II; others were adopted by governments of the old regime), but their scale and ambition was greatly increased.[6]

Later generations of Egyptian intellectuals would often talk of an implicit "social contract" in Egypt in which the regime provided welfare benefits but asked people to surrender democratic freedoms. They likely did so for a powerful reason: to tell authoritarian leaders who were scaling back on socialism that if they could not provide welfare benefits, they should provide democracy instead. But the idea of the "bargain" was projected retroactively. It is true that at its height, the regime was both socialist and authoritarian, but the image of an antidemocratic "bargain" ignores the regime's rhetoric. Nasser and other Egyptian leaders claimed to be fulfilling rather than abandoning democracy. Older systems that had focused on parliaments, multiple parties, and elections, had resulted in ineffective and corrupt leadership, they claimed. Egypt's emerging system, these rulers asserted, was one that placed power in the people's hands, not through multiparty elections but by unifying the people and granting them ownership. What we will describe as "state corporatism" in part 2 was presented to the Egyptian people as a system that brought them into the running of the state.

The regime's foreign policy—the "Arab" part of "Arab socialism"—also reflected its ambitions. In 1956, Egypt faced down two European powers and

Israel and emerged with a diplomatic victory. Posing as a champion of the newly emerging "non-aligned movement"—those countries allied neither with the United States nor the Soviet Union in the Cold War—the Egyptian regime was seen favorably by rising generations of political activists pressing to overcome the legacy of European imperialism, particularly in the Arab world. Between 1958 and 1961, Egypt formed a union with Syria when the leadership of the latter country requested it.

By the 1960s, however, the string of policy successes associated with the ambitious statist program had begun to lose their luster. Egypt's industrial production had increased but it had done so to meet the needs of a limited domestic market, and most firms could not compete internationally. The state's welfare commitments—in terms of housing, employment, and the provision of basic commodities—were gradually becoming more onerous and could no longer be met simply through redistribution. Egypt's foreign policy ran into problems as well: a disastrous military confrontation in June 1967 with Israel led to Israeli occupation of the Sinai Peninsula (with its oil fields then being developed by Israel while it controlled the area) and closure of the Suez Canal (a major source of foreign exchange for the Egyptian state), which in turn drove Egypt toward greater dependence on the Soviet Union for its defense needs. In the late 1960s, signs of popular discontent appeared, with demonstrations from students and strikes by workers supporting demands for accountability and meeting unfulfilled promises for prosperity and strength.

THE CRISIS AND RECALIBRATION

By the late 1960s, with a faltering economic record, a stinging military defeat by Israel, and rising activism among students and workers, the regime showed signs of stress, including deep internal divisions and rivalries among leading individuals and institutions. The regime's response over the next decade was to take a number of steps that effectively reconfigured the state without transforming it. The partial economic and political liberalization seemed less a product of farsighted design than a series of short-term moves leading uncertainly and unevenly in the new direction.

Some aspects of this new direction were manifest in the late 1960s as President Nasser and the ruling party tentatively laid out some themes in 1968 that involved promises of greater democracy and accountability; the regime also downplayed some of the more radical suggestions about socialist transformation. But these signals were confusing. When the Judges Club, a social organization, endorsed the 1968 call for political liberalization with a statement that seemed critical of the regime's past behavior, regime leaders waited for a year and then dismissed a large number of sitting judges and brought judicial structures more firmly under its control. The president denounced the existence of "centers of power" that had grown up within the state apparatus and were impervious to societal needs and popular pressure, but he seemed to use this as a way of targeting potential rivals, especially in the military and the Arab Socialist Union.

In September 1970, in the midst of the regime's maneuverings, Nasser died unexpectedly. He was succeeded by his vice president at the time, Anwar al-Sadat. A loyal member of the regime, and one of the remaining members of the Free Officers still active in politics, Sadat's position as president at first seemed insecure. But he used some of the tactics of Nasser's last years—trimming the Arab Socialist Union and denouncing "centers of power"—in order to weed out rivals. In May 1971, he proclaimed a "corrective revolution" in order to defend the regime while embarking on limited reform. Without repudiating Nasser and Nasserism, he took steps against some of Nasser's measures, such as reining in the security services, reinstating some of the dismissed judges, and releasing political prisoners, in an apparent effort to broaden his political base.

What began as a series of tactical steps by Egypt's leaders had a cumulative effect on the structure of the Egyptian state, moving it in a somewhat more liberal direction in a number of dimensions. Over the course of the 1970s and 1980s, the regime sought to jettison some social welfare commitments and diminish others. In economic policy, it allowed for greater private and international investment. The overall effect was not so much to dismantle the Egyptian state's economic role but to allow significant private activity alongside of it.

There was a measure of political liberalization as well. The Arab Socialist Union, the sole political party, was disestablished; a nominally multiparty system was allowed to form (with what eventually became the National Democratic Party dominating the political system and oversight of the press transferred to a newly created upper house within parliament). Other small opposition parties were permitted, and even the Wafd was allowed to reemerge. Opposition media, such as newspapers, were also permitted.

In the 1970s and 1980s, the Muslim Brotherhood, too, was allowed to reemerge; while it was discouraged from formal political activity, it nonetheless provided a counterweight to leftist groups, especially on college campuses. Other religious groups—especially those that stayed away from politics—were also permitted. Indeed, the state's increasing difficulties meeting its welfare commitments left an open space for the formation of self-help groups and charities, many with a religious coloration, who sought to assist students, the ill, or the poor.

The course of this limited liberalization was uneven, and the Egyptian regime, both under Sadat (from 1970 until 1981) and during the presidency of Hosni Mubarak (1981–2011), periodically bared its full authoritarian teeth when either its control of the state or the control the state exercised over society was challenged. This was most notable in 1981 with a wholesale crackdown on dissent across the spectrum, or in the 1990s, when the system used its harshest tools against Islamists.

Over these four decades of growing pluralism, limited liberalization, sporadic reversals, and periodic crackdowns in Egyptian political life, the Egyptian state apparatus began to decentralize its operations. The military was gradually edged out of certain aspects of its political role; the security services continued to play a part in policing political life, but the regime seemed to find ways to limit each one, and even to play them off as rivals against each other. A limited measure of judicial independence was restored, with administrative courts (responsible for cases in which the state was a party) sometimes taking a strong role in protecting citizen rights. Structures used to ensure presidential control were loosened and a powerful new constitutional court managed to emerge.

The overall effect of this state restructuring was to produce an apparatus that was still quite large and sprawling but much less centralized. The period of the 1960s—in which the presidency and a small group of former and current military officers kept tight control of most structures—gave way to a system in which different bureaucracies and institutions (the religious establishment, the judiciary, the security services, the military, state-owned media) had significant autonomy within their own realms (with some controlling property or business enterprises, some even showing some fiscal autonomy). Yet if they had some internal autonomy, they were expected to hold to a generally pro-regime line in their policies and behavior. Appointments to key positions were often made by the president, and if a structure seemed excessively independent, its top personnel could be changed to bring in more loyal figures (as happened with the command of the military in the 1980s or the constitutional court in the early 2000s).

UPRISING AND AFTERMATH

The evolution of this more complex political environment may have contributed to the regime's faltering in 2011. On the one hand, the limited liberalization allowed new groups to emerge and organize, but generally left most feeling that they were shut out of any contest for political authority. This encouraged an upsurge in protest activity in the early 2000s, as we will see in part 2. On the other hand, important state bodies had some limited autonomy from the regime, and were uncertain about harnessing themselves to a presidency that sometimes hemmed them in and was the target of popular mobilization. In the uprising of January and February 2011, as protests mushroomed, key state bodies appeared to waver, and many experienced pressure within their own ranks.

In February 2011, President Mubarak was finally forced out of office by a military cowed by mass protests that severely hampered the regime's ability to steer politics. The military seized temporary control of the state and rushed through a process designed to incorporate a measure of democratic participation while still securing the role of state institutions; when elections led to a parliament dominated by Islamists and a presidency won by Muhammad Morsi, a Muslim Brotherhood candidate, state institutions—along with most non-Islamist political forces—swung in opposition.

The period of 2011–2013 saw not only a contest for power among Egyptian political forces (expressed in competitive elections, street protests, and other forms of political mobilization) but also an attempt by key state institutions to fend off revolutionary pressure. With the 2013 overthrow of Muhammad Morsi, they were able to reassert themselves more fully. In the years after that overthrow, the regime was able to edge most political and social actors out of Egyptian public life, beginning with the Muslim Brotherhood but extending to virtually all other organized forces. The highly centralized control of the 1960s was revived, this time without the commitments to socialism and populism that characterized the official rhetoric of the past. Additionally, there was no attempt at mobilization of the population through a state party or even the emergence of broad patronage networks that emerged after the 1970s. We will examine the tumultuous post-2011 period more fully in chapter 9.

We now return to the question that opened the chapter: Where do strong states come from? In Egypt, the state's strong presence in economic, political, and social life is striking. It was clearly not imposed by external actors, though external actors were very much involved in setting the context and shaping the opportunities and constraints in which state building occurred. Much of this state building was intentional, but it was not always seen as such by the regime. Except at specific periods (the early nineteenth century, the immediate postindependence era, and the 1950s and 1960s), the Egyptian leadership does not seem to have had a comprehensive state-building vision, and even in those periods, their decisions often had unintended consequences. At other periods, more short-term or tactical thinking seems to have prevailed, though that does not mean that the choices made by leaders had no consequences.

In short, states emerge out of long-term historical processes; they are the product of concerted human action but are not narrowly determined by individual wills. Rulers and regimes steer states but they do not always do so easily or effectively—and that is the matter we will turn our attention to in the next chapter.

Chapter Three

BETWEEN STATE AND REGIME
The Evolution of Egyptian Authoritarianism

Why are authoritarian systems built the way they are? Many scholars have explored why authoritarian rulers construct regimes the way they do. In this chapter, however, we argue that the question itself can be partially misleading. We adopt a different approach by exploring the idea that authoritarian systems are not only built on purpose by rulers; they also evolve in ways that rulers do not plan. In other words, this chapter will build on the analytical perspective of the previous one by arguing that rulers build states but not as they please; they make imperfect and often short-term efforts to deal with long-term trends. And we will also see in this chapter how regimes have struggled to control the state apparatus that became so far-reaching in Egyptian society.

STATES AND REGIMES

In the previous chapter, we focused on the evolution of the Egyptian *state*: the set of governing institutions in Egypt. But we were also attentive to the Egyptian *regime*, a term that is a bit harder to define precisely. It is hard to define because, like other terms we use in this book (like "revolution" and "democracy"), it has both a more specialized usage as well as one that is employed among nonspecialists. The latter generally use it to refer to authoritarian rulers or systems—we talk often of the "North Korean regime" or, in the case of Egypt, the "Mubarak regime," which we use to refer to the period when Mubarak was president, but we do not usually refer to the "Obama regime" in the United States, or the "French regime" to refer to those governing that country.

Scholars use the term a bit more precisely to refer to the system or the set of rules that determines who wields state power. But less consciously, scholars often slide between using the "regime" to mean the system as well as the ruling group, and they even (as in general usage) often refer to it by the name of the individual ruler (especially an authoritarian one).

Maybe that murkiness is partially the point. As we said in the introduction, scholars do not like to use murky terms when they analyze and explain; they want to have a good idea of what they are saying. But in this chapter, we will turn the murkiness of the term "regime" to our advantage. What has changed over the years in Egypt is the degree to which we can speak of a regime as distinct from the state. Sometimes there is a distinction between state and regime that seems fairly obvious—there has been a clear set of people and structures who are overseeing, without having the ability to micromanage, the entire state apparatus. This distinction was illustrated by the Mubarak years, when top officials in the presidency, the ruling party, the security apparatus, and a few key institutions were clearly in general command, but when many state institutions (the religious establishment, the judiciary, state-controlled higher education) were headed by regime loyalists but still somewhat autonomous. Other times, however, the border between the regime and the state is harder to draw—such as when power has been centralized; when the same people monopolized a small number of top positions; and when those on top made whatever formal and informal rules they wanted. These blurred boundaries are most evident in the Nasserist period of Egyptian politics.

This chapter is thus based on the idea that if we want to understand Egyptian politics, we need to look not merely at the state as a whole (as we did in the last chapter) but at who is on top of it and how they rule—that is, we need to look at the regime. And above all, we need to be alert to the nature of the regime—which individuals and offices comprise the regime—and how the way it commands, steers, and manages the state apparatus has changed over time.

In the previous chapter, we examined how and why the Egyptian state was built over a considerable period of time. Now, we are turning our attention to the Egyptian regime over a shorter period (the past half century) and focusing most of all on the past two decades. And we will do so not so much to examine policy—what the regime has done in the society and the economy (that will be the subject of parts 2 and 3)—but to focus on what the regime is and on the relationship between the regime and the state itself. Who are Egypt's top leaders? Is there a system that describes where they come from and how they rule? In what ways and how much have Egypt's top leaders been able to control or use the state? How did the regime get to be what it is?

The relationship between the regime and the state as a whole has actually not drawn a lot of attention from scholars, many of whom have been more interested in how authoritarian regimes rise and fall, especially when they give way to democratic ones. But scholars have often paid less attention to how regimes operate or how one authoritarian regime might evolve into another. Many scholars are less interested in how the regime commands the state since they often seem to assume that under authoritarianism, the regime uses the state however it likes. So when they do explain how regimes operate, they often start with the intentions of regime leaders—if there are elections, for instance, students of authoritarianism often assume these must serve some purpose for these leaders (such as forcing their opposition out into the open, where they can be regulated, or perhaps organizing regime supporters in ways that benefit loyalists). If there are strong judiciaries, the assumption often goes, they must be there to serve the long-term interest of the regime in some way.

They are not completely wrong to make such assumptions. Scholars try to explain so much in terms of the ruler and the regime's interests for good reasons. We have seen highly personalized authoritarian regimes—ones led by a single, dominant leader who seems to be able to command the entire state apparatus. Saddam Hussein's Iraq and Mao Zedong's China were places where the leader could command state forces to do his will—and, if these state forces resisted or even showed sluggishness in responding to directives (as was sometimes the case under Mao), rulers found ways to subdue them.

Such answers are sometimes helpful, but not always. This level of control is often difficult for rulers to maintain—especially in Egypt, which has a state with very strong and deeply rooted institutions. Indeed, the relationship between regime and state has evolved over time. Egypt is hardly unusual. There are many cases of authoritarian regimes—such as that which existed in Germany before World War I—that have strong institutions with some ability to act on their own, and some that are sticklers for following legal procedures rather than waiting for instructions from the ruler. So seeing authoritarian politics largely as the projection of a single ruler or group of rulers is sometimes accurate, but usually does not adequately capture the broader relationship between the state and the regime.

Before we proceed to an examination of the Egyptian regime and its relationship with the state, we should pause on another term that Egyptians have imported into their political lexicon—the "deep state."[1] Does Egypt have one? We think the term is helpful in explaining how many Egyptians experience their rule, but it makes understanding various regimes' efforts to manage the state unnecessarily mysterious.

The phrase was coined in Turkey to refer to a group of top officials (generally military, security, and judicial personnel) who operated outside of regular channels to guarantee what they saw as the fundamental pillars of the political system, even if it meant overturning the results of the electoral process. In that sense, it comes close to the term "regime" as we are using it, though it is also born of the suspicion that the real regime is hidden from public view. From Turkey, the term was adapted for use elsewhere (even the United States during the Trump presidency) because it resonated with the feelings of those in a variety of societies (such as Algerians, who referred to *le pouvoir* [the power], a group of top leaders who dominated from the shadows) that there is a regime behind the scenes that does not so much follow the rules as make them—indeed, breaking and remaking them according to their needs. It has even been used in some democracies by those who feel that top officials try to undermine democratically elected leaders so they can exercise power as they like.

We do not dismiss these ideas out of hand. The term "deep state" is difficult to pin down precisely but it does seem that something of the kind has operated in Egypt at times—senior officials have sometimes operated as if they have ultimately responsibility for, and control of, the state apparatus regardless of formal procedures or constitutional rules. We prefer the term "regime" to "deep state," however, since it is both clearer and more widely used. We just need to keep in mind that the "regime" might sometimes operate a bit less openly and formally.

Whether we speak of a "deep state" or a "regime," we should not simply equate either with the entire state. In Egypt, there is clearly a very wide state as well as a deep one—a Ministry of Supply that spreads into every provincial market; a set of courts that adjudicates disputes between husband and wife, landlord and tenant, employer and employee; a set of neighborhood mosques that are regulated by a Ministry of Religious Affairs; a Ministry of Education that tests students on the basis of textbooks it produces; and so on. These bodies are sometimes far too extensive and far-flung to be closely controlled.

Or, to put it in more formal terms: the Egyptian regime shapes and steers the state but its ability to control many aspects of it varies. Regimes do not build every structure from scratch; rather, they find a group of mechanisms and institutions in place that answer to a country's top leadership but that also have their own distinctive ways and even, on occasion, wills of their own. There has been significant variation over time in how much the regime can micromanage the state.

For instance, Egypt's current judicial structure dates back to the nineteenth century; the presidency, by contrast—central to all regimes that have governed in recent years—dates only to the mid-twentieth century. Judicial structures have struggled to attain some level of fiscal independence as well as some control over appointments within their own ranks. There are moments at which the presidency—which is at the apex of the regime and sometimes identified with it—has reshaped the courts in some fundamental ways. But at other times, courts have made decisions that have not been dictated by the regime. The judiciary has changed in its autonomy in incremental and evolutionary ways, not always by design.

So while there is a regime that governs Egypt, the state's various components are sometimes at odds with each other, and the regime's centerpiece, the presidency itself, has played a shifting role in shaping and steering them. Not only does the state's ability to act coherently vary; the regime's mastery of the levers of the vast state apparatus is at best clumsy. And at critical moments (most notably but not exclusively during the 2011 uprising), the regime's ability to control Egyptian society and politics has been challenged.

When push comes to shove, the Egyptian presidency has always had ways to override any law or procedure and impose its will. But push rarely comes to shove, and critical state institutions have realized a degree of internal autonomy, such that social and political forces can sometimes hem in a leader's options or act independently of his will. The presidency manages the state apparatus by appointing individuals to key positions (such as the country's prosecutor general or the chief editors of state-owned press outlets), co-optation (doling out higher salaries, plum appointments, or other benefits to key individuals or institutions), and fostering institutional duplication (with an array of courts to use if one proved unreliable, overlapping security services, and so on).

In this chapter, we will proceed in two steps: after a brief overview of the evolution of regime-state relations, we will turn our focus to some key state institutions: the judiciary, the media, and the military. In the process, Egyptian authoritarianism will be shown in comparative terms to resemble less the personalistic kinds of rule often associated with that designation than the versions that emerged in southern Europe in the middle of the twentieth century: regimes that were authoritarian, to be sure, but that did not try to control everything. In fact, it was a political scientist specializing in Spain who popularized the term "authoritarianism" to refer to such systems.[2] In Spain and some other authoritarian systems in Europe and South America, the Catholic Church retained some degree of autonomy from the different national regimes, possessing control over important educational activities and a great deal of influence over social policy. Some key state institutions—for example, the judiciary—were allowed to arrange their own affairs as long as they remained generally loyal to the regime. Such systems—those in Portugal from the 1930s until the 1970s, for example—were often seen as ideologically on the right because they were socially conservative and sought to crush leftist forces. Egypt's regimes have shifted among various ideological camps (varying in the degree that they are socialist, liberal, or religious) and they have repressed a variety of groups (leftist, religious, and nationalist), sometimes favoring others. So the comparison is inexact. But it does suggest that there is not a uniquely Egyptian political form in which authoritarian regimes guide large states, but instead a pattern that has appeared in many different places.

RECENT HISTORY OF REGIME-STATE RELATIONS

Prior to 1952, Egypt had a political system in which there was a strong monarchy but also an elected parliament. The parliament generally determined the composition of the cabinet, meaning that policy was determined by a tug-of-war between the king and the largest party (the Wafd). On several occasions before 1952, the king either suspended the Constitution or tried to sway electoral results to exclude or weaken the Wafd. Other state institutions (like al-Azhar or the judiciary) had some limited autonomy but often got pulled into the power struggle. When, for instance, a new administrative court system was established and then headed by one of Egypt's most influential and prestigious legal figures (`Abd al-Razzaq al-Sanhuri, whose legal influence spread throughout the Arab world), the Wafd viewed it with some suspicion because of al-Sanhuri's personal ties with a small rival party. Similarly, al-Azhar was sometimes seen as close to the palace.

But both the monarchy and the Wafd—as well as competitive elections for the parliament—were abolished after 1952. Whether what happened in 1952 was a revolution—Egyptians still argue today whether to call the events of that year a coup or a revolution—it certainly brought about a change in the regime, as a group of army officers (the "Free Officers" described in chapter 2) assumed control over the entire political system and then built a presidential system to replace the pre-1952 order.

And the years after 1952 also brought more gradual changes in the state structure. Indeed, we have already seen how during the 1950s and 1960s the state greatly expanded in scope, assumed direct control over much of the economy, eliminated political parties (except for a single ruling organization), and greatly expanded welfare benefits. In short, it became a towering presence in the Egyptian economy and society.[3] During that period as well, the Egyptian state was also reconfigured in such a way as to be brought under the control of the regime. In fact, the regime's control grew so strong and direct that it became difficult to speak of a distinct state apparatus.

Gamal `Abd al-Nasser, the former army officer, held the presidency. Heading many state institutions were a group of friends, allies, and associates, many from the Free Officers group that had built the new regime after overthrowing the old one in 1952. This gave the regime a bit of a military coloration, and the military was clearly a powerful institution. The regime also built a strong internal security apparatus that established a reputation for intrusiveness and ruthlessness. The military was headed by `Abd al-Hakim `Amr, the internal security service by Salah Nasr. Both were former members of the Free Officers.

But it was not only friendship and force that allowed the regime to dominate the state apparatus. The regime founded various new structures that allowed it to wield power more effectively. The sole political party, the Arab

Socialist Union (ASU), was headed at various times by `Ali Sabri, another Free Officer, and by President Nasser himself. Its total control of the parliament allowed the regime to control legislation and any oversight of the cabinet. Membership in the ASU was necessary to practice some professions; the party also owned the daily press. The ASU did not control all structures, but even those that escaped it (such as the religious establishment) saw the regime appoint officials it trusted to positions of authority.

In this way, the regime maintained formal democratic mechanisms: there was an elected parliament; there were periodic referenda in which citizens were asked to approve official policies—and they always did with few dissenting voices.

Yet the regime's control began to loosen in the 1970s. The Free Officers themselves grew older; those who were still active became embroiled in power struggles. When Nasser died in 1970, his successor, Anwar al-Sadat, came to suspect some of the structures (such as the ASU) where potential rivals might be strong, and he moved to cut some down to size (eventually allowing the ASU to be succeeded by a dominant party, the National Democratic Party (NDP), that coexisted with some newly formed opposition parties). He began to speak of a "state of institutions" and allowed some important state structures to have greater autonomy.

The regime still steered the state, but no longer was it able to micromanage it. There was no moment in which the regime systematically rebuilt the Egyptian state, but the rulers gradually found tools—sometimes through trial and error or for initially short-term reasons (like sidelining a potential rival)—that allowed them to maintain overall control. And state institutions could find ways to carve out autonomy or press for more.

Beginning in the 1970s and extending for several decades, the tools available to the regime to steer the state became more subtle.

First, key senior appointments were often in the hands of the president (or occasionally senior actors in the executive such as the prime minister of members of the cabinet). The chief religious officials in the country—for instance, the head of al-Azhar, the minister of religious affairs (responsible for overseeing mosques and pious endowments), and the grand mufti (responsible for giving opinions about Islamic law to state bodies)—were all accountable in such a manner.

Second, these sectors (or important actors within them) could be coopted with benefits. For instance, the regime could weigh in with favors for journalists when it wished to have its candidates win in the state-licensed journalists' association.

Third, there were overlapping authorities within each sector (different court systems that were often at odds with each other or different security services that vied for dominance in a specific domain), and even crossing them (so that courts and security bodies sometimes found themselves clashing over a case). This allowed the regime to play state agencies off against each other or favor one that was proving more useful at a particular time.

Fourth, the legislative process—with legislation drafted in ministries but approved by a parliament dominated by the ruling NDP—could effectively operate only under regime oversight. And finally, in cases where it was deemed necessary, the state had repressive security bodies that the regime could call upon to do its bidding.

In the late Mubarak period—the years after 2000—the nature of the regime and its relationship with the state evolved still further. Several trends came together to reshape the system in some subtle ways.

First, years of economic liberalization had allowed the emergence of wealthy businessmen, some of whom had or sought political influence. We will explore these economic changes in part 3, but for now we note that some patronage networks emerged tying wealthy business leaders to important state structures (such as those involved in construction or finance).

Second, some patronage networks found a place to operate under the umbrella of the NDP—the dominant ruling party that had been created out of the old ASU. We will examine the ASU and its legacy more fully in part 2. For our present purpose, it is worth noting that the older structure had some pretensions to mobilizing the population behind an Arab socialist ideology. In truth, the ASU's ideology was flexible and its mobilization half-hearted at best, but the NDP did not even pretend to have much of an ideology beyond loyalty to the regime and its policies. Indeed, the NDP seemed more interested in taking up political space and guaranteeing a parliamentary majority than to governing or mobilizing, largely through patronage networks built more on personal ties than on ideas or policy positions.[4] Over time, President Mubarak's son, Gamal Mubarak, led a group of business leaders and intellectuals into some prominent positions within the party, and some business leaders seeking official connections sought NDP positions or parliamentary seats under its banner. With that development, the party became more of a gathering place for influential Egyptians who did seek to influence economic policy in particular. The effect on elections was odd—many of the newly influential politician-businessmen were elected as independents and then joined the NDP in parliament after, rather than before, their election. In other words, influential leaders, often with business backgrounds, would show their personal influence by winning elections *before* signing up in support of the regime, generally expecting that their standing would give them more political weight.

Third, the growth of the business community, the rise of loyal but still somewhat independent figures, and the growing significance of some civilian structures (the parliament and the NDP among them) made for more power centers within a regime that seemed a bit less coherent.

And the shifts in the regime were accompanied by an attenuation of its ability to control the state in a coherent manner. The result of this process was a partially fragmented state, one made up of many bureaucracies, agencies, and bodies that were coordinated and dominated by the regime while still enjoying some autonomy. Within each realm, state bodies sometimes owned valuable property, had control over hiring decisions (and, as in many societies, children often followed their parents' professions), and could offer benefits to employees (such as housing projects, help with health care, or membership in private clubs).

The Egyptian cabinet came to represent a gathering of this fragmented state, with each ministry headed by an individual—appointed, to be sure, with the formal approval of the parliament, but effectively serving at the pleasure of the president—from the sector in question. Over time, the minister of justice was always a senior judge; the minister of culture was a leading artist; the minister of defense was a senior officer; the minister of foreign affairs was a senior professional diplomat.

This pattern of regime-state relations allowed the regime to steer the state as a whole, but it also led to an unexpected result: in 2011, when the regime came under strong popular pressure, leading parts of the state discovered that they had an independent will and either failed or simply chose not to protect the presidency. In January and February of that year, as demonstrators gathered in Tahrir Square in the center of Cairo and in other locations throughout the country, they rallied around several cries, among them, "The People Want the Fall of the Regime." The surest sign of that fall would be the departure of longtime president Husni Mubarak, which was finally secured on February 11.

In that way, the stunning events of 2011 comprised a popular uprising. But the state institutions that had shown some autonomy from the regime were themselves left largely intact. In the 2011–2013 period, sharp contestation among political groups occurred—expressed in rival demonstrations, elections, vigorous public debates, and even occasional violence—over the question of how the political system should be redesigned. That struggle, which resulted, among other outcomes, in electoral victories for Islamists and their brief domination of the parliament, a constitution-writing body, and the presidency, showed no sign of abating by the summer of 2013. At that time, the military led a coalition of state bodies (backed by many political movements and members of the public) to overthrow the Islamist presidency.

In subsequent years, a new regime was consolidated—but we postpone the full story of the 2011 uprising and the post-2013 regime for chapter 9. For now, we turn our analysis of regime-state relations to three sets of institutions (judicial, media, and military) to understand how the relationship between the regime and the state it sought to control evolved in practice.

The Judiciary

Egypt's current judicial institutions were built in several waves.[5] The late nineteenth century saw the construction of a set of courts based on the French system (ruling on a modified version of French law codes). These courts handled most cases, with two broad exceptions. First, "personal status" cases—generally covering family law like marriage, divorce, and inheritance—fell under the jurisdiction of a distinct set of courts based on Islamic law (for Muslims) or the dictates of certain religious authorities (for Christians and Jews). Second, cases involving foreigners, or even a foreign interest, were tried by "Mixed Courts" consisting largely of judges from Europe and the Americas (with some Egyptians joining them) because of limitations on Egyptian sovereignty.

When Britain was occupying the country, it found ways to avoid Egyptian courts for cases it found too sensitive—it set up special courts, for instance, to try offenses against British troops. It also declared martial law during World War I to shield colonial authorities from any kind of judicial oversight.

When Egypt became independent in 1922, the government strove to negotiate an end to the Mixed Courts, finally securing their abolition in 1949. During the following decade it also abolished the religious courts, folding their work into the regular court system (but still using religious law as the basis for family matters). Generally, the Egyptian courts seemed free from political interference and judicial bodies gained increasing autonomy over their own affairs. In 1946, legal activists even secured the construction of a new system of administrative courts, designed to ensure that citizens who had a claim against a state body or official could receive a fair hearing. A judicial council, staffed mostly by senior judges, oversaw most of the judiciary's administrative and personnel affairs.

Yet even as the judiciary as a whole retained some autonomy, the country's top political leaders had ways of avoiding the courts when they felt they needed to. In 1939, the leadership declared martial law, dusting off the tool the British had brought to the country in 1914. Subsequent governments expanded these emergency powers; over the past seven decades, Egyptians have enjoyed only brief respites from this "state of emergency" (as martial law came to be called). So when the regime wanted to do things that were outside the normal law—such as detain people without trial or ban groups it distrusted—it often had the ability to do so by bypassing rather than pressuring the judicial apparatus. At first these tools were not often used.

In 1952, however, after the new regime came in, it forged some innovative tools and began using them much more freely. It established a series of special courts to try politicians of the old regime and some of its new opponents (such as the Muslim Brotherhood). It suspended the Constitution and persuaded the administrative courts to go along with its legal measures on the grounds that the country had entered a revolutionary situation. And it used its unchecked power to ban political parties and take other politically repressive measures. In 1954, fearing that the administrative courts would begin ruling against the new rulers' measures, regime supporters stormed the courts and the office of its president, forcing him to resign; a number of judges were dismissed with him.

But that direct attack by the regime on the administrative courts proved to be the exception. For the most part, it allowed the judiciary autonomy in ordinary cases. And ways were found to mold the law to authoritarian ends. Over time, legal figures supportive of the regime wrote constitutions and laws that allowed for nationalizations of much of the economy and the creation of a one-party state. When the regime deemed repressive measures necessary, it could transfer cases to military courts, construct exceptional courts, or simply act completely outside the law with few repercussions.

In all these ways, the judiciary remained part of the state but outside of the regime. While it was not under the regime's direct control, however, most of the time it posed no deep challenge to the regime.

In the late 1960s, however, the regime faced rising popular pressure from some students and workers protesting its policy performance. The country's rulers, fearing a loss of control, moved to rein in any potential challenger. Judges, while state employees, had never been organized in the ASU, and some regime figures, wishing perhaps to control the judiciary more tightly, pressed for their inclusion. In the wake of the 1967 war with Israel, as popular support for the regime seemed to be diminishing, some judges took advantage of the Judges Club, previously a social organization for judges, and used the body to advocate for political reform and to resist inclusion in the sole political party. In 1969, the regime responded forcefully with three measures (referred to collectively as the "massacre of the judiciary"), all taken by presidential decree. First, it dismissed over one hundred sitting judges, generally targeting those who had been active in the Judges Club. Second, it created a new "Supreme Court" that would sit at the apex of the judiciary and consist only of judges appointed by the president. Third, it created a new "Supreme Council of Judicial Organizations," headed by the president. The overall effect was to place the judiciary directly under regime control.

But over the next fifteen years, that control gradually relaxed. In the 1970s, most dismissed judges were rehired. Judicial and legal figures charged with drafting legislation to replace the presidential decrees managed to write a law for the Supreme Court (transforming it into the Supreme Constitutional Court) that gave the body a strong say over its own composition. While the chief justice of the court remained a presidential appointment, the Supreme Constitutional Court managed to persuade the president to follow a tradition of appointing the most senior member. And the Supreme Council of Judicial Organizations generally had its authority transferred back to bodies that were headed by judicial figures rather than regime officials. Those bodies also generally followed the principle of seniority rather than loyalty to the regime when making appointments.

In that sense, the regime moved back to its previous approach. It allowed the judiciary independence but wrote authoritarian laws and built in escape hatches (exceptional courts, states of emergency) when those laws were not enough. When the regime moved to repress a resurgent Muslim

Brotherhood, for example, it moved the resulting cases to military courts. When regular courts began acquitting those who showed evidence that they had been tortured, the regime moved their cases to exceptional courts.

And the regime could still manipulate the judiciary through subtler means than those it deployed in 1969. The Ministry of Justice could assign favorites to lucrative work overseeing public-sector companies or second them for work in other Arab countries where there were more material benefits. Some judges criticized such practices and tried to revive the Judges Club as a structure that could call for reform and an end to emergency rule. The regime sometimes dangled out incentives (higher salaries, more resources) to co-opt judges, showing them that if they avoided rocking the boat they could benefit. The result was to set off tensions among judges, between those who wished to press publicly for reform and those who saw such efforts as dangerous and politically, rather than legally, motivated.

In 2011, during the mass uprising against the regime, the judiciary largely stood aside, though individual judges made their inclinations clear and many participated in public debates. More significantly, most of the political struggles of the next several years were carried out in part in a legal and constitutional language that allowed the courts to play a significant political role. And that they did, dissolving a parliament and a constituent assembly, meting out harsh sentences to opponents of the post-2013 regime, and serving as a battlefield on which contending political forces would ultimately clash. We will return to the judiciary's role in post-2011 politics in chapter 9.

The Media

The Egyptian media showed a similar evolution from greater to lesser control—with the regime again stopping short of allowing total freedom. In Egypt before 1952, print media (newspapers and magazines) were in private hands. Many had political inclinations toward various parties (and some were quietly subsidized by political forces), but regulation was light. In post-1952 Egypt, however, print media were nationalized, the regime established new newspapers, and journalists were required to join the ASU. Broadcast media were monopolized by the state, with the result that all media were state media—and the regime had tools (ownership, censorship, party discipline) to control almost everything published or broadcast.

Media restrictions loosened slightly in the 1970s. Oversight of state-run media was transferred from the ASU to a newly created upper house of parliament. Formal censorship was eased, so that state-run media were now controlled a bit less directly—generally by allowing those in key editorial positions loyal to (and sometimes selected by) the president freer rein within their domains. Opposition parties were allowed to publish newspapers, first on a weekly basis. There were still mechanisms of control: they were kept financially viable through advertisements by state-owned enterprises; they were printed on state-run presses; and when they became too critical they could be harassed in various ways, sometimes to the point that they ceased publication. But a series of court judgments actually widened opposition newspapers' room for maneuver, especially from the 1980s on.

Far more significant, however, was the entry of new media. In the 1990s, pan-Arab newspapers (often edited in London or elsewhere) were circulated widely and Arab satellite broadcasters were able to attract an Egyptian audience. A few independent Egyptian newspapers arose in the 1990s; these multiplied in the early 2000s. Some were commercially quite successful as Egyptians flocked to independent media. The regime still had powerful tools. For instance, it could harass individual journalists (and did); it could complain to the countries hosting the satellite broadcasters (which were generally run by foreign states or members of ruling families); and it could threaten to block distribution or remove state advertising. But in the first decade of the twenty-first century, Egypt's media environment was far more cacophonous than it had been during the 1960s.[6]

Social media added a new layer of cacophony as Egyptians took to Facebook and SMS messaging with enthusiasm. Security agencies could (and did) monitor what was said on these platforms, and they eventually found tools to manipulate discussion on social media, but the task was much more complicated and uneven than it had been at the height of the Nasserist era.

The Military

Like the judiciary, the Egyptian military has a long institutional history, and it also has a corporate sense of mission that identifies it with the Egyptian state. Indeed, in its public-facing ethos—and likely internally as well—the military carved out a powerful, existential role for itself in the life of the Egyptian nation: Egyptian officers often talk of their role as protecting the society against all threats.⁷

But if both the judiciary and the military have a strong connection to the state, they have had different relationships with the regime. At times, the military has been a pillar of the regime; at others, it has brought the regime down. And at still other times, it has formed the regime.

In the second half of the nineteenth century, Egyptian rulers—then nominally under the sovereignty of the Ottoman Empire but effectively independent—were prevented by weak public finances and European pressure from constructing an extensive military apparatus. When fiscal pressures led to delayed salary payments and when other resentments about ill-treatment boiled over, officers formed an alliance with civilian critics of the ruler. Colonel Ahmad 'Urabi emerged at the head first of the military and then of an alternative national leadership. What came to be called the "'Urabi Revolt" (or Revolution) eventually led the ruler of the khedival state to flee. He obtained British backing that returned him to power, but with the country now occupied by British troops. 'Urabi and his leading supporters were placed on trial and the army nearly dismantled. Thus the Egyptian military's first political intervention of modern times ended not only in defeat but with harmful results for the military as an institution.

The second military intervention, in 1952, ended quite differently, with officers coming to form the backbone of the regime. Since that time, many Egyptians have referred to their political order as a "military" system, but that phrase is both exaggerated and masks the various political stances the military as an institution has adopted vis-à-vis the regime.

When Egypt became formally independent in 1922, and especially in 1936, when it signed a treaty of alliance with Great Britain, the Egyptian regime decided to expand the army somewhat, recruiting officers through a military training academy that was open to the middle classes. Those officers, who came of age in a time of rising political agitation, formed the backbone of the officer corps during the 1948 war over the creation of the State of Israel. Some of them charged that they had been sent into battle by a regime that had not provided them what they needed to win. Eventually, in 1952, a select group (the Free Officers) overthrew the parliamentary monarchy. While at first claiming that they wished only to reform the political system, the Free Officers gradually began to term their movement a "revolution." They formed a "Revolutionary Command Council" that ruled the country unimpeded for two years and then dissolved itself, with its leader, Nasser, then elected to the presidency.

From 1952 to the mid-1970s, the regime was comprised of figures from the military's senior ranks, but the military as an institution did not rule. Many ministers, leading officials, and, of course, the president himself came from the military. But the results were not always conducive to the military's stated mission of protecting the country; the officer corps became politicized and acted according to personal loyalties, adversely impacting the military's performance in interstate conflicts.

And indeed, after 1967—when the defense minister and chief of staff, Field Marshall 'Abd al-Hakim 'Amr (a former Free Officer), was accused of plotting a coup in the wake of the country's defeat by Israel—and especially after Nasser's death in 1970, the regime slowly diminished the role of army officers in many governmental spheres not connected with the military's core mission. This was not a full exit. Both of Nasser's successors as president, Anwar al-Sadat (a former Free Officer) and Husni Mubarak (who rose to the position of commander of the Air Force), hailed from military backgrounds. And retired officers often filled key positions—as provincial governors, for instance, or as the heads of public-sector companies. But the regime's civilian face was given greater emphasis. Top positions were increasingly filled by technocrats; economic policy was increasingly determined by economists and private-sector business leaders; other parts of the state (such as the judiciary) saw a greater number of leadership positions filled by people without military backgrounds; and the president surrounded himself with more civilian than military figures.

The overall result was to reshape the relationship between the military and the regime, with the former supportive of but no longer playing so active and visible a role in the latter. No longer was the military the backbone of the regime; the officer corps saw its political role diminished (though it never quite disappeared). Within its own realm, the military was able to run its affairs with considerable autonomy. The officer corps formed a closed environment within the larger society, with their own clubs, substantial perquisites, and favored residential neighborhoods. The military budget was kept outside of any mechanisms of civilian oversight, and the substantial American assistance program (dating back to the mid-1970s but substantially increased after the Egyptian-Israeli peace treaty of 1979) was devoted primarily to the military. In that sense, the military lost influence over many day-to-day political matters but gained autonomy over its own affairs.

And it was this military that found the ability to speak forcefully with its own voice when the regime was threatened by the popular uprising in January 2011. And it was the military as an institution—not individual officers or secret rings of officers—that acted. That month, the military's top command ousted Mubarak from its own supreme decision-making structure, the Supreme Council of the Armed Forces (SCAF). When it announced that Mubarak had stepped down on February 11, suspending the Constitution on the same day, the SCAF assumed the position of interim president in a system with the authority to issue interim constitutions, promulgate laws, and appoint and dismiss ministers. From both a practical and a legal standpoint, the SCAF *was* the regime until a new president was elected and a new constitutional order put in place.

That order slowly took shape in 2011 and 2012—but it was not one that excluded the military, which continued to play a leading political role even as a civilian president was elected and a new constitution was written. With the overthrow of Muhammad Morsi in July 2013, however, the military took on a new role. To be sure, the interim president was from the country's Supreme Constitutional Court, and a new constitution was written by a collection of judges, civilian officials, and political actors. But it was clear that the military was overseeing the process. To preserve its position, the military vetoed constitutional clauses that might diminish its authority (such as one that would have barred military trials for civilians), and ultimately endorsed the decision of its new head, `Abd al-Fattah al-Sisi, to run for the presidency. In that sense, the military was more than the regime's backbone and recruiting ground, as it had been in the 1950s and 1960s. It was now taking on the duty, as an institution, of reconstituting a new Egyptian regime.

THE EGYPTIAN REGIME TODAY

We began this chapter by observing that the fuzziness of the distinction between regime and state is sometimes itself worthy of attention. And we have seen that in practice in the evolution of the regime in Egypt. During the 1950s and 1960s, the regime seemed to control most aspects of the state in a way that was difficult to disentangle; over the subsequent decades, state bodies often gained in their ability to form independent agendas within their own realm—the judiciary in legal affairs; the media with public debate; and the military in security affairs—though this took place in the context of continuing authoritarianism and without threatening the regime itself.

In 2011, however, the system came apart. As various Egyptian groups mobilized, key parts of the state apparatus remained on the sidelines; more interested in protecting the state than the regime, they were willing to cast the ruler aside. In 2013, as Egyptian society showed increasing polarization between Islamists and their opponents, various parts of the state apparatus—including the police and other security and intelligence forces, the judiciary, state media, and the official religious apparatus—all came together under military leadership to endorse regime change and try to build a new regime. That process has succeeded to an extent—it has returned a military figure to the presidency, who in turn has sought to control the entire state apparatus. Yet the system being built since 2013 is not a recreation of that which existed in the 1950s and 1960s. We will return to a full consideration of its nature to chapter 9.

PART II
Egyptian Society

In this section, we will be going over some familiar ground: the story of state control and partial retreat that we told in part 1 will now be examined by placing Egyptian society rather than state structures at the center. In other words, we will add to the analysis of the Egyptian state by examining Egyptian society. But in the process, we will hardly leave the state behind.

Indeed, we will look first in chapter 4 at how the Egyptian regime used the state apparatus in the middle of the twentieth century to structure Egyptian society in a pattern seen elsewhere and often dubbed "corporatism." Seeing the Egyptian attempt that way will alert us to some commonalities with other countries, particularly in Latin America—not simply how corporatism operates but how it can fray for a variety of reasons. The Egyptian experience is not identical to that of Latin American societies (which themselves show great variety). However, since those regimes and societies faced similar questions and issues, elucidating a comparison between the two will also show what happens when state corporatism frays. The outcome in Egypt was, by and large, distinct. In Latin America the decay of corporatism was associated with a variety of regime changes (with bouts of authoritarianism and some moves toward democracy). But in Egypt the regime stayed in power, loosening its grip in some areas without losing it. Why? Chapter 4 will therefore begin by probing the comparison and then proceed to an analysis of Egyptian corporatism—how it was built and operated, and how it decayed somewhat. In some ways, the story will be told from the vantage point of the regime.

In chapter 5, our vantage point will shift slightly, from that of the regime to various social actors. We will also pick up the story at a later date—namely, the 1990s, when an unevenly liberalized authoritarian system seemed well established but when various groups rose up inside and outside the decayed corporatist structures and discovered oppositional and critical voices and a limited ability to resist the regime. That resistance, and the regime's efforts to retain control, dominated much of the politics of the 1990s and early 2000s. The dynamic changed dramatically in and after 2011. However, we will reserve that part of the story for the book's final chapter.

Part 2 will conclude with an examination of religion in Egyptian politics, society, and economics in chapter 6. Religion is clearly an important part of Egyptian life, and it is woven into each of the other sections. But it is significant enough to warrant a separate examination, even though it cuts across the three divisions we have imposed on our understanding of Egypt: there are political, social, and economic aspects to religion, and we will examine each in turn. By treating it this way, we would seem to imply that there is something distinctive about religion in Egypt, and indeed there are some distinctive elements. But there are also commonalities with other societies (designation of an official religion, for instance, is quite common throughout the world), so we will not drop our comparative focus.

Chapter Four

THE RISE AND DECAY OF SOCIAL CONTROL— AND THE PERPETUATION OF AUTHORITARIANISM

How—and how much—can authoritarian regimes control society?

After the military coup of 1952, Colonel Gamal 'Abdel Nasser and a group of fellow military officers who had dubbed themselves the "Free Officers" began to champion an extensive social and economic agenda, including land redistribution, nationalization, and investment in public services. These state-led development policies ushered in an era of tight social control that was not just about reforming and developing Egypt's economy. The regime followed different tactics to crush existing or rising social forces and to induce others to toe its line. The Free Officers' regime championed an "alliance of the working forces of the people" to encapsulate a broad spectrum of social sectors ruled by the evolving military-bureaucratic elite that led the state apparatus and used it to dominate the entire political system.

COMPARATIVE CORPORATISM

Of course, this was not the first regime to follow such a path. Egypt's post-1952 regime adopted a general approach, termed "corporatism," that has been identified in many other settings. The concept of corporatism offers a perspective for understanding how authoritarian regimes organize society into groups, secure their obedience and loyalty, and channel their demands.

Corporatism is not always authoritarian; there are variants that have worked in democratic contexts, though they tend to be much looser and less dominated by the state.[1] Authoritarian corporatism—or "state corporatism," as it is often called—works by officially established monopolistic and hierarchical patterns of interest representation. In other words, the society is organized into a set of organizations that have each secured domination over their respective sectors (for instance, with a single, state-licensed labor union). These are then coordinated by the state, which thus takes on a strong role by sponsoring the formation of various social groups, granting them a monopoly over representation within their sectors, shaping their internal organizational structures, and channeling their demands through official institutions. Social actors, therefore, seek to harmonize relations with their respective groups, classes, and sectors, and their organizations control their demand making and interaction with public institutions.

When it works, corporatism can allow the regime to control politics. But this control can decay; corporatist systems can lose their grip for a variety of internal and external reasons. Constituencies formed by regimes can discover their own voices and mobilize on their own, working to secure gains (such as higher wages) outside of official channels. The collection of carrots (like economic benefits) and sticks (such as suppressing dissidents) might not work as well over time—especially at times of fiscal crisis, leading to a loss of official control. Regimes might feel forced to make concessions (higher wages; more democratic rights) or crack down (more repression) in order to maintain their position as their tools begin to fray. The decline of these corporatist structures usually represents a critical juncture at which authoritarian regimes face a choice between two divergent trajectories: they can democratize, recognizing their loss of control over social groups, or they can double down through the use of greater repression to suppress rising demands from previously advantaged groups.

In Latin America, populist leaders were not able to maintain their dominance forever; the sectors whose members they mobilized often began to strain at the controls placed on them. State-managed labor unions, for instance, took on an agenda of their own, leading to widening strikes, demonstrations, political crisis, and sometimes regime collapse. Sometimes the collapse of populist rule was followed by a military regime that attempted to demobilize the population by dismantling unions, suppressing political opposition, and preventing demonstrations. Sometimes gentler and more competitive regimes could be built that allowed democracy to continue within bounds. The first (authoritarian) path was not permanent either and generally gave way to democracy in the last part of the twentieth century.[2]

In Egypt, some decay occurred when the regime began to falter in its policy performance. But Egypt represents a puzzling case because the regime avoided either of the choices described above. It neither democratized nor doubled down using repressive tools. There was a post-corporatist liberalization process, but it was not accompanied by full-fledged democratization—yet neither did it trigger more repressive tendencies and exclusionary policies to suppress popular demands.

When we compare the Egyptian experience with the corporatist arrangements that prevailed in Latin America throughout the 1930s and 1940s, we immediately uncover some clear similarities—but also some critical differences that are especially apparent in hindsight.

This chapter will show how the Free Officers' regime differed from various populist regimes in Latin America—most notably, populist corporatist regimes (the Peronist regime in Argentina of the 1940s and 1950s; radical populism in Mexico after 1917; and populist Brazil from 1930 to 1964). The Latin American regimes depended heavily on massive participation, popular mobilization, and inducement (rather than demobilization and depoliticization) to sustain their grip on power. In other words, they tried to mobilize supporters much more thoroughly. They used corporatism to mobilize these supporters, not demobilize the society. The Free Officers *appeared* to do the same (they held mass rallies and plebiscites), making them appear populist to many observers at the time. But in reality, outside of those symbolic steps they actually discouraged political organization.

Therefore, while Egyptian corporatism looked a bit like its Latin American counterpart as it was being built, it was far more authoritarian and less interested in mobilizing the population. Indeed, it was never as fully committed to organizing its supporters as some other varieties of state corporatism—such as those in Mussolini's Italy or Velasco's Peru. In Egypt, state-corporatist mechanisms were occasionally used to stage mass rallies or turn out loyal voters, but their real purpose seemed to be to control and manage more than mobilize. Thus, when the corporatism that was built in the 1950s and 1960s began to run into trouble by the late 1960s and early 1970s, it left a very different residue that made either full democratization or heightened repression both unlikely and unnecessary. But, rather than lead to democratization or deepened dictatorship, it was followed by a mild political opening in Egypt after the early 1970s, one that re-formed the social coalition underpinning the regime and maintained the corporatist pattern of interest representation.

But if it eschewed both democracy and deepened dictatorship, how did it sustain itself? How did the regime sustain authoritarianism when it relaxed some controls in the 1970s? Since it had never really encouraged mass mobilization, the regime could draw on three coping strategies that its Latin American counterparts did not have or would not have found as useful to organize its relations with social groups.

First, the regime continued to use legal and extralegal measures to control society. The harsh legal environment and the arbitrary enforcement of rules offered the regime a tool to monitor and regulate the activities of social groups. The regime also sought to underscore a division between a moderate and radical opposition, allowing those who accepted the basic contours of the system an open (if circumscribed) political role.

Second, Egypt's leaders co-opted the top echelon of corporatist organizations, widening the schism between the leadership and social bases of these organizations. This allowed the regime to shore up support and undermine the bargaining power and mobilizing capacity of different social groups.

Third, the regime created a pressure release valve by offering a venue for opposition groups to express discontent without undermining the regime's control. The party system provides an excellent vantage point from which to see how the regime evolved and adjusted to the decay of corporatism.

Though these measures collectively marked a significant shift from the noncompetitive corporatist structure bequeathed by the Free Officers' regime, the inclusion of political opposition remained limited and reversible. The regime continued to incorporate new actors and pit them against each other. For instance, as Islamists grew in influence in Egyptian society, the regime not only found ways to play Islamist against non-Islamist forces but also to divide the Islamists by treating them differently (some were allowed to operate socially as long as they did not dabble in politics; some were allowed limited influence as a way of undermining the radicals). In this way, the regime created a more divided oppositional structure, allowing more parties in the political sphere while at the same time excluding significant opposition forces, most notably the Muslim Brotherhood. Although the Brotherhood had been formally integrated into the parliament and the professional syndicates since the late 1980s, the regime repeatedly resorted to the legal system to treat the Brotherhood as an illegal group or informal opposition and to prohibit the formation of any religious party.

Contrary to the experiences of some Latin American countries, pluralist policies in Egypt reflected more an evolution of the regime than a sudden change in its nature or structure. The Egyptian experience suggests that political liberalization and corporatism have not been diametrically opposed patterns of social representation. Both ways of organizing social interests coexisted, switching positions of relative precedence in successive epochs and across various sectors and policy areas. Thus, the system evolved in several ways until the uprising of 2011, when it came under very strong social pressure that led first to unstable and inconsistent moves toward democratization before its reverting to increased authoritarianism—but this last part of the story we will reserve for chapter 9. The present chapter focuses on the Free Officers' regime and how it deployed a demobilizing strategy to control popular demands and to undermine the autonomy of diverse social groups.

We move first to a more detailed definition of corporatism as a framework of interest representation that differentiates between the corporatist framework in Egypt and its counterparts Latin America. We then move to explore the initial attempts of the Free Officers' regime to incorporate the popular sectors (i.e., workers and peasants). We also show the regime's strategy to control and dominate professional syndicates that were opposed to their incorporation into one overarching federation. Finally, we explain how the regime gradually opened politically while stopping well short of democracy, which involved the introduction of pluralist (albeit restricted) party politics that went in tandem with the decline in old corporatist arrangements.

CORPORATISM AND INTEREST REPRESENTATION

Corporatism refers to a formal and limited system of representation wherein interest groups are controlled and regulated by the state. It is a way for the state to decide how society should be organized and to regulate which groups can form and who will speak for them. The goal is to have one organization representing one sector and for the state to coordinate among these large, officially recognized groups. Of course, regulation of social activity is common. But in pluralist societies, there might be many groups—regulated or not—existing in the same sector of society or seeking to organize the society in crosscutting ways. In the corporatist model, the state plays a more active role, not only in organizing or regulating social groups, but also in recognizing and identifying groups' role in the decision-making process, deciding which ones are allowed to operate, determining who can lead them and how they can function, and granting each organization a monopoly over its sector. So a single trade union confederation might be allowed while ethnic groups are barred. The state, therefore, creates a corporatist framework through: (a) *structuring* interest representation, which involves the official recognition of groups' occupational categories and the monopoly of representation within their respective categories; (b) *subsidizing* groups by transferring public funds or imposing compulsory membership fees; (c) *controlling* leadership selection, demand making, and financial resources, which makes the leadership derive legitimacy from the state, rather than from organizations' members.[3]

Corporatist relationships are thus based on two pillars: "inducements" and "constraints." Structuring and subsidizing groups' organizations represent benefits for them in exchange for their acquiescence to the state's control. The corporatist strategy in Latin America was part and parcel of regimes' economic orientation throughout the 1940s and 1950s, which revolved around the introduction of a state-led development strategy known as import substitution industrialization (ISI). Under ISI, states encouraged industrialization in areas where countries had imported finished products. The policy was common among developing states during this period, and it sometimes led to significant industrialization, generally built up with some state support, such as providing encouragement to investors or the implementation of tariffs to protect the new industries. It also created winners (those with jobs in factories, industrialists) and losers (wealthy consumers who had to pay more because of tariffs; farmers who found that state support shifted from agriculture to industry).

The ISI policy—relying on industry rather than agriculture—both allowed and encouraged regimes to undermine landed elites, channel societal demands, and restructure economic relations in industry and agriculture. In Egypt, as in other countries pursuing ISI, the regime sought to expand its social base by mobilizing broad mass support of hitherto excluded workers. The new Egyptian regime discovered that peasants, who had been excluded as well, could benefit and be brought into its support base by a land reform program at the expense of the old landed elite.

The leaders of Egypt, like their Latin American counterparts, thus followed a mixed strategy of "inducements" and "constraints" by granting a monopoly of representation to some organizations and suppressing others. This strategy helped the regime to undermine old elites, outflank more radical organizations, and promote those favored by the government.[4]

The installation of strong corporatist frameworks during the 1950s depended on four main factors to reshape power structures in Egypt and Latin American societies. First, the organizational strength and ideological unity of the ruling elite was a crucial factor that determined the ability of corporatist arrangements to successfully control society. Second, the preexistence of autonomous political parties and interest groups structured along noncorporatist lines in civil society affected the potential resistance to, or support for, the state's attempts to subsume society. Third, the intensity of societal polarization affected both coalitional possibilities available to the state elites and their will to exclude and repress particular constituents in society. Finally, the reach of the state—its coercive capacity and economic role—affected the rulers' ability to redistribute wealth, incorporate excluded groups into new corporatist structures, and control the rising demands of the newly incorporated groups.[5]

But this is where Egypt also began to diverge from its Latin American counterparts. Contrary to the path taken elsewhere, corporatist policies in Egypt did not aim at creating mass organizations to mobilize supporters, stimulating class conflict, or instigating political mobilization along rigid ideological lines. The society that the regime operated in had not been strongly organized to begin with, and some potential opposition (such as from those whose wealth was based on the export of raw materials and import of finished products and who were therefore likely to be harmed by ISI) had lost some international support (namely, with the end of the capitulations).

Corporatist organizations still served as instruments to support the regime's economic policies and push through social reforms. The state sought to marginalize forces that supported the precolonial arrangements (i.e., landowners) and to co-opt sectors that would sustain the state's new ISI development strategy (i.e., workers and peasants). But it did not need to mobilize its own supporters in any but symbolic ways because the policy encountered few powerful opponents (especially after Nasser's harsh crack down on the Brotherhood, as detailed below).

The Free Officers' regime enjoyed elite unity but lacked the practical ideology and solid organizational bases needed to atomize rival groups. There was an official ideology embodied in the National Charter of 1962 to justify the nationalization of industrial sectors, but the doctrinal elements were not related to any set of social/political principles. "Arab socialism" stressed social harmony, downplayed class struggles, and delegitimized any challenges to the regime's authority. The belief in the state's ability to guide far-reaching social and economic change had a leftward tilt but it was reinforced by a nationalist and patriotic discourse. These vague ideological proclivities were translated into both a direct economic role for the state and a strong position for workers and peasants in the planned economy.

The state's strong role in the economy allowed it to install a new pattern of power relations in society that expanded beyond economic matters. The Free Officers outlawed political parties and eliminated any densely organized or hostile associational networks. Media organizations were nationalized so no dissident voices were heard. A single political party was formed that contained and coordinated all organized groups, ensuring they all toed the official line.

Control extended to the religious space, where the new regime confronted the Muslim Brotherhood. Following a brief honeymoon between the Free Officers and the Brotherhood, the mood turned sour. The regime accused the Brotherhood of attempting to assassinate Nasser after one of the group's member opened fire on him during a public speech in October 1954. An initial wave of repression intensified greatly: thousands were incarcerated with or without trial, and a number of leading Brotherhood figures were sentenced to death by military tribunals.

Repression was not the regime's only tool, however. Professional associations (the Bar Association for lawyers, professional syndicates for medical doctors, and so on) had taken on an overt political role (instead of merely focusing on narrow professional matters) under the old regime, often taking up the nationalist cause against a continued British role in Egyptian politics. Professional syndicates, therefore, represented a potential ally to mobilize an educated middle class around the Free Officers regime. But they also signified a potential threat by organizing masses around ideas and demands that the regime was not willing to accommodate. Thus, the post-1952 regime aimed not to disband the syndicates or treat them with raw repression but simply to depoliticize them and place them in the hands of supporters. The regime's strategy centered on co-opting the syndicates' leadership, securing changes in their internal bylaws (such as allowing public-sector lawyers—who, as government employees, were more likely to be loyal—into the Bar Association), and undertaking arbitrary—and often retributive—measures to emasculate the professional elites and keep them acquiescent to the regime's policy.

The system made the regime seem very solid indeed. The stick was branded effectively to intimidate, while the carrot was used to co-opt. But both approaches met with trouble. On the first, we have seen in the previous section how the repressive apparatus—especially internal security bodies—came to be seen as a state within the state and a potential threat to the regime. But it is the second that concerns us here. The corporatist carrot was based on two contradictory processes: investment in production and consumption of welfare goods and public services. Over the long term, this led to competing demands.

ISI required the state to squeeze much of the economy to invest in and reward new industries. Political loyalty required the regime to supply social services, subsidize basic commodities, and generate employment. The state had to offer some material rewards, such as employment security, better working conditions, free education, and health insurance, to attract workers' and peasants' support.

Some similar strains emerged in Latin America, leading to political crisis. Unions that had supported a given regime began to push against corporatist control. Industrialists who profited from public investment and tariffs began to feel the regime was no longer able to provide for economic growth. In short, as cooperation with the state began to bring groups less reward, they began to push against state control and regulation. And the resulting crisis led to breakdown—often resulting in deepened authoritarianism, especially over the short term.[6]

When a similar set of problems arose in Egypt, they appeared in less pressing form. The problems were real but there was a much-reduced threat of opposition, as the regime had hardly mobilized the opposition and still controlled corporatist arrangements. Those arrangements came under pressure; there were some strikes by workers, calls for reform from professional associations, and demonstrations by student groups in the late 1960s in particular; but while the threat to the regime was notable, it was not existential. The groups were still readily amenable to manipulation from above through an amalgam of legal inducements and constraints. The Egyptian regime did not need to atomize social opponents and control rising popular demands as there were few strong or autonomous occupational sectors with robust corporate traditions of their own (we have already seen how there was an effort to ensure that professional associations did not play such a role). Worker and peasant organizations were only vehicles for alliance building and there were no diverse patterns of sociopolitical mobilizations. But the Free Officers' regime, finding its policies under pressure, realized that it had to take preemptive measures to ensure that latent opposition did not become manifest, that professional associations did not become radicalized, and that wide constituencies did not form groups outside of the state's corporatist structures of control, like the Muslim Brotherhood.

By the end of the 1970s, the political regime battled economic hardship to sustain the corporatist arrangements. The result was an attempt to move from the clearly defined controls of corporatism to a limited relaxation, as Egypt's rulers worked to calibrate the degree of repression, control, and incentives by sector to contain, prevent, co-opt, and manipulate various constituencies. This was not one-way liberalization—the regime occasionally imposed a more centralized and uniform version of corporatism to crush dissent. Following severe riots in 1977, for example, which were spearheaded by workers and students in response to the removal of subsidies on bread and other essential food elements, the regime engaged in open struggles with all political opposition, several occupational groups, and a number of religious organizations. But even such a reversal could itself be reversed. Such was the case in the mid-1980s, when the regime reverted to a more selective strategy of coordination with political opposition and carefully avoided all efforts to refashion groups' organizations into a coercive system of representation.

In the following sections, we investigate these two periods in more detail. We look first at how the Free Officers' regime built a system to incorporate workers, peasants, and others without truly mobilizing them (from

1952 until the mid 1970s). Then we explore how the regime dealt with the pressures on, and shortcomings of, these arrangements in the following decades.

PREEMPTIVE EFFORTS AT RESTRUCTURING SOCIETY: INCORPORATING WORKERS AND PEASANTS (1952-1975)

After the installation of the Free Officers' regime, the enactment of corporatist politics was gradual, appearing in retrospect to be a series of steps taken for tactical reasons and therefore somewhat inadvertent overall. The ongoing process of restructuring society vacillated according to the immediate priorities of the new regime, between co-optation and preemption on the one hand and coercion and repression on the other. The regime organized a series of all-encompassing national rallies to capture the support of the popular classes benefitting from its socioeconomic reform programs (like land redistribution), to co-opt potential dissidents, and to repress stalwart opponents. The Liberation Rally (with its slogan "Unity, Liberty, and Work") was created in 1953 to replace the old political parties outlawed by the regime, preempt new ones, and organize popular mobilization in support of the regime.

The National Union succeeded the Liberation Rally in 1956 after Nasser became president. Its establishment was a more serious, rather than preemptive, attempt to structure political life. The Union led a new phase of strong state involvement in the economy, which was reflected in its slogan of "Socialism, Cooperativism, and Democracy."

Finally, all efforts to establish efficient political institutions to facilitate decision-making processes culminated in the creation of the Arab Socialist Union (ASU) in 1961. The regime wished to reorganize society and align it with the leftward policies proclaimed by Nasser (including widespread nationalizations) in 1961. But as it moved left, it also repressed active communists, so it needed its own structure to mobilize society and to isolate adversaries it described as "reactionary" or "feudal." The president dealt with the ASU as an extension of the central administration. The ASU was run by Nasser's own loyal political allies and penetrated villages, urban districts, and educational institutions. Membership in the ASU was also essential for appointment to any local, regional, or national assembly, or the board of any union, cooperative, or professional association.[7]

As the new regime consolidated itself, it gradually transitioned from one headed by the Free Officers to a presidential one dominated by Nasser, a process that began in the mid-1950s. The president also headed the ASU, making it the centerpiece of the entire system.

The regime regularized this new system with a new law (Law 32 of 1964) that tightened the state's control over the voluntary associations and continued to organize state-society relations until it was finally replaced the late 1990s. The law obliged all social associations to inform the Ministry of Social Affairs (MOSA) in advance of the dates of the meetings of their general assemblies and boards of directors. The law extended the authority of the MOSA by stipulating that "the special administrative authority has the right to terminate any decision taken by association's authorities if it violates . . . the public system . . . or the moral system."[8] The MOSA, therefore, had the right to license, dissolve, accept or reject members of social associations and their boards of directors, and to veto any decision they made. Moreover, it had the prerogative to judge certain acts by members as criminal offences that could lead to imprisonment for up to six months.

How did the new system operate at its height? To answer this question, we will examine three sectors in detail in turn—labor unions, agriculture, and professional associations—studying how the arrangements came into being, how they worked, and how they came under pressure by the 1970s.

Dynamics of Labor Co-optation

The Egyptian regime had to work to bring labor on board. While some Latin American countries, such as Mexico and Peru, managed to sustain the support of an already existing and relatively powerful labor movement, the Free Officers' regime came in without any such alliance. In Mexico, for instance, organized labor took part in the revolution of 1917; by the 1930s, the regime consolidated its power by turning first to labor for its social base and then to land reform to mobilize peasants, allowing it to circumvent older economic and political elites. The corporatist organizations of popular sectors became constituent parts of the dominant party, the former seen as being naturally integrated into one harmonious polity under the authoritative leadership of the statist party.[9]

The co-optation of labor movements in Egypt, however, was not an easy task. The movements' contentious relations with pre-1952 Egyptian governments, coupled with the existence of other political forces that had reached out to labor (partisans of the Wafd, the Brotherhood, the communists), led the regime at first not toward an alliance but a mixture of coercion and repression, responding to events as it arose.[10]

Rather than being greeted with an open hand, labor first felt the new regime's fist. Only two weeks after the military takeover in 1952, workers went on strike and worked to organize an independent federation in a textile factory in Kafr al-Dawar, outside Alexandria. The regime responded harshly by executing two workers' leaders, signaling the regime's intolerance of any disruptive behavior. The new leaders, however, took the immediate precaution of implementing favorable new laws for the workers, by which they sought to send a message that it was not entirely hostile. Continuing with this carrot-and-stick approach, the regime introduced laws that banned strikes but guaranteed job security and better working conditions. However, another two thousand workers demonstrated in the Cairo suburb of Imbaba in 1953 for improved working conditions, defying the regime's tacit insistence that it would provide benefits but obtain full obedience. The regime responded with a harsh crackdown and widespread arrests. The repression was followed once again by concessions to further guarantee workers' job security. By the end of this cycle of repression and concession, it had become almost impossible, from both a financial and a bureaucratic standpoint, for an employer to dismiss a worker without a very strong reason.

This set of tactics evolved into a strategy in which unions were gradually brought into full-fledged corporatist structures—obedient but privileged—between 1957 and 1964. The creation of the Egyptian Trade Union Federation (ETUF) in 1957 streamlined the organization of unions by placing them under the umbrella of one of 121 newly established federations. Between 1959 and 1964, a set of laws were laid down regulating trade union organizations and all aspects of employment. The Unified Labor Code of 1959 created the pyramid structure of the trade unions, with company unions at the bottom clustered together according to field of activity in national unions. The national unions formed the middle layer of the pyramid, while at the top sat the ETUF. The new national unions were empowered to negotiate and ratify collective work contracts. A new post of minister of labor was also created and given the power to dissolve any union opposing the Constitution.[11]

In addition, the Trade Union Law 62 of 1964 regulated employment and membership in various occupational sectors. The law "reduced the weekly working hours in industrial establishments to 42 hours, doubled the minimum wage, introduced a social insurance scheme, obliged the government to provide administrative jobs to all university graduates, and guaranteed worker representation on the management boards of all the public-sector companies."[12] These inducement measures were followed by the reinforcement of stringent state control. The same laws that required ASU membership for union candidates and banned labor activism could also be used to penalize and deny ASU membership and the opportunity to run for union positions.

The regime's strategy of co-optation and coercion paid off after Egypt's defeat in the 1967 war with Israel. The military failure produced an ideological disillusionment across the country that manifested in mass marches organized by student activists. The workweek increased from forty-two to forty-eight hours without compensation and paid holidays were canceled in the name of sacrifice for the "battle." But while there was some unrest among workers, the regime managed to persuade industrial workers of Helwan (a major factory town just south of Cairo where many of Egypt's new industries were located) to disengage from the marches. With worker participation staved off, the regime managed to isolate the student movements.

But just as they had proved their usefulness in the midst of a grave crisis following military defeat, the new arrangements came under stress. The regime's economic development plans and public-sector enterprises were beginning to run into difficulties. As we will see in part 3, the regime felt compelled to adopt a measure of economic liberalization. The new policy, dubbed *infitah* (opening) was pursued unevenly. But any liberalization would mean the possibility of whittling away benefits given to workers and small farmers in order to attract investment and lift state control. For instance, Law 43 of 1974 on joint ventures eroded workers' rights of profit sharing and worker representation on boards of directors. Workers in those public enterprises that entered into joint ventures with foreign capital automatically came under the law governing private-sector companies.

These economic policies indeed triggered protests, the most violent of which took place in the predominantly textile-manufacturing area of Mahalla al-Kubra in March 1975. In 1977, food riots broke out throughout the country after the regime tried to liberalize prices by lifting bread subsidies.

With corporatist arrangements still in place, the regime had legal means to curb the radicalization of labor organizations. It restrained workers' actions by purging the confederation leadership and reduced the number of federations. A new union law (Law 35 of 1976, modified in 1981)[13] tightened the control of the ETUF and the minister of labor over the activities, finances, and the formation of trade unions.

Union leaders were incorporated even more deeply into the state: they were folded into state bureaucracy and given the right to participate in the discussion of all legislation regarding social and economic development. Most members of the confederation's executive committee were leaders in the ruling party; the president of the confederation is generally an *ex officio* member of the cabinet, serving as head of the Ministry of Manpower and Vocational Training. The Socialist Public Prosecutor's Office had to approve higher-ranking leaders.[14]

The effect of this was to prevent organized labor from becoming a bastion of opposition. But it also widened the schism between leadership and the rank and file, eroding leaders' accountability to their constituents. The regime created from top union leaders self-recruiting elites that kept the unions' decisions in line with the regime's political orientations.

Thus by the late 1970s, corporatist structures were still in place but they were no longer operating smoothly.

Depoliticization of Agricultural Cooperatives

The Free Officers' land reform measures, which focused on dividing large estates into small parcels and distributing them to farmers, were widely heralded as a mark of the regime's commitment to redistribution and care for neglected parts of the Egyptian population. But the program did not stop with giving peasants land; it also compelled the establishment of the agricultural cooperatives for farmers to get access to vital inputs (such as fertilizer) and market their crops. The effect was to make the state a powerful actor in agriculture and to support the ISI development strategy by determining what was grown, setting prices, and securing agricultural inputs to bolster the homegrown ISI industries being promoted.

Unlike the Mexican regime, which organized peasants in leagues in each state (seeking both to mobilize and control them by keeping them separate from urban workers inside the party's bureaucratic organization), the Egyptian elites never planned to create a strong peasant confederation; the regime's efforts were restricted to folding them into its economic plans.[15] While the Mexican leadership united the peasantry leagues into a National Confederation of Peasants in which all beneficiaries of agrarian reform in the *ejidos* (small parcels) had compulsory membership, the Free Officers did not aim to strengthen the cooperative movement organizationally for fear of creating an independent power center in the countryside that would challenge the regime's authority. Indeed, the regime took some precautionary measures to offset any potential threat that might have come from the cooperatives. These insured that rural Egyptians would be organized through state-sponsored institutions—but not in a manner that put them in any position to make demands.

The first step came with the enactment of a law in 1955 that gave the cooperatives' supervisory staff the right to evict recipients of land for "mismanagement of their holdings." The cooperatives controlled the distribution of loans, seeds, fertilizers, livestock, and agricultural machinery to farmers. This supplying function of the cooperatives served as an effective tool for government intervention.[16]

Second, the regime enacted another cooperative law in 1969 that severely reduced the representation of small peasants on village cooperative boards. Before this law, the majority of seats were reserved for peasants possessing less than five *feddans* (a *feddan* is very close to an acre and a five-*feddan* plot was sufficient for a family farm). The law raised the ceiling to ten *feddans* and literacy became conditional for membership. That effectively meant that cooperatives were unlikely to become a way to unionize a group of poor or middle-income peasants. The final measure was taken in the same year and prevented the ASU from conditioning candidacy and controlling elections to parliament. These steps allowed rural notables (some of whom had been on the defensive since the state's land reforms) to reassert themselves, fragmenting the cooperative movement in the provinces.

In addition, cooperatives organized farmers on the local level, but they were never allowed to establish any independent national structure that could pressure government agencies administering agricultural policy. An attempt was actually made in the 1970s, exploiting the loosening associated with the *infitah*, but it was not led by peasants and ultimately went in a different direction. The leadership of the Egyptian Confederation of Agricultural Cooperatives—now dominated by provincial notables and associated with the reemerging Wafd Party—tried to create an autonomous space that challenged the state's policies of land commercialization and agricultural production.

The regime could not tolerate this effort and turned it back, abolishing the confederation in 1976. It also stripped the local cooperatives of their functions, which were transferred to the newly established agricultural banks.[17]

Unincorporated Professional Associations: Excluding and Dominating Syndicates (1952-1970s)

Egypt had a rich network of associations and organizations for members of various professions—doctors, lawyers, engineers, for example—and these were often given official recognition as "syndicates." In the pre-1952 period, many syndicates had been sites not only for narrow professional matters but also for discussions and mobilization, especially around nationalist issues such as the presence of British troops in the country. The regime followed a more heavy-handed strategy with these associations as their autonomous status and their legacy of political struggle represented a potential threat to the new regime's monopoly over political organization. Contrary to trade unions and rural cooperatives, professional syndicates were never organized into a general federation. Instead, the regime found tools for each one that allowed state management of professionals, though in a manner that varied at times by profession.

First, each syndicate was governed by its own bylaw—one written not by the association itself but as state legislation. That meant that the regime, with its monopoly over the legislative process, could oversee how the association was run. This allowed the regime to tinker with the law in a way that could often bring the associations under the influence of its supporters.

Second, syndicates controlled entry into their respective professions. With the syndicates under regime control, that meant that they could be used to require members to toe the line—or leave the profession. A dissident journalist, for instance, would not be protected by the Journalists

Syndicate; instead, she would be policed by it. Syndicate membership could also be flooded with regime supporters. Socialist policies gave the regime strong influence as the state became the employer of most professionals. The syndicates were obliged to admit all graduates from universities to work in state bureaucracies, and new state employees were expected to support the regime within the syndicate they joined.

Third, while the syndicates were not grouped together, each one was folded into the ASU, the sole political party. This move was taken in several steps. After the Free Officers took power in 1952, all syndicates were forced to postpone the annual meetings of their general assemblies, and thus their elections, for years. During this period, the syndicates' officers were appointed by the government in a clear violation of the syndicate laws and a constitutional tradition recognizing free association. In 1958, President Nasser issued a decree requiring that candidates who intended to run for syndicate elections had to be members of the ASU. In addition, each syndicate had to establish an ASU committee that worked closely with the ASU federation. This enabled the regime to exclude active and nonconformist individuals and to contain the syndicates' activities. By 1964, the ASU had monopolized the syndicates, censored their public statements, and prohibited open deliberations in their meetings. In comparison to the trade unions, the diverse and relatively small membership base of the professional syndicates made the pattern of manipulation and control easily extendable.[18]

Fourth, if an association showed signs of independence, it could be threatened with dissolution. Sometimes the threat was categorical and ideological. At its socialist height, for instance, the regime portrayed professional syndicates as "bourgeois strongholds and dangerous anachronisms in a socialist society" and as "factions that split society."[19] But far more often the threats were tactical and targeted. The Bar Association for lawyers and the Journalists Syndicate were dissolved in 1954; in both cases, this was in response to the stand the syndicates took during the Naguib-Nasser power struggle and their condemnation of military rule. The regime suspended their activities and appointed a "guardian" syndicate council that remained in place until 1958. All syndicate councils were dissolved in 1971 after Sadat took power in an attempt by the new leadership to break the power of the ASU and purge syndicate presidencies and governing councils.

Finally, the regime could intervene in syndicate elections. Compulsory membership in the party (first the National Union, and then its successor, the ASU) was the essential tool to impose restrictions on candidates. The party's endorsement of particular candidates was an effective tool to control syndicates' activities.

The system gave a strong corporatist flavor to Egyptian associational life in the 1960s into the 1970s. Corporatism began to fray elsewhere, however, and the professional associations were no exception. The dismantlement of the ASU, for instance, initially led the regime to adjust by requiring candidates running for council membership to get the approval of the socialist public prosecutor to continue monitoring syndicates' members.

But as time went on, it was clear that a more sustained—if confusing and sometimes contradictory—reconfiguration was occurring for all the groups we have examined (workers, farmers, and professionals). Corporatism hardly died but it was often under strain and constantly reconfigured. It is to that story that we now turn.

RELAXING CONTROLS AND THE EVOLUTION OF AUTHORITARIANISM (1976-1990S)

From the late 1970s to the 1990s, corporatism was diluted as varieties of pluralist politics (in which society is organized in multiple, competing groups that are not micromanaged by the state) came into being, supplementing rather than replacing past arrangements.

Similar developments were on clear display in other regions like Latin America. These included the end of ISI; the way in which constituencies mobilized by the state took on a bit of their own will; and the fact that political parties now had some political space to woo away co-opted groups. These trends operated in Egypt as well, but generally more gradually and gently. ISI ran into trouble (as we shall see in part 3), but Egypt avoided the sudden economic crises that sometimes afflicted Latin American countries. Constituencies had never been fully mobilized by the Egyptian regime, so the corporatist arrangements did not give way to intensely contentious politics. Political party pluralism existed, but it was sharply constrained, especially when it came to parties' ability to link up with organized constituencies.

Elsewhere, the exhaustion of the ISI era is often held to have intensified social polarization and undermined state capacity to meet rising demands on the part of previously privileged groups, provoking the military to intervene on the pretext of restoring stability and order. Economic factors seem to lead down a single path according to this analysis. But Alfred Stepan has offered a more nuanced account, insisting that historical and political variables can lead to different paths in a similar situation. He has argued that the legacy of the corporatist period had varying consequences for subsequent periods of political and economic development. In his explanation for why some Latin American countries took a repressive turn while others did not, he notes that the legacy of "populist corporatism" rendered civil society more or less amenable to bureaucratic authoritarianism "because populist rulers themselves may have endowed organized interests with sufficient power and resources to prevent or defeat later efforts to install a more repressive regime."[20] So Venezuela and Mexico followed a gentler path than Argentina and Chile.

In that sense, the Egyptian case vindicates Stepan. But Egypt followed a third path that differed from Latin America. The distinctive way in which corporatism was built in the country meant that it did not fall into intense crisis or collapse. It frayed as the regime itself evolved (as described in part 1) and allowed for limited liberalization as the economic policy it supported ran into trouble.

What we saw from the viewpoint of the state in part 1 we will now examine from the viewpoint of social actors. They experienced the period as a loosening rather than an abandonment of corporatism and a series of measures taken by the regime to devise new ways to manage social groups—often authoritarian, to be sure, but avoiding the harsh demobilization of Chile or Argentina or the more populist approach of Venezuela or Mexico. With the regime's declining ability to offer welfare benefits, faltering instruments of control, and willingness to tolerate limited (if disorganized) opposition, various groups (from labor unions to professional associations) attempted to push for more autonomy and to form alliances with opposition groups (the Islamists, for instance, moved into professional associations, as we will see). And the regime pushed back by invoking some old instruments and inventing new ones that aimed at manipulation as much as rigid control.

In the following sections, we show how the organizational legacy of trade unions, peasant cooperatives, and professional syndicates hindered the emergence of independent and well-organized forces to pressure the regime to democratize. We will then tie this discussion to a consideration of electoral politics, showing how a very limited move toward party pluralism was managed in an attempt to isolate Islamists and allow other voices to be heard without developing into a genuinely pluralist or competitive system that could threaten the regime's control.

Controlling Trade Unions and Intermittent Unrest

Labor unions may have found the least favorable terrain on which to operate since the economic liberalization being pursued and made their demands for job guarantees or pay raises seem to serve as an obstacle to making industry more efficient or attracting investment. Those overseeing economic policy feared that if they satisfied workers, they would make state-owned enterprises more expensive to run and less likely to attract private investors. Workers generally proved to be manageable for the regime—but managing them made workers trust the regime less. As a result, the post-1975 regime took measures to maintain or recreate some corporatist controls in order to choose union leaders and stave off mobilization. But when workers engaged in wildcat strikes or when independent unions threatened to form, the regime would occasionally use gentler tools, such as offering workers limited benefits so they would follow their designated leaders. The result was an unsteady swing from control to concession.

This pattern unfolded in the last quarter of the twentieth century. In 1978, the regime issued a law on "The Protection of the Internal Front and Social Peace." While the law was used to disqualify candidates from trade union elections, the result was leadership dominated by regime loyalists unable to defend workers' rights throughout the 1980s. Frequent government intervention in union elections further emphasized the gap between the rank and file and the top hierarchy. These interventions took the form of a direct endorsement of candidates affiliated with the ruling party and the disqualification of oppositional figures.

In response, workers initiated some sporadic strikes and protests independently of the confederation, albeit with limited effect. In 1984 the state began implementing a provision of the insurance law that doubled workers' required contributions to pension and health insurance plans. At the same time, the regime moved to raise the prices of certain subsidized foods.

The result was a series of isolated strikes and demonstrations around the country. In 1989, large sit-ins erupted at a major state-owned enterprise, the Helwan Iron and Steel Company, as workers demanded a pay increase. In these incidents, the labor confederation took the side of the government and condemned workers' disruptive actions. This triggered worker animosity toward union committees; in their view, their supposed leaders were taking sides against them. This gave rise in turn to a dualistic system of representation with the emergence of informal groups alongside official union structures and fragmented labor organizations, hindering the formation of strong labor movements.

The mounting political awareness and independent actions among rank-and-file workers pushed the government to promulgate laws to weaken the link between workers and unions even further. First, Law 12 of 1995 barred public-sector workers that had been on fixed-term contracts since 1978 from seeking candidacy and representing unions. Second, the unified labor law passed in 2003 eroded the few remaining labor benefits from the Nasserist era. For example, the labor minister had previously maintained the right to force some firms to hire workers from specified vocations according to their date of administrative registration. The unified law abolished this benefit on the grounds that economic liberalization required that firms and business owners have the right to hire their own workers. Moreover, the unified law offered a degree of leeway to employers when it came to dismissing workers easily if they failed to carry out any of their "basic duties." The law further restricted workers' political rights by dictating the dismissal of workers in case of engagement with contentious action without getting prior permission from the management.[21]

Although concessions were essential to maintaining the support of labor unions during the ISI era, economic liberalization pushed the state to roll back employment guarantees, welfare benefits, and subsidies. While it sometimes made short-term or tactical concessions, the state failed to offer other incentive structures to maintain the loyalty of workers. The lack of institutionalized channels for bargaining, coupled with diminishing state resources, undercut the state's attempts to gain worker support. So rather than satisfying workers as a group, officials turned to co-opting the top echelon of the labor confederation, ensuring that workers' official leaders toed the line. Militants who sought to move outside of official structures were repressed. The regime lacked the economic capacity throughout the 1980s and 1990s to co-opt labor opposition or to mobilize workers across the country, but the legacy of populist corporatism debilitated the movement and undermined its mobilizing capacity.

Rural Dispossession and the Inception of New Confederations

Peasants had a similar experience to that of their urban working-class counterparts: economic liberalization led the regime to jettison some of the benefits it had accorded to them in the past in favor of older (or in some cases newer) means of corporatist control. But unlike the earlier era, it allowed wealthier rural Egyptians a greater influence over policy, even taking steps that some felt reversed the land reform measures of the socialist era. In short, while the regime was more responsive to some demands, it succeeded at keeping the peasant population demobilized.

In response to pressures from several European countries to renew international cooperative agreements with the Egyptian government, the regime initiated a new cooperative law that came into effect in 1983. But the step actually maintained official control over cooperatives. Both the Ministry of Agriculture and the local governors were given broad prerogatives to appoint cooperative leaders, veto the decisions of elected councils, supervise their financial inflows, and dissolve cooperatives by administrative order.[22]

In the mid-1980s, the value of land increased significantly while rents remained fixed. Landlords started to lobby for an increase in rents and for the right of owners to sell land that they had rented out, a prerogative that had previously been restricted in order to protect tenant farmers. Landlords eventually won that right, showing that the regime was willing to accede to their requests and was unconcerned about the reaction from poorer Egyptians. And they were right: the land reform policies of the earlier era led to material benefits for peasants but no ability to organize or translate their economic gains into political power.

Thus, the peasants' federations adopted a conciliatory posture toward the new government policy. Contrary to their counterparts in some Latin American countries, who were more willing to engage in political confrontation, peasant leaders in Egypt hoped that cooperation with the regime would bring concessions.

Professional Syndicates and the Rising Power of the Muslim Brotherhood

Professional syndicates tussled more consistently with the regime and managed at times to loosen corporatist structures far more than workers or peasants. They even forged strong ties with—or proved a bastion for—opposition groups, especially of an Islamist bent. But the regime also responded forcefully, tinkering with new tools and finding new ways to control the associations as well as cooperative allies within them. The result was a lively battleground, one that absorbed energy and occasioned drama but led to little political change.

The Bar Association, traditionally known for its vocal and firm political stances in the pre-1952 period, was the first to discover its political voice in mid-1972 when it decried the steps the regime had taken to entrench new authoritarian tools in legal form. But it did not restrict its criticism to legal analysis. In 1977, for instance, the Bar Association issued a statement supporting the right to peaceful strike action, arguing that food riots that year were due to the absence of effective political parties as indispensable channels for popular expression. The statement also warned the government against using the riots as an excuse to impose more restraints on political liberties. The Bar Association stood against the regime's attempt to rein in the Journalists Syndicate by transforming it into a "club" rather than a "syndicate" (the new body would have to focus on social matters rather than professional licensing and representation). The lawyers also attacked the regime's foreign policy after the ratification of the peace accord with Israel, eventually leading the regime to dissolve the Bar Association board in July 1981.[23]

Syndicates turned into an arena for ideological conflict among various forces (the Brotherhood, Marxists, and also Nasserists, who called for the regime to renew its commitment to socialism and Arab nationalism), and the members of the Wafd (who denounced the authoritarianism of the post-1952 system) in their struggles to attain more representation in syndicate boards.

Contest among these groups continued, but in most associations, Islamists gradually rose to the top. Unlike other groups—which tended to take the form of loose associations of like-minded people—Islamists in general, and the Brotherhood in particular, showed organizational discipline and an ability to draw on members with considerable experience in student politics; they also developed ways to supplement their ideological appeal with dedicated associational work, communicating to their colleagues that they were willing to work for the collective benefit and were not merely seeking a narrow political platform.

So when the Doctors Syndicate and the Engineers Syndicate finally followed the Bar Association into political activism in the mid-1980s, the Brotherhood often took the lead within these organizations. The Brotherhood gained a foothold in the Doctors Syndicate in 1984, winning 7 out of 25 council seats. It then gained an absolute majority in the Engineers Syndicate in 1987, winning 54 out of 63 council seats.

But the Brotherhood's ascendency within the syndicates occasioned sharp countermeasures. The regime responded with Law 100 of 1993, requiring (unrealistically) high turnout in syndicate elections; if the required number of voters did not cast ballots, the syndicate could be placed under sequestration and a board appointed by the regime. Non-Islamist forces who had been edged out by the Brotherhood's rise supported the law and openly joined the regime's effort.

These adversarial relations culminated in a direct confrontation between Brotherhood-led boards and the regime beginning in January 1995, when eight prominent Brotherhood members of the Doctors Syndicate's council were imprisoned. A few months later, the regime levied charges that some Brotherhood members were using the syndicates as a cover for their involvement in a terrorist campaign.

In the Engineers Syndicate, divisions arose in 1995 between the syndicate's higher council, dominated by the Brotherhood, and the Islamists' opponents, who formed what they called the "National Engineers' Front." The latter successfully secured a court order under the new law (Law 100 of 1993), placing the syndicate under judicial supervision and wresting the organization away from the Islamists. In May 1995, the police forced their way into the syndicate to enforce the court ruling, which escalated the confrontation between the Brotherhood and the regime.[24]

RESTRICTED PARTY POLITICS AND DIVIDED OPPOSITION

In other countries, the decay of corporatism and the introduction of more contentious politics among formerly controlled groups was often expressed through party politics and electoral competition, as opposition movements and politicians courted the support of disaffected groups. In Egypt, the regime kept a very close eye on the party system and electoral processes to ensure that the very limited opening it allowed did not lead to the same result. In 1976, Sadat, who had moved gradually to dismantle the ASU since it harbored his rivals, orchestrated a very limited form of party politics by authorizing the establishment of "platforms" within the ASU to represent diverse political views. This was an extremely narrow expression of pluralism: each group needed to elect at least twelve deputies to the legislature to be legally recognized, sharply limiting the new freedom. The leftist group created the National Progressive Unionist Party. The right-wing group formed the Ahrar Party. The ASU retained the centrist position. Over time, these platforms assumed the profile of full parties and the ASU was completely dismantled—or rather, the major platform within it (the one fully supportive of the regime) was folded into the new National Democratic Party (NDP). The NDP henceforth absorbed the ASU leadership and its deep connections with the state bureaucracy and official structures.

Even as it allowed parties to emerge, the regime enforced strict legal conditions to prevent the emergence of popular and potentially destabilizing opposition. Law 40 of 1977 set the parameters for party creation. According to that law, political parties could only be established if their programs, goals, and policies were distinct from each other and in line with "public order." The law prevented "the establishment of any [party] that could possibly appeal to a widespread regional, religious, or working-class constituency." A Committee for the Affairs of Political Parties was established to regulate party activities as well as to license new parties according to the law, which was so vague that it gave the committee wide discretion to reject parties and restrict their political activities. The committee was comprised of six regime-linked individuals: the minister of interior, the minister of justice, the state minister for affairs of the People's Assembly, and three judicial figures appointed by the president's minsters. Some parties resorted to the courts to overturn the committee's rulings, sometimes with success. But with the existing restrictions, political parties remained weak and vulnerable to the regime's divide-and-rule strategy, which prevented the formation of a strong opposition coalition and maintained the NDP's dominance. No party was able to build a true constituency and most found themselves tied up in legal restrictions, divided by rivalries, and bereft of resources. As such, they were hardly able to reach out to disaffected groups.

CONCLUSION

Corporatism was used in Egypt after 1952 to build a constituency for the regime and to give it instruments of control, but not to mobilize the population or bring into being forces or organizations beyond the regime's control. The mobilization of the popular sectors did not include the encouragement of autonomous organization from below but sought instead to foster controlled organization from above.

The liberalization measures that began in the 1970s and accelerated in the early 1990s was motivated by economic complications following the end of ISI and the fraying of corporatist arrangements. Those measures altered relations in Egyptian society and moved the sate away from its role as the main dispenser of resources and services.

This meant that corporatist arrangements designed in the earlier period could not work as easily. The dramatic crises that afflicted Latin American countries did not occur in Egypt, and the regime found itself managing protracted problems rather than facing sudden threats. In so doing, it had to find new tools, revive old ones, and cope with shifting circumstances. Corporatist organizations were no longer so closely tied to the state and many began to lose some of their visibility.

And new organizations also found space to operate, undertaking certain activities where the state no longer could. A new generation of NGOs and advocacy organizations, particularly social service organizations and human rights groups, proliferated in the 1980s and 1990s. And it is this story that we pick up in the next chapter.

Chapter Five

CIVIL SOCIETY ORGANIZATIONS
Limited Political Agenda and Mounting Resistance

How and why did Egyptian society become organized—especially in ways that resisted the state-corporatist controls imposed in earlier decades—in the 1990s? What happens, especially for civil society actors, their interactions, and their political roles, when society organizes under liberalized but still authoritarian conditions?

Beginning in the 1980s and accelerating in the 1990s, Egyptians formed a myriad of new formal and informal organizations. The introduction of liberalization measures, limited as they were, created conditions in which civil society organizations, community development associations, and religious voluntary associations could emerge. Indeed, the 1990s witnessed a marked increase in the diversity and strength of civil society organizations (or CSOs, meaning any organization composed of members of the society and distinct from a government body). This took place not only through the expansion of the number of NGOs (we use the term "NGO" to refer to those CSOs that focus on advocacy or community-based development), but also through a growing level of political engagement among social movements and older professional syndicates (chartered by the state but composed of members of various professions). Why did this happen and what were the results?

Here, we shift some of our focus from regime strategy, which was at the center of the previous chapter, to social dynamics. We also move partially beyond the large, formal organizations to smaller, informal, and grassroots ones. The context is a common one in which more liberalized autocratic regimes try to delineate the boundaries of civil society activity. But we do not assume that regime actions are the beginning and the end of the story. We also consider how different social associations pushed the boundaries laid down by the regime to assume a more political role. Over time, the more organized society in Egypt developed a repertoire of ways to contest policy, politicize some service provision, and challenge the authority of the ruling party.

But these efforts were not met with unalloyed success. Throughout the 1990s and 2000s, the regime continued to restrict the function of diverse NGOs, and CSOs more broadly, through a mix of legal codes and regulatory frameworks that fostered rivalry among some and prevented others from operating altogether. Both strategies secured more flexibility and allowed the regime to sustain authoritarian rule by pluralizing the associational landscape while co-opting opposition and curtailing independent action or popular mobilization, but this made for a steadily shifting set of arrangements. And, as we will see in chapter 9, it facilitated an uprising that challenged the regime in 2011.

References to "civil society" in Egypt are fairly new, as is the widespread usage of the term. Many scholars familiar with the phrase had been reluctant to use it. After a wave of democratization that began in South America and southern Europe in the 1970s and 1980s before spreading to the former Soviet bloc in 1989, the concept of civil society—and its relationship to democracy—rose greatly among both scholars and activists. And yet it did so in a way that made it seem as though the concept's application to Egypt could be premised only on exaggeration or overly hopeful thinking that the country was bound to follow the path of those other, more liberal societies.

Many came to believe that an effective political role for civil society had to be centered on the struggle for democratization or against authoritarianism and its legacies. Proponents of this view hoped that a rich, diverse, and active civil society could promote a healthy "civic culture" among citizens.[1] The close connection between such citizen activity and the notion of "civility" suggests an idea of what a "good" society looks like, rendering the former term positive and hardly neutral. In this sense, the politics of civil society suggests rationalization, social cohesion, pluralism, the inclusion of a greater share of the population, and the fulfilment of values such as liberty, tolerance, and equality.

Beginning in the 1990s and early 2000s, these positive connotations led many Egyptian intellectuals and activists to latch onto the concept of civil society in order to celebrate their own efforts. And the regime, too, used the concept to promote its mobilization of its supporters and to strengthen its ties with business associations, as well as to compensate for its provision of poor public services due to austerity measures. "Popular organizations" (*jama'iyyat ahliyya*) had long existed and were described as such, but it wasn't until the end of the twentieth century that new terms like "civil society" and "NGO" entered Egyptian discussions. In this book, we use "civil society" in a more analytical way (as defined at the outset of this chapter), but we should keep in mind that the term is laden with multiple meanings.

These terms have also been used by a host of actors with different agendas. Islamists, for example, used them to fight for a legal share of public space. (In this book we use the term "Islamists" to refer to those individuals and groups who seek to increase the role of Islam in Egyptian politics and society; if groups or organizations are religious in nature, like a charity, academy, or mosque, but do not have such a broad social and political agenda, we call them "Islamic.") A large array of advocacy groups with varying reform agendas used these concepts to expand the boundaries of individual liberty and freedom and sometimes to denounce Islamists' role in Egyptian society (suggesting that Islamists were not "civil" but religious). Not only CSOs but the very idea of civil society was thus subject to rivalry among various actors in competition over power and resources. Within the sphere of civil society as normally defined—social organization outside of the state—this broad competition led to a sharp polarization between the two main camps, Islamist and non-Islamist (though of course many remained outside of this divide and a few managed to straddle it). Each attempted to organize their followers, posing as the authentic voice of Egyptian society. This polarization has generally dominated the political interactions between oppositional forces and the relations between diverse associations and social networks in Egypt.

Social organizations in Egypt have long included Islamist (as well as other religious) associations and pious communities eager to express themselves and communicate their vision of a virtuous, moral, and good society. Religion, charity, and politics have never been separate realms in Egyptian society. Rather, they regularly reinforce one another, continually constitute the boundaries of social and political activities, and usually trigger a regime response aimed at policing the boundaries for political activity (especially for social organizations that could turn political). In the period in question—from the early 1990s until the 2011 uprising—Christian organizations began to expand along with Islamic ones, as did organizations that possessed a moral vision but not an explicitly religious one.

Despite its multiple meanings, it is still possible to situate Egyptian civil society in a comparative frame. The nature and contours of civil society vary from one place to another, but in Egypt CSOs proliferated and NGOS (ones that were far more likely not merely to organize but to see themselves as part of a broad political effort to build a "civil society") did as well. In the previous chapter, we emphasized a bit more how the regime shaped the society than how the society responded (though we did cover the latter). In this chapter, while we will not forget the regime, we will focus a bit more attention on the agency of civil society actors. The way organizational environments function depends, by and large, on the way people use them and the meanings they attribute to them at the micro level. In this chapter, we seek to show what actually took place in the realm of civil society, to elucidate how religion has been woven into Egyptian society (a point considered more fully in the next chapter), and to probe whose interests CSOs represent and what strategies they adopt to serve these interests.

We do this in three steps. First, we map domestic social forces and the forms they take, their activities, and the political content of their agendas. Second, we move beyond individual actors to trace the coalitional power of CSOs and the horizontal relations among different societal actors. By comparing the Egyptian case to Latin America, we can assess the idea that civil society can have positive influences on democracy, tolerance, and civility. Third, we will begin to see some ephemeral and tactical coordination among ideologically distinct social groups, which helped politicize certain issues and enabled these groups to make claims on authority in the years leading up to the uprising of January 2011, thus setting the stage for our consideration of post-2011 politics in chapter 9.

PROLIFERATION OF CIVIL SOCIETY ORGANIZATIONS AND MAIN SOCIAL PLAYERS

The concept of civil society is usually used loosely, either as a framework for identifying the main actors of state-society relations or as an analytical tool to explain the forces challenging authoritarian power and propelling transitions to democracy. The boundaries of civil society are hazy and drawn differently by different observers, particularly since application of the "civil society" label sometimes involves an exercise in moral judgment (which organizations are "civil") as much as a simple act of taxonomy. There is debate about what ought to be included in civil society as a sphere of self-regulating groups with "corporate identities" independent of state control yet governed by its laws.

In Egypt, moral judgment, ideology, and scholarship were not the only things at issue: the question of an organization's very identity effectively governed what law applied to it. Most nonprofit and nongovernmental associations were governed by Law 22 of 1964, which divided them into two categories: *jama'iyyat ra'aya* (welfare organizations that specialize in at least one particular activity) and *jama'iyyat tanmiya* (development organizations, known as community development associations [CDAs], that are restricted geographically and provide different services to local communities). But not all nonprofit and nongovernmental associations fell within these two broad categories; many other CSOs fell under different legal rubrics, sometimes because they wanted to find the most permissive regulatory framework for their activities. Some registered, for instance, as companies, while others avoided registration altogether. Even the two categories defined by the law effectively masked political objectives, religious views, and strategies. For example, advocacy groups aimed at influencing state policies and religious organizations (Islamic and Coptic) had some political interests. In other words, social activism and social service provision are not independent from a strategy to ensure a tight and cohesive activist movement among advocacy groups or to attract potential political supporters (as has been the case with the Brotherhood).

Indeed, the law—by being more permissive toward social and charitable work than political activity—effectively encouraged the blending of CSOs and politics. Groups whose agendas that included political aspects found it much easier to operate as CSOs than to organize or link with political parties. In the absence of other platforms for political expression, CSOs became venues for political contestation between different groups that hitherto were excluded from power and unable to mobilize mass support around their political programs. In mapping the field, we consider a series of CSOs: local community development associations, Islamic nonprofits, Christian organizations, advocacy groups, and business associations.

Community Development Associations

CDAs accounted for approximately 25 percent of the total number of registered nonprofit and nongovernmental associations in the 1990s. While we consider them CSOs, they were actually semiofficial organizations that were heavily dependent on the Ministry of Social Affairs (MOSA) for their funding and staffing. Indeed, the vast majority of these associations were established by MOSA and continued to function as executing entities for its projects. Their leadership was drawn from the state bureaucracy and included employees of local and village councils, cooperatives, and, in some cases, MOSA itself. Other CDAs represented a reaction on the part of Islamists (the Muslim Brotherhood in particular) to political exclusion, rampant corruption, poor economic development, and social inequality. By claiming to side with the marginalized and less privileged segments in society, providing some social services through Islamic organizations and Islamic welfare projects, and criticizing the corrupt leadership, the Islamists gained societal penetration and built wide support bases through a considerable number of CDAs. They did so not so much by offering a comprehensive political alternative to the existing polity, but by simply rejecting and opposing the existing regime and its institutions.

Islamic Nonprofit Associations

These comprised nearly 43 percent of all nonprofit and nongovernmental associations during the 1990s. Because of their possible association with the Muslim Brotherhood and other oppositional movements, they were heavily scrutinized by state authorities. But even under the watchful eye of the state, they were more organized than other groups because they secured wide popular bases, access to resources, and enjoyed relative autonomy from state funding and Western donor agencies. In order to avoid suspension and harsher treatment, Islamic associations registered as CDAs; this allowed them to extend their activities to different areas and offer more social services to low-income communities. Islamic associations maintained a relatively privileged position, as they were financially independent from MOSA and remained outside of the minster's oversight. Indeed, the law was generous in allowing mosques and other religious organizations to accept funding without state permission.[2]

The enactment of liberalizing economic policies, the rollback of the state's ability to provide social services, and ongoing fiscal pressures that weakened the state's ability to provide employment created favorable conditions for social welfare and charitable organizations to sustain their work and serve wide segments of society. And many Islamic organizations had the sense of mission and the practical experience to take advantage of these circumstances.

Islamic associations also moved beyond purely localized activity to build a complex network of health, orphanage sponsorship, and educational services across the country. This created a wide constituency that cut across different social classes, as these services reached not only the urban working class and the poor within the informal sector, but also attracted clientele from the middle and upper-middle classes.[3]

The regime struggled to keep these networks out of politics. One of the oldest, most well-established Islamic associations, al-Jama'iyya al-Shar'iyya, grew sufficiently successful that it became subject one of the state's most conspicuous attempts at suppression. Dating back as far as 1912, and with more than 360 branches across the country serving roughly 3 million members, the organization's charter suggested it was an apolitical civic organization aiming at spreading Islamic awareness and providing social and economic services to the needy and deprived segments of society. But it was often suspected of supporting the Brotherhood and other Islamist groups. In order to preserve the organization's charitable activities while preventing any political role, MOSA dissolved its board of directors several times. The association in turn filed cases against the ministry and its appointed board.[4]

Christian Organizations

Like their Muslim counterparts, Egyptian Christians, the vast majority of whom belong to the Coptic Church, established a series of organizations that grew and flourished in the late twentieth century for the same reason—there was both a supply of donors wishing to help and growing gaps in what the state could provide. But the political context was far different.

These were among the most professional and affluent nonprofit organizations in the country. They comprised nearly 10 percent of all NGOs during the 1990s. The al-Sa`id [Upper Egypt] Association for Education and Development, the Coptic Evangelical Organization for Social Services, and the Coptic Association for Social Care were the most prominent Coptic organizations in the health and education sectors. Like their Islamic counterparts, Coptic associations enjoyed a considerable level of financial autonomy from the state due to the article in Law 32 that excludes donations to religious institutions from MOSA supervision.

The regime was of course not worried about these groups' links with Islamists, but it did show unease with their connections with foreign donors and Coptic communities abroad, especially with the pressures migrant communities tried to exert on the regime to change its discriminatory policies toward Copts in Egypt.

Advocacy Groups

Advocacy groups come the closest to having a political agenda. They are primarily made up of professionals and activists dedicated to human rights, women's rights, and other causes. They generally aimed to influence public policies instead of offering services directly. Most of them registered as CDAs but some sought other, less-restrictive legal rubrics. Many were engaged in constant confrontation with the regime because of their inherently political goals and their efforts to gain some influence over the decision-making process.

These groups were often successful in attracting domestic and international attention. But because they served abstract principles rather than specific beneficiaries, they were limited in their ability to reach out beyond elite circles. And even those groups with similar agendas were often divided by rivalry. In their comments on human rights organizations and other nonprofit associations working in the field of democracy in Egypt, Ray Bush and David Seddon maintain that "the state is the main beneficiary of the absence of a united front for democracy and human rights as local nongovernment organizations fight among themselves over . . . how to access donor funds and what the appropriate strategy should be to promote even a limited political liberalization."[5] Although the lack of a unified political project poses significant challenges, advocacy groups have been the most outspoken of the NGOs and have engaged in fierce and direct confrontation with the regime and elements of the state.

The Egyptian Organization for Human Rights (EOHR) is a prominent example. MOSA denied licensing to the EOHR since its inception in 1989, despite the group's status as an active branch of the Arab Organization for Human Rights. This lack of legal status, although repeatedly—and unsuccessfully—challenged in court, allowed the regime to persecute EOHR members when they publicized reports on torture and random arrest. Organizers found themselves charged with disseminating information that harmed Egypt's national interests, accepting foreign funds to do harm to Egypt, and receiving illicit donations without government authorization.[6] Under such pressure, the EOHR split after 1995 and many of its leaders left to establish their own organizations.

The government further restricted the activities of NGOs by issuing Law 84 of 2002, which replaced all previous legal opportunities for the registration of NGOs. Chapter 3, article 48 of the regulation implementing the law approved activities as those aimed at realizing continuing human development, whether the educational, health, cultural, or social; economic or environmental services; consumer protection; and raising awareness about constitutional, legal, or human rights.[7] Moreover, chapter 2, article 24 expressly prohibited organizations from engaging in activities that could be deemed political or that threatened "national unity" or disrupted "public order or morals."[8] An organization that breached these provisions—which were admittedly vague and thus subject to arbitrary interpretation—could face immediate dissolution. In reaction to the state's harsh measures, many independent human rights groups developed alternative organizational forms, registering as private companies, legal firms, or medical clinics.

Business Associations

The business community took advantage of the liberalized environment as well. With the state's turn away from socialism, business leaders were not necessarily marginalized in the political arena as individuals. The goal was not to challenge the regime but to create a wide space in which to consolidate and coordinate efforts to influence and sway policy in ways that were generally beneficial to business interests.

There had been growing dissatisfaction since the early 1970s with the inefficient and bureaucratic nature of preexisting corporatist occupational groups that had dominated associational life in Egypt. This led to several parallel efforts to fashion new channels of representation to reflect the increasingly differentiated nature of the country's business community. This changing composition, especially after the implementation of the *infitah* policy of economic liberalization (see part 3), combined with business leaders' ability to bear the financial cost of association and coordination, led to the emergence of various business associations. Moreover, the changing strategies of political domination and economic development led the regime, now much more open to the private sector, to tolerate business associations, even to see them as potential allies.

Two older groups, left over from the pre-1952 era, still existed: the Federation of Chambers of Commerce and the Federation of Chambers of Industry. These groups had been refashioned under tighter state control as agents of economic regulation after 1952. Now, with the enactment of economic liberalization measures, they were granted more space to express private-sector demands. The ruling National Democratic Party came to offer these associations space inside the party as a way to garner support for its policies.

For their part, many middle-sized provincial merchants wished to establish political connections with the party as a way to gain access to government help, to compete with larger metropolitan firms, and to acquire financial and investment facilities. The Federation of Chambers of Commerce was thus an attractive vehicle, both for these merchants and the regime.

The same was true for the Federation of Chambers of Industry. Transformed in the post-1952 period into agency of the Ministry of Industry to support state policy and coordinate among public-sector companies, the federation found a more independent voice in the *infitah* era. It succeeded in formulating common demands that brought together the managers of large public establishments and diverse owners of small private firms. These demands centered not only on administrative decentralization and a greater reliance on market forces, but also on eliminating the socialist heritage of worker participation in management, profit sharing, and job security. Yet even the pro-regime Federation of Chambers of Industry could not realize all of its goals. The state refused to give up all of its instruments for controlling it. Without absolute autonomy, the federation still had to approach the state's key bankers, planners, and economic ministers for consultations on public policy, where it only sometimes found a receptive audience.

Emerging alongside these older bodies was the Egyptian Businessmen Association, which took advantage of the opportunities for pluralism in the business sector and the erosion (though not the elimination) of corporatist arrangements. The association represented a new coalition of over two hundred of the largest private firms in foreign trade, manufacturing, construction, banking, and consulting. It established itself throughout the 1990s and 2000s as the major coordinator of big-business demands and as the principal bargaining agent of the private sector vis-à-vis the state and foreign capital. The association welcomed the regime's interventionist policies aimed at transferring private investment from commerce and trade to manufacturing and the industrial sector and directing more foreign investment toward joint ventures with local firms.[9]

POLITICAL STRATEGIES OF CIVIL SOCIETY GROUPS AND THE ABSENCE OF NETWORKING

Thus far, our analysis suggests that civil society has assumed a more significant role since the early 1990s not merely through the proliferation of organizations but also when different groups form links and coalitions, find broader constituencies, or even develop explicitly political agendas that align them with specific actors or orientations. And while that happened in Egypt, the process was slow and subject to resistance on the part of the regime. When it did occur, it led to polarization rather than a cohesive civil society standing against the regime (as advocates of change in the Soviet bloc felt in their case). In other words, civil society grew but remained divided, limiting its ability to affect change.

Throughout the 1990s and 2000s, Egypt's civil society sector was fragmented and largely apolitical. The vast majority of CSOs focused on socioeconomic development activities and carefully avoided engaging in political issues, with the exception of a few isolated cases. While Egypt's CSOs provided much-needed social services, the state's co-optation and/or harsh restrictions prevented them from serving as hubs of wider political mobilization. More ambitious NGOs fell under an especially watchful eye. It is not just a question of whether CSOs bolstered or challenged state power or regime legitimacy; more important is whether they could link up in support of any common causes. Internal and intraorganizational rivalries and turf wars obstructed the formation of a more cohesive vision. CSOs—particularly advocacy NGOs, which, as the most vocal sector, sometimes challenged the boundaries of permissible political behavior—could sometimes speak boldly, but they could not strategize, mobilize, or move from seminars and newspaper columns to coordinated political action.

When they tried to link up—and they were successful in some cases—the polarization of Egyptian society between Islamists and non-Islamist forces rapidly became apparent. Egyptian civil society was less likely to produce a unified political agenda and articulate a clear democratizing mission—despite its growing significance—than some of its counterparts in Latin America and Eastern Europe. Mutual distrust between advocacy groups and Islamic organizations thwarted any attempts to form coalitions and capitalize on common ground to achieve collective goals. Islamists suggested that NGOs served effectively as agents of alien, secular discourse and clients of Western donors, while non-Islamists NGOs accused Islamists of adopting a double standard by taking advantage of the growing space for civil society to build uncivil organizations.

The rising role of religious organizations was hardly unique to Egypt. Latin American societies in the 1960s and 1970s—when the region was dominated by authoritarian regimes—faced similar polarization. Leftist groups of various kinds pushed not merely for democracy but redistribution. Others, inspired by the religious teachings of the Catholic Church, saw such groups—many of which were irreligious—as a danger to their conservative social values and a threat to social peace.

But attention to polarization reveals something distinctive about the Egyptian case. In Latin America, two factors led to less polarized outcomes.

First, the Latin American religious public was led by an independent structure, the Catholic Church. In Egypt, by contrast, the religious establishment was part of the state itself; al-Azhar, the country's leading Islamic institution, had less autonomy than did the majority of Catholic institutions in Latin America. To be sure, some independent voices arose inside al-Azhar, but these were often monitored by the institution's leadership and by state security agencies. The regime was largely successful at co-opting the religious establishment to retain popular legitimacy and ensure its supremacy of power. Additionally, casting the Brotherhood as a threat not merely to the regime but to the official religious establishment kept key figures aligned with the state against the opposition.

Second, in Latin America some voices arose within the church itself (though this varied by country) to articulate an agenda of political liberation and social justice that could lead to a degree of rapprochement with some on the left. Up until the late 1960s and the early 1970s, few clerics in Latin America were concerned with economic conditions and social justice. In 1968, a conference of bishops in Medellín served as a turning point for advocates of liberation theology, who sought to challenge authoritarianism and take a stronger stance against human rights violations committed by the state. Clergymen supported economic and political demands and became agents of social awakening and vocal advocates of calls for democratic political representation and social justice. In Paraguay, for instance, the Catholic Church was the strongest institution to challenge Alfredo Stroessner's authoritarian regime, and indeed, the Paraguayan church became one of the most vocal Catholic institutions in Latin America. It served both as a carrier of, and medium for, reformist ideas and called for liberation from oppressive and unjust socioeconomic structures during Stroessner's reign. It did not merely speak; it also organized a network of rural Christian base communities, which grew to become one of the most important peasant movements in Paraguayan history. The regime resisted these efforts and did manage to co-opt predominant conservative groups within the Catholic hierarchy.[10] But the ability to develop an oppositional language within the church proved contagious. In Chile, the Catholic Church also led the social opposition to Pinochet's rule, marking a significant departure from its previous institutional mode of elite accommodation. The church offered a protective milieu that helped political parties and social organizations to reconstitute themselves gradually as autonomous entities with means and ends. The Chilean church's ecclesiastical base communities were crucial to the construction of structures that could mobilize in opposition. The major mechanisms for these base communities were the local vicariates, which served as intermediary channels across neighborhoods and helped politicize economic grievances and challenge authoritarian rule.[11] And in Brazil, the Movement of the Friends of the Neighborhood in Nova Iguaçu, with the help of the Catholic Church, established strong horizontal ties across civil society that strengthened the forces struggling for inclusion, participation, and, eventually, democracy from below. The participatory practices of these base communities predisposed their members to demand participation and representation in the political process at large.[12]

In Egypt, this happened to a far lesser degree. Some Islamists became friendlier to the talk of human rights and democratic change, while others took up the issue of social justice (though most respected property rights and were therefore limited in their willingness to adopt leftist causes). Attempts to find commonality across various social divides did take place (producing some limited results, as we will see in chapter 9), but these remained fairly embryonic.

We will return to the role of religion in Egypt in the next chapter. For now, it is enough to note that polarization was considerable and diminished the degree to which a unified civil society stood against an authoritarian regime. But we have also seen in this chapter that for all its limitations and divisions, civil society was hardly a passive recipient of the state's control policies. Although it neither provided the engine of social and political change nor found traction in its struggle for democratization, civil society constituted a terrain for contestation with the regime.

And it also brought attention and controversy to the regime's instruments of control, making those mechanisms themselves objects of increasing contention. Civil society groups created pockets of resistance by organizing some political events or single-issue campaigns that offered crucial loci for excluded social groups to become the most vocal opposition, assuming roles that ranged from defending the economic interests of workers and farmers to calling for the replacement of incumbent regimes. Shifting the balance between different social groups challenged the regime's ability to manage and organize society and widened the circle of social groups denouncing the regime's encroachments on human rights and the unaccountability of political authority.

So the struggle that began slowly and inauspiciously in the 1970s gradually grew; by the early 2000s, civil society leaders were frustrated but more active and inventive than they had been before.

GROWING POLITICAL RESISTANCE AND DIVIDED SOCIAL GROUPS

By 2004, social actors and political opposition forces started to look for alternative venues for political participation, play a more active political role to challenge the regime's restraining boundaries, and overcome the obstacles discussed above. With an aging president, early struggles over succession, including maneuvering around the president's son as a possible future president, growing political experience among opposition groups, and a spirit of experimentation among activists seeking to construct new movements and organizations that would not fall into the divisions and limitations that characterized past efforts, two new initiatives stand out. The organization known as "Kifaya" (Enough!) came into being to gather activists from across the political spectrum around the effort to prevent the president's son, Gamal Mubarak, from succeeding his father. And industrial workers and other categories of state employees began a series of strikes in 2006 in which they called for wage increases and job security. Just as important, they worked to create new, independent trade unions outside of the old structures, thereby gathering some broader public support for their efforts. We now turn to each of these to understand how social groups organized themselves in nonhierarchical and decentralized structures to coordinate their efforts and put pressure on the regime. The effect was not so much to dismantle older arrangements as to challenge them and demonstrate the possibility of change. And both efforts engendered some success, however ephemeral, in bridging divisions among Egypt's polarized opposition. Despite the weakness and loose structures of these networks, civil society did manage to create some new ways of contesting the regime and its policies.

Kifaya: A United Opposition Front Outside the Domain of Electoral Politics

When Kifaya emerged in 2004 under the slogan *la lil-tawrith, la lil-tamdid* (No to Inheritance, No to Extension), it broke a period of social acquiescence and focused public attention on the possibility of hereditary rule raised by rumors that Gamal Mubarak might succeed his father. Within a year of its establishment, Kifaya had gained some eighteen hundred signatures on its founding statement. The movement declared the necessity of reforming the "repressive despotism" permeating all aspects of Egyptian politics. It also called for a termination of the monopolization of power and for promoting the rule of law as the supreme source of legitimacy.

The rise of Kifaya as an opposition movement marked a significant political development for two reasons: first, it broke the regime's policy, which was implemented in the early 1990s, of shutting down formal politics. Second, it integrated various political factions.

The movement grew out of the committees organized in support of the Palestinian Intifada of 2001. The Popular Committee to Support the Intifada (PCSI) included members of rival political factions—the Muslim Brotherhood, Nasserists, and socialists—as well as activists from professional syndicates and NGOs. The PCSI offered these actors a living experience of how they could overcome ideological differences and translate a shared sympathy for the Palestinians into a mass campaign. The committee provided a space for continuous collaboration among activists, offering opportunities for self-learning in negotiation and the tactics of overcoming ideological divisions in the interest of achieving joint goals.

The mutual collaboration between activists and Islamists in the PCSI laid the groundwork for further collaboration in opposing the U.S. invasion of Iraq. Various CSOs and the Brotherhood coordinated in a 2003 conference in Cairo held under the three slogans "No to Capitalist Globalization and U.S. Hegemony," "No to the Occupation of Iraq and Zionism in Palestine," and "No to Authoritarianism in the Arab Region." A conference the following year brought more active cooperation from the Brotherhood, with its supreme guide giving a presentation. The conference's organizing committee was equally divided between members of the Brotherhood, the Nasserists, and the Left.[13]

During the 2000s the collaboration between different ideologically inclined social groups was not organized within formal, hierarchical political channels or CSOs, such as political parties or human rights NGOs. On the contrary, activism and political action occurred within loosely established horizontal networks with no hierarchical leadership structures whose membership was often fluid and interchangeable. This form of collaboration emphasized the value of individuality and the possibility of differentiating and retaining a given group's independent program.[14] It was a form of coordinated effort for particular short-term goals and specific demands, one that shaped a principle upon which any alliance between rival political groups has subsequently been forged. That is, any attempt to form a strategic coalition by organizing it into hierarchical structures and diluting the differences in its political program triggered further polarization between the Brotherhood and it rivals.

Kifaya facilitated the expression of disenchantment with the regime's policies and brought confidence that collective action could bring attention to specific causes. The results were unprecedented—but also limited. Groups could only coalesce around a lowest common denominator. Defections, rivalries, and co-optation by the regime (which was initially caught off guard) meant that Kifaya produced a series of statements, press conferences, and rallies, but nothing that was sustained or that moved beyond a few urban centers. The organization could not build on its limited agenda or construct any organizational framework.

Kifaya, always a coalition, split into two rival groups in 2009. Mohammed El-Baradei—an Egyptian Nobel laureate—formed the National Front for Change. With support from some prominent figures and intellectuals, the National Front could not break out of its elitist image. It did gain some momentum in June 2010 after the police murder of a young blogger, Khalid Sa'id. His death attracted great attention among Egyptian youth. A Facebook page—"We Are All Khaled Sa'id"—was set up after his death, offering Egyptians an unusual forum in which to expose their outrage about government abuses.

Labor Unrest: Establishing Independent Committees and Unsettling the Corporatist Bargain

The regime had long treated workers' collective action as primarily a security concern. Despite a court ruling in April 1987 stating that the right to strike is constitutionally protected and legalized by the Unified Labor Law 12 of 2003, the regime effectively restricted strikes and they were only permitted with the authorization of the executive committee of the Egyptian Trade Union Federation (ETUF). When workers tried to break free of such corporatist structures, the regime reacted as if it was responding to a security threat, with the police forcefully repressing almost all of the unofficial strikes in the steel, textile, and railway sectors in the 1980s and 1990s.

But beginning in December 2006, Egypt experienced an unprecedented wave of labor protests in the country's biggest weaving and spinning factory. The factory, located in the town of al-Mahalla al-Kubra, employed nearly a quarter of all public-sector textile and clothing workers. The strike, in which workers demanded a bonus from the government (as the owner of the enterprise), marked the start of a new form of contesting state authority and challenging the institutional foundation of state corporatism.

The strike occurred outside official union committees, whose job, ostensibly, was to manage action and represent workers in negotiations with the authorities. Workers developed new contentious tactics, ranging from street protests and wildcat strikes to extended sit-ins at factories and official buildings, such as the parliament and the cabinet's headquarters. Al-Mahalla workers established "strike committees" and elected their own representatives to negotiate with authorities and to speak to the press. Five thousand company workers had resigned from the state-controlled Textile Workers' Union by March 2007. In September of that year, they went on strike again, calling upon the government to raise the national minimum wage and asking for the removal of corrupt managers and union officials. Although the textile sector instigated various rounds of anti-regime strikes, real estate tax collectors jumped on the bandwagon to ask for equal pay with their counterparts affiliated with the Ministry of Finance. Such seemingly unlikely political activism culminated in the establishment of the Independent General Union of Real Estate Tax Authority Workers in April 2009. Tax collectors won official recognition of their union as the first independent organization unaffiliated with the ETUF since 1957.[15]

The strike attracted the support of political activists from diverse sectors. On March 23, 2008, a small group of young Egyptian activists, calling themselves the April 6 Youth Movement, created a Facebook page to protest skyrocketing inflation and to call for solidarity with the workers of al-Mahalla. Thousands joined the call, transforming in just a few weeks an initial wave of solidarity with the workers' action into a nationwide general strike.

The erosion of the traditional corporatist bargain, the mounting co-optation of top leadership figures, and decreasing levels of repression paved the way for previously co-opted constituencies of workers to begin challenging and renegotiating the terms of their relationship with the state. But unlike some of their counterparts in Latin America, supporting conditions—such as a legacy of powerful labor organizations, historical memories of activism, and networks of supporters—were far weaker for Egyptian workers, and they were operating on more difficult terrain. Even so, they were a critical part of an emerging struggle against authoritarianism, illustrating that regime and state institutions did not have a monopoly on political action. And in that sense, for all its differences from the celebrated cases of "civil society" forcing regime change in Latin America and the Soviet bloc, social actors in Egypt did discover a voice and an ability to act, especially in the early twenty-first century.

CONCLUSION

Because civil society can coexist with softer types of authoritarianism, the mere existence of a civil society is not in itself a sufficient condition for democracy. In Egypt, the period examined in this chapter saw the slow emergence of groups that, as they found limited ways to organize and work together outside of regime control, were able to contest the state's authoritarian rule. In that sense, the question of whether "civil society" exists in Egypt had received a positive answer by the early 2000s.

But we learned two things from this examination. The portrayal of civil society as an independent entity separated from the state can leave us insufficiently attentive to important factors: the divisions within society; the way that the state can still structure civil society; the importance of a legacy of mobilization (in Latin America) or its weakness (in Egypt); and the way that even decayed state corporatism can leave regimes with important tools of repression and manipulation.

The second lesson is that academic observers are not the only ones who learn. The civil society actors examined in this chapter shaped Egypt because they learned lessons about how to organize, which forms would be successful and which were likely to fail, how to build coalitions; they searched for new tools, appropriate slogans, and successful techniques. Failure here could be a harsh teacher indeed. And of course regimes learn as well. The Egyptian regime, initially caught off balance by Kifaya, found ways to diffuse the new movement.

In the first decade of the twenty-first century, the cycle of experimentation and learning among civil society actors and between regime and opposition seemed to pick up speed. And indeed it did, culminating in the tumultuous uprising of 2011, to which we will return in chapter 9.

Chapter Six

ISLAM AND RELIGION IN EGYPTIAN STATE, SOCIETY, AND ECONOMY

In Egypt, religion has emerged as such a vital arena for politics that it merits special attention. Islam, the religion of the vast majority of (but not all) Egyptians, is woven into the state apparatus and public life in a manner that affects politics, society, and economy. It may seem strange to have a chapter on religion in a book about politics. It is indeed odd—but for an odd reason.

Religion is not an arena where scholars often look to analyze politics. Much about religion is a matter of personal faith (and in fact, in English, we often use "religion" and "faith" interchangeably). We speak of "church" and "state" as separate realms. So most books on politics do not say much about religion and come to it only when it is clearly a public matter relevant to politics and policy. Many earlier generations of scholars subscribed, either implicitly or explicitly, to the presumption that secularization was an aspect of modernity and that it will naturally increase as societies become more modern.

But that view is fading globally. Whether or not religion and politics should be separate, they rarely are. The overlaying of religion and politics is actually neither unusual nor is it fading in most of the world. Almost all countries' constitutions have something to say about religion. Some protect worship or belief from state control. Some instead, or in addition, proclaim official religions, stipulate a religious role in education, protect religious values, or give official status to some religious institutions. Most regions of the world have had governing parties or regimes that cite or pledge to honor religious values—whether Germany's Christian Democratic Union; India's Hindu nationalist leadership; the U.S. Republican Party's reference to Judeo-Christian heritage and its proclamation that "if God-given, natural, inalienable rights come in conflict with government, court, or human-granted rights, God-given, natural, inalienable rights always prevail";[1] or the position of Morocco's king as "commander of the faithful." The British monarch serves as the head of the Church of England; Ireland is constitutionally Catholic; and Norway constitutionally Lutheran. In Latin America, religion has not been limited to the private sphere but routinely recurs in a variety of vital public debates, on everything from family life to social justice.

Egypt, then, should not seem so unusual. Religion is an arena in which Egyptians sort out norms and rules rooted in religious beliefs; it is thus clearly linked to politics and society. Islam is the official state religion. Most Muslims have understood their religion to focus not only on belief but also practice, and the country's Islamic heritage thus bequeaths a rich tradition of legal guidance to Egyptians—a system of legal rules whose relevance to politics and law in a modern state has been the topic of debate for over a century. And other religions have adherents in Egypt too, raising complicated questions about these religions' status in public life and the legal system.

And religion is also an arena for economic activity—or rather it is so much a part of social and political relations that it naturally is linked to economics as well. When Egyptians approach marriage and family relations or look for a job or housing, they often find themselves involved in networks and practices that have religious dimensions. And we will see that over the past century, a general revival in religious consciousness and organization has expressed itself as fully in the economic as in the social realm.

So while religion and politics often intersect, there are some distinctive elements in the way they overlap in Egypt. First, the state encompasses religious authorities in particular ways. The Egyptian state folds these structures into its legal apparatus and bureaucracy in ways that are sometimes extremely clear, but other times subtle. For example, the Ministry of Religious Affairs represents a clear way the Egyptian state can encompass religious organizations, whereas in other cases, the state uses legal provisions supporting "public order" in a manner that protects religious sensibilities, a more subtle method of incorporating religious structures into the legal apparatus. So the state shapes religious authority and practice in some profound ways. But the converse is just as true: because it is folded into the state, religion influences the behavior of important state officials and structures. In short, in Egypt the state incorporates religion but cannot control all aspects of it. As a result, religion remains a factor in large parts of Egyptian social life that can be steered and often managed but not minutely controlled by the regime.

Second, religion and economics overlap in some distinctive ways. Encountering a tie between economics and religion might be especially surprising. Most modern conceptions of the economy, be they liberal, socialist, or nationalist, focus more on the material than the moral aspects of life, with the result that they draw relatively little attention to beliefs and norms that might inform the allocation of resources. Currently dominant neoclassical economic theory proceeds by assuming that markets are culturally and socially neutral. Those markets are thought to be made up of self-interested individuals or firms that follow price signals embodying the forces of supply and demand. Market exchange is conducted anonymously at an arm's length. In such a setting, religion has not generally been seen as significant for the functioning of a modern economy, except in smaller pockets of society where markets are not really operating, such as where there are religious obligations, charity, or pious community organizations building houses of worship or providing for the poor. But in places like Egypt—and many other parts of the world—markets are imperfect, information is scarce, transaction costs are high, and formal institutions are often weak and unreliable. Religion, defined as norms and customs that inform people's patterns of behavior, does play a role in the functioning of real existing markets by influencing how individuals behave, creating markets for religious products, and opening opportunities for those who claim to be operating in accordance with moral and religious strictures in the economic realm.

Thus, viewing religion as separate from politics or economics, as simply a matter of personal belief, is more often a hindrance to understanding than a helpful assumption. Discovering that religion is an important force in Egyptian politics should not be surprising; it is often important in many other societies.

Finally, Egypt is distinctive—though hardly alone—in that religion seems to be growing more presence in the political realm, not less. We have noted elsewhere in this volume, and will further explore in this chapter, the increasingly public nature of religious belief, practice, and organization in Egypt over the past half century. And in the past decade, controversies over religion and politics have moved to the center of Egyptian political life, with the rise of a president from the Muslim Brotherhood to power that triggered intense debates over religion in law, media, and education; harsh suppression of Islamist groups; and even spates of sectarian violence directed against Christians. Smaller religious communities—such as Jews, Baha'is, or even Shi`i Muslims—have been involved in similar controversies.

And that brings us to the real reason we devote a separate chapter to religion—not because it is a separate subject, but because it ties together so much of what we are exploring. Religion is so woven into Egyptian society, the structure of the state, politics, and even the economy, that it is integral to all these other areas. And that is what we mean when we describe religion as an "arena for politics."

Of course, religion does involve intensely private matters like belief and faith, but it is about more than that, and we have seen in the preceding chapters how it generates political controversies, structures some social and economic interactions, and serves as the basis for various political movements. The goal of this chapter, therefore, is not to carve out a distinct subject of "religion" but to trace more directly what we have only glimpsed in a piecemeal fashion thus far: how religion operates in the various realms we have looked at and, above all, to see how Egyptians wrestle over religious issues in unmistakably political ways.

In this chapter, we will follow much of the story we have told in previous chapters, a story of state formation and authoritarianism, but also incomplete state control and authoritarianism that sometimes operates uncertainly and unevenly. We will first track the role of Islam in the period that preceded the installation of the Free Officers' regime in 1952. We will also consider some movements outside the state—the Muslim Brotherhood and the Salafis, as well as one of the non-Muslim groups in Egypt—namely, Jews—and how they fit into the broader political framework.

Second, we will explore the way that Islam specifically and religion in general have been folded into the Egyptian state apparatus, such that when Egyptians seek to study or practice their faith, they often encounter a state body. We will focus most of our attention on Islamic institutions, but we will also consider how Coptic Christianity—the biggest religious minority in Egypt—is folded into official institutions and state policy. Our efforts to incorporate Egyptian Jews and Christians into our understanding are not designed to be comprehensive; our goal, rather, is it to explore how the themes that draw our attention in this chapter apply to non-Muslims.

But after examining the historical emergence of this far-flung collection of state actors and official bodies (or organizations connected to the state), we will turn our attention to the many ways in which state domination falls short of the full story—how an "Islamic revival" in Egyptian society (sometimes abetted by regime policy but hardly controlled by the regime) emerged from the 1970s onward, and how religion has become part of the social fabric and prevailed in public debates from the 1990s onwards. In this section, we will be attentive to how other groups—Muslim groups that do not fit easily into official structures (Salafis and Shi`a, for instance) complicate the picture.

Finally, we provide an extended consideration of how religion and economy are interlinked, setting the stage for our consideration of Egyptian political economy in part 3.

In this analysis, six key themes will become clear. First, there is a wide consensus that religion in general should play a strong role in public life and that Islam in particular should play a leading role. Second, religion has gained a more powerful presence in Egyptian society, economics, and politics since the 1970s. Third, religion is a strong motivator for many political actors. Fourth, religion gets pushed into many debates by social and political actors who have their own vision and preferences about what religion teaches. Fifth, even where no specific political actor is pushing religion, religion can get pulled into political debates simply because it is so widely present in Egyptian state structures. And sixth, religion often provides political arenas—from educational curricula to constitutional clauses—in which politics is played out.

If we delve into the period before 1952, we find many of the themes and institutions that have been at work over more recent decades. As the modern Egyptian state was built, religion took institutional forms that remain today; Egyptian social movements with a religious coloration (most notably but not exclusively the Muslim Brotherhood) took root in the first half of twentieth century as well. The period since 1952 built on these foundations, but also found religion entering politics in some new and forceful ways, especially when the regime loosened some of its grip and the state found itself forced to reduce its presence in some areas of life. We turn first to the historical background.

RELIGION AND THE EMERGENCE OF THE MODERN EGYPTIAN STATE PRIOR TO 1952

The role of religion is not simply limited to major institutions.

Egyptian family life is legally structured in accordance with official interpretations of religious teachings. In the nineteenth century, Islamic law (and legal aspects of other religious traditions) became associated increasingly, though hardly exclusively, with the family.

In previous centuries, courts of law often adjudicated cases on the basis of Islamic law, with non-Muslims resorting to their own religious authorities for disputes among members of their own communities. Rulers issued directives, rules, and other law-like instructions on matters of particular concern, a practice that religious authorities generally accepted since they saw a ruler's task as maintaining order and protecting the public. With the rise of the modern state, the legal instructions coming from the ruler vastly increased, and the growing complexity of the state apparatus meant that various bodies were giving instructions over a host of economic, technical, social, and fiscal matters. Official bodies arose (or were strengthened) to hear disputes or consider violations of state instructions. These often operated alongside older courts but were increasingly elaborate. By the late nineteenth century, a complex court system had been built (see chapter 2) and the older courts—staffed with religiously trained judges—were progressively confined to the area of family law.[2]

Thus, when Egypt's current court systems were built, they left matters of what became known as "personal status" (which generally referred to marriage, divorce, and inheritance) to courts that had a religious basis. There were many reasons for this. For one thing, European powers had non-Muslim citizens in Egypt who did not wish to be subject to the courts. Equally important, Egyptian Christians and Jews had their own courts, which they wished to maintain for family life; high officials often cared a lot about financial and criminal law but much less about family affairs; and the British (when they oversaw Egyptian governance from 1882 to 1922) did not wish to tread on sensitive matters unnecessarily. There were, of course, other areas of law where the tension between religious and other sources was felt. There has been an evolving debate among intellectuals, legal scholars, and religious officials over the role of religious law in a modern state. And because of the importance of the Islamic legal tradition in the way many Muslims understand their religion, that debate has not been resolved. Indeed, over the past half century, it seems that abstract debates about the relationship between religious sources and legislative drafting in a modern state (with a role for ministries, lawyers, officials, and parliaments) has grown more acute, not less. But much of that debate is very general or focuses on whose interpretations should prevail. It is largely in the area of family law that the focus moves from such general issues to more detailed questions of which laws are actually on the books, and it is here that efforts to draw on the Islamic legal tradition move from abstract to minute provisions.

But the result is not the exclusion of the state from family life and family law. Instead, Egyptian state institutions (such as the parliament) have determined through legislation which interpretations of Islamic family law will be applied. They have modified that law, for instance, to adopt interpretations more favorable to wives' divorce rights under pressure from some women activists. Non-Muslims can practice their own law—so long as their religious denomination is officially recognized. Those who are not a member of a recognized religion are governed by the official Islamic code by default. The separate religious courts were abolished in the 1950s, so judges trained in Egyptian law at Egyptian law schools—rather than religious scholars—apply whatever law is deemed relevant to a case.

Moreover, the historical context of World War I and the formal dissolution of the Ottoman Empire in 1924 meant that Egypt—which had been formally part of that empire—became a major center of attention for the building of strong national states in the Arab and broader Muslim world. Various intellectuals and social movements from different ideological backgrounds wrestled with the implications of the collapse of the Ottoman Caliphate. A multifaceted movement of Islamic reform or modernization had been taking shape in the late nineteenth century; it continued through the mid-twentieth century to work to reconcile Islamic principles with perceived Western values of progress and development. But growing national resentment against the colonial role of Britain, France, and Italy, as well as the obvious limitations these countries' presence in the region placed on self-government—with consequences for economic development and the living conditions of ordinary people—made it increasingly difficult for intellectuals to reconcile the role of Europe as a stimulus for progress. From the late 1920s and throughout 1930s, a broad nationalist movement (mixing secularists, liberals, religious reformers, and orthodox clerics) increasingly came to understand Islamic civilization as a powerful framework for identity in an anticolonial struggle that could reclaim the Egyptian state's authentic identity. This religiously tinged fight against colonialism often was strong enough to overshadow nationalists' different visions of what an independent Egypt should look like.[3]

During the 1940s, the intensified struggle in Palestine, ineffectual efforts to remove the British from Egyptian politics, and increasing cases of corruption among senior political leaders and the palace pushed some thinkers and social groups to go beyond a reformist Islamic vision to explore more radical ideas. On the left, some intellectuals and political organizers showed a greater interest in Marxism. For its part, the Muslim Brotherhood articulated a more radical Islamist project that went beyond social reform to call for the establishment of a state founded on Qur'anic principles.

Throughout 1930s and 1940s, the Brotherhood grew stronger, building a nationwide organization alongside that of the Wafd. And indeed, the Wafd, while continuing to mobilize supporters in elections, no longer seemed able to offer any inspiring vision to those in its social base, a coalition between the urban middle class, the middle-class landowning notables, religious minorities including Copts, and the more nationalistic elements of the great landed aristocracy. The Wafd coalition had been able to bring these disparate groups together, but that became increasingly difficult in the contentious 1940s. For instance, threatened by the Brotherhood's ideology, Coptic leaders launched a campaign to "revive the Coptic nationalism to counter the radically Islamist thought of *Ikhwan* [the Brotherhood]."[4] Among intellectuals, religious values were beginning to edge out liberal ones, with the king and the Wafd using Islamic symbols and rhetoric in their discourse and deploying traditional religious institutions to outbid each other.[5]

Early Roots of Salafism

The Brotherhood was not the only organized Islamic group, even if it was the most politically prominent one. Formal Salafi groups and other organizations dedicated to preaching and charity are as old as the Muslim

Brotherhood (and a few are even older). Indeed, the same dynamics that led to the Brotherhood's rise also propelled the Salafis—namely, a desire for religious authenticity, an interest in social service, and a feeling that religion was the best guide for realizing a better society. In some ways, there was a regional trend at work: various ideas that might be called "Salafist," originating from a range of Arab countries, from Syria to Saudi Arabia, were forming; the Brotherhood itself originally saw itself in part as a Salafist group. But while there was formal Salafi organizations and movements, there was no overarching structure like the Brotherhood. Indeed, the concept of Salafism carried different meanings over different historical epochs.

Salafism is a broad term that encompasses a wide array of different approaches. In general, "Salafi" is a label used by various thinkers and groups who believe that prevailing interpretations of Islamic religious teachings have been corrupted and that Muslims should turn back to original Islamic texts and practices to properly understand their religion. In the late nineteenth and early twentieth centuries, the term was used mostly by those who believed that such a return to original sources would make progress (in a manner that sometimes mirrored liberal ideas of that term) possible. Instead of being constrained by centuries of legal scholarship, it was thought that Muslims had to return to the basics—and that such a turn backward would lead them forward.[6]

But especially since the 1950s, the term is used for literalist schools of thought that focus on purifying details of religious doctrine and practice.

Salafism is thus more of a general religious approach than a rigidly structured movement, but it has grown influential in parts of Egyptian society, with some leading Salafis forming organizations in order to pursue their preaching and social activities. With their focus on correct practice, they were often viewed as nonpolitical, more interested in study and in debating the correct way to eat or pray rather than vote or lobby. And indeed, some Salafi teachers did view politics as dangerous or likely to be divisive or distracting.

The Muslim Brotherhood Turns Political in the 1940s

The Muslim Brotherhood emerged out of the same religious and intellectual environment as other groups, such as the Salafis, that were religious in inspiration; its purpose was, like theirs, to increase the role of Islam in public life and to propagate its understanding of proper Islamic belief and practice. But the Brotherhood also built a formal, structured, and hierarchical organization that made it resemble other nonreligious actors (such as political parties and movements). In this way, the Brotherhood stood out from among other participants in the loose trend of religious reform, eventually becoming the political force that we examine in other chapters of this book.

The Brotherhood was founded in 1928 as a movement designed to reform Egyptian Muslim individuals, families, and society. Its initial leader, Hasan al-Banna, was an inspirational figure to a growing number of followers who saw his organization as a way to improve themselves and their society through a revived Islamic spirit. Initially focusing on self-improvement, preaching, and charity, the movement established a strong presence in Egyptian society, particularly in urban settings.

The period in which it emerged—the 1930s and 1940s—was one of rising political mobilization in Egyptian society coupled with periodic elections. The Brotherhood was drawn into political life as powerful politicians and movements saw it as a potential ally or constituency, and the Brotherhood itself saw politics as one avenue to pursue its goal. It did not organize itself as an electoral movement or a political party, but it did begin giving some training to some of its younger members in a special unit in the 1940s. That unit—which evolved into a paramilitary group—was justified in the leadership's eyes by the need to prepare a new generation to fight British imperialism (with British troops still present in Egypt) or defend Palestinians (as conflict brewed on Egypt's eastern border between what became the Jewish State of Israel and the Arab, predominantly Muslim, population of Mandatory Palestine). That step marked the Brotherhood's move beyond politics and into paramilitary action, as the new unit attacked British targets, organized volunteers to fight in Palestine, and even attacked Jewish targets and Egyptian political leaders it thought were too close to the British. The Egyptian government at the time banned the Brotherhood (and, when the prime minister who took that step was assassinated, Egyptian police retaliated by assassinating the Brotherhood's leader).

In 1952, when the Free Officers overthrew the Egyptian regime, the Brotherhood applauded the move, but the new rulers and the Brotherhood soon split. In an increasingly authoritarian atmosphere, the Brotherhood represented a potential challenge, and the new regime used a series of harsh tools—special courts, mass detentions, forced exile, and torture—to suppress the movement. Largely driven into hiding, exile, or prison, embittered members who stuck with the movement engaged in a debate about the correct strategy (and even ideology): Was it to create a new Islamic society that would fight and replace the current regime (deemed un-Islamic)? Or was it to persuade Egyptian society and even its rulers—most of whom claimed to be Muslim—to move slowly and gradually toward a more righteous path? The way Brotherhood leaders (and other Islamists) answered these questions had a profound influence on Egyptian political life, as shown in previous chapters.

Non-Muslims in Egypt Before 1952: The Example of Jewish Communities

In the first half of the twentieth century, the connection between religion and national identity underwent some subtle changes that would have a significant legal and political impact on subsequent decades. Those able to claim foreign citizenship during much of this period strove to maintain it because this allowed them to claim exemptions from aspects of Egyptian law under the capitulations (see chapter 2); there were some religious communities—especially, but not exclusively, those with many members who had migrated from European states—who, in a juridical sense, were thus often not Egyptian citizens. Others, like Copts, were overwhelmingly Egyptian. The nationalist movement that united many Egyptians in the struggle for political independence tended to accentuate this distinction not merely in law but in public discussions and personal identity. The Wafd Party presented itself as unifying Muslims and Christians (with the latter largely restricted to Copts, almost all of whom held Egyptian citizenship, spoke Arabic as a first language, and were spread throughout the country). Christians with foreign citizenship, concentrated in major cities and sometimes speaking languages other than Arabic (such as Greek, Armenian, Italian, or French), and non-Christian minorities fit uneasily into this idea of the national community. Jews, who straddled this division, will draw our attention in this section (we will later turn our attention to Copts in the post-1952 period).

Various Jewish communities have resided in Egypt since ancient times. In the nineteenth century, they were joined by Jewish immigrants from other places in the Ottoman Empire and a small number from European states. Some acquired Egyptian nationality through the Egyptian Citizenship Law of 1929, which extended citizenship to former Ottoman subjects residing in Egypt since the start of the Protectorate in 1914. Others retained foreign citizenship, benefiting from the capitulations that granted them extraterritorial status, and a few remained stateless.[7]

For the most part, Egyptian official bodies showed no interest in Jewish religious belief and practice, allowing Egyptian Jews to operate communal organization and, as non-Muslims, practice their own family law with courts staffed by religious authorities. Yet such religious tolerance operated alongside conceptions of nationality, Egyptian identity, and, over time, Zionism (the program of Jewish nationalism to construct a homeland in neighboring Palestine), factors that ultimately undermined much Jewish communal life in Egypt and led most Jews to leave for other countries.[8]

Many Jews participated in public and political life—for example, through the popular movement of 1919 or representation in the legislatures. Some business leaders participated in emerging industrial and financial initiatives that took place between the two world wars. But the Jewish community as a whole, as well as its constituent subgroups, retained a strong corporate identity.[9] In 1934, a group of Jewish journalists and writers began to publish the first Arabic-language Jewish newspaper, and the following year they founded a youth club, Jama'iyyat al-Shubban al-Yahud al-Misriyyin (the Association of the Egyptian Jewish Youth). Their main target was to raise awareness among the Jewish community of its heritage and to promote a sense of Egyptian patriotism (while local Zionists aimed primarily to educate Egyptian Jews in the spirit of Jewish nationalism[10]). The association declared its support for Egyptian nationalists against British rule, joined the national call for the evacuation of British troops from the country, and rejected British guarantees or protective measures for Jewish positions in Egypt.[11]

The growing tension in neighboring Palestine heightened divisions among Egyptian Jews about their political preferences—and focused the attention of other Egyptians on Egyptian Jews' position toward Zionism and Palestine. The outbreak of the Arab Revolt in Palestine in 1936 enhanced the idea of Arab unity and strengthened nationalist zeal among a variety of governments, political movements, and religious actors throughout the Arab world. The rising tide of anti-Zionism (which sometimes triggered anti-Jewish feelings) in nationalist circles devoted to the Palestinian cause was closely tied with the broader national struggle against British colonial authority in Egypt and against European imperialism in the Arab region at large.[12]

As Palestine headed toward open military conflict in 1947, Zionist Jews in Egypt were opposed by some official community leaders and a communist movement that had attracted support from some Jews by stressing "the loyalty of the Jews to their Arab homelands" and the importance of finding peaceful solution to the conflict in Palestine.[13] Within Egypt, the United Nations decision in December 1947 favoring the partition of Palestine at the end of the British Mandate ignited anti-Zionist sentiments, triggering attacks on Jewish properties and residential areas. In 1948, Egypt entered the war in Palestine, where it supported the Arab population against the newly declared State of Israel; the national press and public debates thereafter dropped any distinction between Zionists and Jews. Even before entering the war, the Egyptian government declared a state of emergency followed by martial law that extended censorship and led to the detention of hundreds of Zionist and communist Jews (as well as several opposition groups comprised of Islamists, communists, and nationalists). Forced underground, Zionist activists maintained clandestine operations.[14]

The wartime government issued a decree that allowed sequestration of the property of any person "who was interned in Egypt and of anyone residing outside Egypt whose activities were deemed prejudicial to the safety and security of the State," as well those who had merely been placed under surveillance. Since the wording was broad and did not offer a clear-cut legal definition of who was eligible for such surveillance or asset confiscation, the decree could be, and effectively was, applied indiscriminately. Between May 1948 and early 1949, "significant Jewish private, commercial and communal assets were seized and placed in the custody of the commissioner of sequestered property."[15] Although some restrictions on the Jews were lifted by the Wafd government in 1950, a significant number of them left the country between 1948 and 1950.

In 1950, the Egyptian Nationality Law was amended to allow it to "be withdrawn from any person involved in actions in favor of states that were at war with Egypt or with whom Egypt had broken off diplomatic relations." In 1954, a group of Egyptian Jews were enlisted by Israel in an effort to bomb American and British targets in Egypt, part of an effort to make the country appear unstable and beset by Muslim Brotherhood and leftist violence, thus making the British and Americans less trusting of Egypt's new regime. When the plot was uncovered, it led to a complete breakdown of the distinction between Zionism and Israel, on the one hand, and the Egyptian Jewish community on the other. In 1956, a joint invasion of Egypt by Israel, France, and the United Kingdom (generally referred to as the "Suez Crisis" in English but known as the "Tripartite Aggression" in Arabic) marked a final break in government relations with local Jews and a policy direction that treated almost all Jews as Zionists and suspect. Government measures ranged from detention and sequestration of businesses and property to formal expulsion orders and deprivation of citizenship (through a set of complicated legal changes).[16] Only in the 1970s, when the number of Jews had dwindled to the hundreds, were some of these measures reversed.

The evolution (and emigration) of Egypt's Jewish communities exhibited specific features but reflected broader trends. Other communities, some with deep historical roots in Egypt but with non-Egyptian ethnicity or citizenship, began to dwindle in number with the end of the capitulations, the advent of less pluralistic approaches to national identity, and waves of nationalization that left noncitizens exposed to sequestration of their property. In religious terms, this meant that in the second half of the twentieth century, in the official and broader public sphere, Egypt had a dominant Sunni Muslim majority and a significant Coptic minority, with other religious sects retaining their vestigial official status but largely disappearing from public life.

THE STATE: OFFICIAL RELIGION AFTER 1952

We now turn to the religious edifice of the Egyptian state—and the politics surrounding it—as it has operated since 1952. We focus primarily on the Islamic religious establishment, but we will turn our attention to the Coptic Church as well, with some references to smaller religious communities.

Al-Azhar and the Islamic Religious Establishment

At the apex of the state apparatus overseeing religion is al-Azhar. Founded in the tenth century as a mosque where religious scholars taught, al-Azhar has grown to encompass a network of primary and secondary religious schools, a university (with both religious and nonreligious faculties), research institutions, and other assorted structures for teaching and preaching Islam. No single doctrine characterizes al-Azhar (though it is a Sunni institution), and indeed, various schools of Islamic law are taught, and the faculty and graduates have a wide variety of interests and orientation. But its leadership has tried to hew to what it views as a mainstream approach, protective of a heritage of Islamic learning but flexible enough to be appropriate for the modern era. Al-Azhar accepts international students and has some branches and activities outside Egypt, sometime imbuing it with a sense of global mission and enhancing the institution's prestige domestically. While part of the Egyptian state, al-Azhar has varied in the degree to which it is close to the regime. In the first half of the twentieth century, various political actors (including the king and some political parties) tried to gain its support. That history, combined with the institution's prestige, led the regime to pursue efforts to monitor and influence what it taught.

That meant that al-Azhar became something of a political prize to be won; when the king faced strong nationalist opposition in the 1920s and 1930s, for instance, he turned to al-Azhar as an ally (see chapter 2). Al-Azhar's status as a state institution, while it had some autonomy, gave leaders tools to sway it. And from the 1960s on, the regime kept a particularly close eye on its leadership, which it expected to toe the official line, bringing it more directly under regime control. Even then, some within the institution could use the regime's reliance on al-Azhar as a kind of limited protection under which they could develop different views.

And the institution itself strove—and sometimes succeeded—in guarding and even increasing its autonomy. In 2011, in the confusing aftermath of the uprising, Egypt's military rulers awarded al-Azhar's top leadership the authority to form its own council to select the institution's leader. The regime's intentions were uncertain, but they may have sought to keep al-Azhar free from the control of Islamists—mainly the Brotherhood and to some extent the Salafis—who had a growing political presence (and even support from many within the institution), and who in fact were about to enjoy a brief period of parliamentary majority. That autonomy allowed al-Azhar to remain aloof during the brief presidency of Brotherhood leader Muhammad Morsi, and even to fend off some pressure from President al-Sisi when he complained about religious teachings and discourse in the country.

But if al-Azhar is at the apex of the system, it does not have a monopoly even over the state's religious establishment. The state mufti (Dar al-Ifta') issues religious legal interpretations when asked by state officials (and must approve death sentences).

The Ministry of Religious Affairs has jurisdiction over all mosques in the country, oversees preachers, and licenses religious charities. It is thus in a potentially powerful position, but it does not always have the resources to monitor the country's religious establishment as closely as it would like—perhaps a majority of mosques in the country feel only very limited oversight.

In a very distinctive move aimed at weaving religion into state institutions—and coinciding with a gradual ideological turn against Arab nationalism and socialism—the constitution adopted in 1971 stipulated that "Islam is the religion of the state and principles of Islamic law (shari`a) are the principal source of legislation."[17] This clause was vague and unattached to any implementing structure and procedure, but it gave a strong foothold to those who argued that Islamic law must play a central role in the Egyptian constitutional and legal order. In general, Egyptian courts have interpreted the clause in a manner that acknowledges the importance of Islamic law but defers to political authorities in determining how to apply it.

The shift in political orientation allowed al-Azhar to play a much stronger role in policing Egypt's moral and cultural spheres, and sometimes even state regulation of economic activities like finance and banking, where religious opinion was solicited to avoid usury. Scholars from al-Azhar have assumed the role of supreme censors by issuing fatwas on an increasing number of public issues and thereby steering public debate. They also intervene to ban certain books on the grounds that they violate Islamic principles, and they screen all material proposed for broadcasting.

The Coptic Church and the State

Other religious groups, most notably Coptic Orthodox Christians (though an array of other Christian denominations are recognized by the Egyptian state, including Roman Catholic, Coptic Catholic—those who retain Coptic rites but have joined the Catholic Church—several Orthodox denominations, and over a dozen Protestant ones), have their own structures that are brought under official oversight, but they also depend on some autonomy from the regime to maintain credibility among their believers.

Institutionally (and in terms of number of adherents), the most significant Christian institution in Egypt is the Coptic Church, which traces its origin back to the beginnings of Christianity in Egypt.

Copts represent a minority in Egyptian society. Egyptian state bodies do not give figures for religious affiliations, but a variety of estimates put Christians in a range from just under 10 to about 15 percent of the population, with perhaps 90 per cent affiliating with the Coptic Orthodox Church. While the church is now the leading interlocutor with the Egyptian state for Copts as a community, this was not always the case. The creation of the Majlis al-Milli (the Coptic Community Council) in 1874 represented a parallel legitimate authority and challenged the church's claim to monopoly of representation. The Majlis was composed of Coptic lay notability—including landowners—and its mandate transcended the focus on spiritual matters to provide social services to the Coptic community, sometimes tangling with the church over politics or even charitable endowments (*waqfs*).[18] While the Majlis was abolished after 1952, lay-led societies created philanthropic networks that continued to operate. In the pre-1952 period, some became involved in the tussles between the church and the Majlis. In recent years, some organizations have pressed for Copts to be included in national life as full citizens and expressed the feeling that the church focuses only on its religious autonomy.

The regime has generally seemed to prefer to deal with the church as a whole and it has developed a relationship with the Coptic pope, or patriarch, in which state recognition and protection are granted in exchange for the church's political loyalty. For instance, under Nasser's leadership, the patriarch "presented the concerns of the community directly to the President and promoted loyalty to the regime among the Copts. In return, Nasser ensured the security of the community and the status of the Patriarch as the Copts' legitimate representative and spokesperson."[19] In addition, the state took an important step involving Christian endowments by transferring the administrative tasks of Coptic *waqfs* to the Coptic Orthodox Waqfs Organization—a body appointed by the church—and dissolving the Majlis al-Milli, thereby eliminating the lay threat to church authority. In 1957,

Nasser issued a presidential decree concerning the new bylaws for the election of the patriarch that endorsed the demands of a conservative ecclesiastical bloc within the church.[20]

But tensions remained and sometimes escaped into public view after Egypt's military defeat in 1967 facilitated expression of the public's rising dissatisfaction with state policies towards the Copts (especially with the prohibition of Coptic television and radio broadcasts and the contentious debate over church-building permits that required approval of the president).[21] In the 1970s, a new president and pope betrayed increasing suspicions of each other. The pope, Shenouda III, openly expressed Copts' qualms about the Islamic revival and condemned sectarian violence, which galvanized the opposition of Coptic citizens. The patriarch also opposed article 2 of the Constitution, which he considered a violation of Copts' fundamental citizenship rights. He denounced the regime's proposed constitutional amendment in 1979 stipulating that "Islamic shari`a is *the* principal source of legislation." The patriarch's confrontation with the regime (and with President Sadat personally) escalated in the late 1970s, culminating in a presidential decision annulling the 1971 decree that "pronounced the appointment of Shenouda as pope"; President Sadat sought not only to depose the pope, but also placed him under house arrest in 1981.[22]

While the confrontation between president and pope eased (with President Mubarak releasing Shenouda and allowing him to resume full duties, and even appear on state television), the relationship between church and state was still fraught. Indeed, since the early 1980s, the sectarian question has increasingly taken on the form of a national security problem thanks to outbreaks of sectarian violence and occasional fears about the involvement of foreign groups and governments. The regime has increasingly deferred to the security and intelligence apparatuses to manage these matters.

In general, the official Coptic leadership and the regime have remained supportive of each other even through the 2011 uprising and since 2013 (with Morsi's short tenure in office a time of great tension).[23] To be sure, this supportive stance was not consistent or absolute. After many sectarian incidents, the pope openly blamed the security apparatus. However, seeking to downplay tensions, the church's leadership continued to stress "national unity." But such a stance often created a schism between the Coptic Church's leadership and many lay Christians who felt either unprotected by the church or beholden to a church leadership that protected their religious institutions and privileges but abandoned their political rights.

Rising discontent with the Coptic Church's alignment with the regime encouraged opponents of the church's political line to act independently of church authorities—a stance that was underscored by the significant Coptic participation in the 2011 uprisings, despite the church's initial rejection of the demonstrations.[24] By contrast, during the Brotherhood's short tenure in office, the church was actively engaged in politics. The pope accused Islamists of marginalizing Copts in Egypt, officially endorsed the demonstrations of June 30, 2013 against the Brotherhood's rule, and declared support for al-Sisi's run for the presidency.[25]

THE SOCIETY

The modern era is not a secular one; it has not washed away religion. Religious institutions remain deeply ingrained in social relations, but not all of those are under control of the state or can easily be steered by the regime. We have seen the institutional development of religion in the Egyptian state and the way that different regimes have sought to use it to persuade and guide the population and appeal to pious citizens. At the same time, Egypt has experienced a growing in the importance of religion in the social realm that has not simply been an instrument of the regimes. The rise of religion has manifested in two important and interrelated ways: an Islamic revival (*al-Sahwa al-Islamiyya*) beginning in the late 1960s, and an increasing number of piety groups focused on producing Islamic culture.

Islamic Revival

From the beginning, this revival confronted the regime with a series of challenges and opportunities, which it managed by attempting to steer the various aspects of the movement, though with mixed success. Following Egypt's defeat in 1967, many Egyptians came to blame the military failure as an indication of the total corruption of the Free Officers' regime; as a widely used phrase from the period put it, the regime "deserted God and so they were let down by God." In many neighborhoods, and especially on university campuses, a new spirit of voluntarism developed, which often took on a religious coloration. Some groups coalesced around the idea of studying religious teachings or preaching them to friends and colleagues.

These various trends collectively became known as *al-Sahwa al-Islamiyya* (Islamic revival). But while this trend toward religion appeared at first to be more about piety than politics, it became clear in the 1970s that politics would be affected. While some studied or organized, others acted. Indeed, one early radical manifestation of this tendency led to a group that came to be called al-Fanniyya al-'Askariyya (the Technical Military Academy) after it launched an attack on that institution in 1974. Another, al-Takfir wa-l-Hijra (Excommunication and Flight), deemed Egypt no longer an Islamic society, effectively attacking the regime's legitimacy in terms that permitted political violence. The most active group was al-Jihad Organization and al-Jama'a al-Islamiyya (the Islamic Group). These more radical organizations rejected any reformist notion of gradual social change. They instead emphasized the role of a strong leader or movement to emancipate people and guide them on the right path toward the establishment of what they saw as a truly Islamic society, replacing the one that merely claimed to be Islamic.

In 1973, Egypt performed more credibly in another war against Israel. But Islamic and religious zeal were revealed to have deeper roots; they were not a mere reaction to recent political events. Rather than fading away, the revival intensified. Even as the most radical groups were repressed, the revival (*sahwa*) became a catalyst for a sociopolitical revolt that reached out to educated youth on university campuses as well as to the wider urban masses. And it was not merely Muslims who participated in the religious revival; there was a similar resurgence of religiosity among Christians resulting in a wave of voluntary and social activity. There was also conflict, especially in areas with mixed Muslim and Christian populations, some abetted by rumormongering, with local disputes over issues like church construction or even mixed marriages sometimes sparking local violence.

Why did the regime permit such a rebellious set of ideas to take root? In many ways, they were an accidental by-product of official attitudes and actions. First, these ideas did not always appear rebellious, especially at first. Egyptian public life was never secular, and indeed the state encouraged a strong role for its favored religious institutions. Some of those institutions provided a protective environment for the emergence of new religious ideas.[26] And in some ways, the groups profited from a context in which the regime's ability to control Egyptian political life was declining, as the authoritarianism of the 1960s gave way to the semi-authoritarianism described in earlier chapters. But the regime also seemed to have derived some benefit from allowing religious groups to organize—they provided a counterweight to other opposition groups (for example, leftist groups in the early 1970s)—and allowing them to operate openly also made it possible to monitor them.

Islamist student associations started to flourish in the mid-1970s, and their activities spread beyond holding religious conferences and seminars on campuses. Islamic student associations organized "Islamic Days" to distribute Islamic books and pamphlets; provided classes on the Qur'an, the Sunna (the teaching and practice of the early community of Muslims in the seventh century), and Islamic jurisprudence (*fiqh*); and established religious camps to foster intensive interactions among Muslim youth during summer vacations. In addition, they initiated a wide range of services, such as providing inexpensive copies of academic books, selling low-cost "Islamic" clothes, and offering separate bus transportation for female university students. They also engaged in political activities and vocalized opposition to the regime's policies.

While this revival took place at a grassroots level, it burst onto the national political scene when an Islamist medical student (who had won a position in the national student union) participated in a discussion with Sadat during a live broadcast in February 1977. In a heated verbal exchange, the student leader blasted the gap between the president's democratic and religious rhetoric and the regime's actual authoritarian practices.[27] That student—'Abd al-Mone'im Aboul Fotouh—later led some Islamist youth activists into the Muslim Brotherhood; after 2011, he left the Brotherhood to run for president.

In sum, the Islamic student associations of the mid-1970s served as an important training ground for a new generation of Islamic leaders who gained experience providing services, disseminating Islamic ideology, countering rival groups on campus, and opposing the regime. Such practical experience left an indelible mark on their communication skills, recruitment capabilities, and mobilizing capacity.

The regime tried to respond by tightening restrictions on student activity. The lenient student charter of 1976 was replaced with a more restrictive version in 1979 that eliminated university-wide student organizations, limited union activities to the faculty level, and, more importantly, allowed the return of the security force known as the "University Guard" to Egyptian campuses. However, the Islamists adapted their strategies to this more restrictive environment and strengthened their control over student politics, with a particularly strong presence in elite technical schools, including the medical faculties and then engineering faculties in the 1980s and 1990s. They also dominated student activities, even after political action on campus was subjected to more stringent government oversight.

In the 1970s, following a degree of limited liberalization, some of the Brotherhood's leadership was released from prison. The growth of religiosity in Egyptian society meant there was a younger generation of recruits to win over, and these newly released leaders hoped to resume their activity. It was in this context that hundreds of thousands of middle-class Egyptian professionals, including teachers, university professors, medical doctors, engineers, and lawyers, migrated to the oil-rich countries of the Arabian Peninsula. With the 1973 oil boom launching ambitious development projects in the conservative Gulf monarchies, Saudi Arabia became the principal destination for more than a million Egyptians. These people later returned with money as well as new consumption patterns, and some had become inclined toward much more conservative interpretations of religion (or found Saudi Arabia and other countries friendly terrain on which to develop their conservative inclinations). This will be discussed at more length below in the section on the economy and religion.

Some of the more radical groups split from the Brotherhood and launched various attempts to build a counter-society, even engaging in attacks against the regime and its pillars, such as the police. In 1981, some of these radicals assassinated President Sadat. But a more gradual, reformist trend dominated the Brotherhood organization (tolerated if not legalized from the 1970s forward), and their message managed to coax in some youthful activists, many of them schooled in university and student politics.

By the time of Sadat's assassination in 1981, the Islamic revival had developed deep roots. As student activists graduated, they moved into the professions and worked to reach a wider circle of youth and others in large cities and provincial towns.

The regime could use various arms of the state to police, monitor, and steer this rising generation of Islamists, but it could not control all of its manifestations. How did Islamists manage to recruit educated youth and mobilize them into politics in the 1980s and early 1990s? One common way of answering this question is to stress economic factors and frustrations—but also opportunities.

The *infitah* economic policy that began in the 1970s widened disparities among social classes and opened up political space in which Islamists could capitalize on prevailing social frustration. The economic frustrations for many Egyptians were—and remain—quite real, but they cannot be the sole explanation for the Islamic revival. Indeed, many of the leaders of the revival were themselves people who made their wealth as a result of the oil boom or took advantage of new markets for religious products among a middle class greatly strengthened by access to jobs or remittances from oil-rich states. After all, many of those left out of this economic dynamic wound up avoiding any kind of social or political engagement, especially in an authoritarian regime where any engagement exposes activists to serious risks (e.g., imprisonment or physical harm).[28]

The Muslim Brotherhood as an organization, infused with young blood and energy, gradually rebuilt itself in the last couple decades of the twentieth century, taking advantage of a limited political opening. It was not allowed to form a political party or even gain any other kind of legal status, but it could operate (with periodic partial crackdowns) and even run candidates for parliament as independents or on the tickets of other parties. The regime strategy was never explicit, but it seemed to allow a contained Brotherhood some space so that it could siphon off supporters from more radical groups but never become strong enough that it could challenge the regime.

What helped turn frustration into activism was the willingness of some leaders of the revival to undertake social activity that resonated with target groups by offering them support and solidarity and even (as will be seen below) organizing some helpful activities. Egypt is hardly unique in this regard. In the late nineteenth and early twentieth centuries, many Christian social activists in Western Europe, worried by rising radicalism and hostility to religion, organized similar activities that provided the basis for many of the Christian Democratic parties that are active to this day. And at about the same time as the religious revival in Egypt, a similar wave swept Latin America as different Christian denominations stepped up activism and some Catholic leaders developed the liberation theology movement throughout the 1960s and early 1970s (see chapter 5). That movement emphasized shared religious values and reinterpreted sacred scripture to denounce authoritarian regimes, criticize exploitative and unequal socio-economic policies, and renew the fight for human dignity.

In some ways, Islamists in Egypt have been less successful than their counterparts elsewhere. For example, activists have not changed the political map or dislodged the regime and its allies, as happened in some Latin American countries like Nicaragua, where the Catholic Church could give some measure of protection to those who sought deep change.[29]

But if they were less able to challenge the regime, their impact upon society and in local politics remained significant. Indeed, Islamic associations offered an alternative platform from which to denounce the regime's corrupt policies and figures. Islam has long provided an important anchor for social debates around issues of justice, economic transaction, morality, and political and social behavior. This meant that the revival could pursue themes that resonated in Egyptian society. For many Egyptians, the idea of detaching social behavior from religious questions is anathema since it would mean that divine guidance and moral values have no role in social life.

And even if there was no powerful, overarching religious institution in Egypt like the Catholic Church, there were still some protected spaces for the revival. For instance, growing social and political criticism by various mosque preachers accelerated the growth of Islamic sentiments in society. Although most preachers started their careers within the traditional religious establishment of al-Azhar and other official religious institutions, some of the most famous preachers in the late 1970s were outspoken critics of regime policies with popularity among wide segments of society. And they found ways to circumvent the regime's control of mass media. Perhaps the most effective means in the 1970s and 1980s—before the advent of social media—were the audio recordings of speeches and sermons that could be disseminated widely via cassette tapes. The Islamic revival even found a voice in official media as long as it stayed away from politics. One of Egypt's biggest media stars in the late twentieth century was Shaikh al-Sha'rawi, whose highly expressive and very accessible sermons had a distinct political message that guided people's behavior and transactions (he was, for example, supportive of Islamic finance). His nonconfrontational political stance toward authority meant that state-run media was allowed to feature him prominently, winning him an enormous television viewership.

ISLAM AND RELIGION IN EGYPTIAN STATE, SOCIETY, AND ECONOMY

The Growing Role of Piety Groups

The increasing number of piety groups and wide involvement in religious gatherings meant that a noticeable growth in religiosity—characterized by modesty in dress, higher consumption of religious literature, and involvement in religious associations or popular ceremonies—was discernable throughout the 1990s. Piety groups organized ceremonies on saints' birthdays. Some mosques sponsored religious lessons and ritualized weekly gatherings for both genders.

Such trends assumed a largely apolitical valance as participants were often more interested in exploring questions of faith and ethical self-fashioning than political issues. But, more subtly, piety groups advocated a form of religiosity that was not entirely limited to the private domain. Rather, they brought religious rituals and ethical obligations to "bear upon worldly issues in new ways."[30] They focused on helping individuals recognize or redefine themselves in terms of Islamic virtues, codes, and traditions. Piety groups and preachers therefore reinvented Islamic discourse by focusing heavily on ethical practices and disciplines through which Muslim individuals could be reformed "as a public self"—in a manner that was socially engaged even if it was not linked to a specific political program.

This focusing on Islamic norms and virtues was not merely about individual belief; it also meant that those participating in the revival were interested in changing social practices. This could take the form of celebrating veiling and the virtue of public modesty, an increased interest in the correct performance of Islamic rituals, or the proliferation of Islamic charities. It also took place through a wide variety of structures and made possible the building of new institutions. For instance, supporters of the revival established "Islamic schools," which aimed to create Islamic awareness by emphasizing the study of religious materials—in fact, already been part of the mainstream curriculum—establishing prayers rooms, making time for prayers during school hours, and hiring religious teachers.

In sum, piety groups, Islamic socialization, and religious media offered a milieu that enabled the reshaping of social practices and the spreading of religious discourse in a new form in different areas. These activities extended across both private and state structures. And the regime could not ignore religious movements that appeared to have wide social influence. The social appeal of *da'wa* (preaching or proselytizing) movements, for instance, or the popularity of *du`a* (preachers) who attracted wide masses by focusing on ethical conduct, were not regarded as apolitical. Instead, the places, individuals, and institutions associated with the Islamic revival were treated by the regime as obvious targets of control and monitoring, especially for signs of political opposition.

Security services stepped up surveillance of women's and men's mosque lessons on the pretext of weeding out extremists and preventing them from using mosques as propaganda outlets. And the regime moved to compel preachers to complete a two-year training program at the Ministry of Religious Affairs in order to get a license for practicing *da`wa* and giving mosque lessons.

Other Groups

Finally, what of those groups that do not fit into officially recognized religious categories? There are several such categories, with some, such as Sufi brotherhoods, not only tolerated but knit into formal structures. (The current sheikh of al-Azhar is also a leader of a large Sufi order; his order and some others occasionally have a significant social presence.) We will focus our attention here not on these politically integrated groups but on those that seem to pose challenges to the authorities in an environment in which religion is not merely a reflection of personal belief but a matter of law—one that touches, moreover, on concerns about public order. Reactions to various faiths and communities have therefore sometimes shifted.

Some communities, like Egyptian Shi`a, are largely ignored. In other countries in the region, Shi`a can choose to have their own family law applied in certain cases, but they have no such privilege in Egypt. Shi`a informally gather in specific locations and mosques. While such gatherings are often allowed, at times of international tension with Iran (an officially Shi`i state) or other concerns about public order, Shi`a can find their gatherings obstructed or their presence treated as alien within Egypt. Unrecognized Christian groups (such as Jehovah's Witnesses) are left out of the official framework altogether. Baha'is are not granted any public recognition either; in earlier decades, this official silence was sometimes neutral, but in recent decades, anti-Baha'i press campaigns have led the group to face an unfriendly atmosphere. After a protracted legal battle, Baha'is won the right to have their religious affiliation omitted from their national identity cards (rather than be registered as Muslims and run the danger of being treated as apostates). But in some ways, this legal victory was more symbolic than practical. The default family law in Egypt is the state-legislated personal status code, which is based on Sunni Muslim law. Egyptian citizens who are not associated with an officially recognized religious group are, by default, governed by that law. And that would extend to atheists, a category that is not only denied legal recognition but often treated as a form of social and moral deviancy by state bodies.

Conversion among religious communities is difficult, though it has been handled in various ways.[31] Conversions among Christian sects sometimes occur; conversion from Christianity to Islam is allowed but often sparks strong concerns that such practices will lead to communal tension, even violence. Conversion from Islam, while it faces no written legal bar, is nevertheless nearly impossible on a bureaucratic level since no state office will recognize it. More notable than the legal complexities, however, is the way such practices are increasingly understood by state authorities, who see conversions not simply as matters of conscience but as security issues that could threaten "national unity" or "social peace."

Despite such evolving state concerns, religion has generally begun to play a larger role over the past few decades. In contrast to the 1950s and 1960s, this role is not simply confined to social life but also extends to economic affairs. In the following section, we will examine three aspects of the increasing overlay of society, economy, and religion in Egyptian life: charity, market exchange and investment, and consumption.

THE ECONOMY

When the Egyptian state retreated from its commitments to offer social services to its citizens; when the regime began to turn away from socialism; and when the possibility for activity outside of state control expanded in the 1970s and 1980s, space opened up for new kinds of charitable associations and community-based groups, many of which had a religious coloration (primarily Islamic but also Coptic). And the oil bonanza in the Gulf monarchies beginning in the 1970s—especially in Saudi Arabia, with its important religious significance—had an indirect effect on the revival of Islamic sentiments among various segments of Egyptian society since it generated resources for community projects beyond state control.

Religion and Charitable Organizations

The most striking institutional developments in Egypt throughout the 1970s and 1980s were an unprecedented wave of private mosque building and the proliferation of a network of "Islamic" hospitals, schools, and welfare centers. A major source of funding for these projects came largely from the voluntary donations of private Egyptians and individual patrons in the Gulf. The larger context for these developments was an intensifying fiscal crisis facing the Egyptian state coupled with international conditionality to slash the budget deficit and to roll back public services. Religious organizations and networks, both Muslim and Christian, stepped in to fill the vacuum. As mentioned in chapter 5, Coptic organizations have been active service providers in Upper Egypt since the 1990s. Coptic NGOs have a noticeable presence in the health and educational sectors and enjoy a considerable degree of financial autonomy in their efforts to serve Coptic communities in less privileged areas. However, Islamic organizations remain the most predominant philanthropic associations in the social sphere.

These new groups did not reach out to wider social segments by igniting class conflict and calling for a society of "owners and workers together." Indeed, few of the new groups had any problem with some Egyptians becoming wealthy as long as they fulfilled the Islamic injunction to give alms to the poor.

In addition to hosting daily and Friday prayers, local mosques served as hubs for a network of service providers that included health clinics, kindergarten classes, private tutors for students, and charity distribution centers for needy families in peripheral areas and low-income neighborhoods. Islamic voluntary associations offered an independent, organized environment for the expression of religious ideas in daily life, creating social bonds and experiences of solidarity that had an independent impact on political interests. These associations offered organizational foundations and logistical support to Islamic groups mobilizing to achieve political objectives, including the Islamic student associations (*jamaat*) and the Muslim Brotherhood, that "prepared a new generation of Islamic leaders who, a decade later, spearheaded the movement's expansion out of the universities into broader arenas of public life."[32] The Brotherhood especially managed to build extensive networks throughout Egyptian society. And its ability to present itself as the political face of a broad swathe of the Islamic resurgence meant that it could tap into unaffiliated but sympathetic networks that served as an electoral bastion for the group during the period of the Mubarak presidency and in the two years after Mubarak's fall.

Religion, Market Exchange, and Investment

Economists like to think of markets as places where anonymous individuals seeking to maximize their own profits follow price signals. But in reality, exchange between buyers and sellers is often facilitated or even enabled by social and cultural affinity; after all, if two individuals have personal ties, they are more likely to trust each other. In part 3 of this book, we will explore more fully the concept of "habitus" and the way it helps us understand economic relations. For now, we should note that habitus refers to the regularized patterns that people adopt in their interactions with each other; it is the way that regular patterns of social behavior emerge. It thus suggests that understanding society (and economics) depends not simply on isolated individuals each pursuing their own self-interest but also on how those individuals act in a broader social context, enmeshed as they are in institutions, networks, and communities. So we pause here to note that habitus in the form of social ties of various sorts, including community and family ties, all function as social interfaces to market exchange.[33] In other words, how people meet, whom they trust, and how they interact, is shaped by the way they are connected socially—the nonmaterial ties that bind them. As explained above, religious norms, identities, and practices in Egypt have always permeated social structures, especially but not exclusively family life. Religion has served as a habitus for business transactions by creating space for cooperation, exchange, and consumption. Religion can play a major role in building trust and sanctioning defection, both as a source of morality as well as a sign of solidarity between members of religious communities. This makes transactions less costly and less risky, especially in imperfect markets where enforcement of contracts is uncertain or inconsistent and basic information is often in short supply (for instance, one party to a transaction might have ties to a state official who knows about a contract that is about to be offered, or businessperson might use their family contacts in order to make deals with trustworthy parties). In such markets, pious groups and networks can step in to develop informal channels for circulating information and sanctioning those who try to cheat or wriggle out of agreements.

Habitus has always been relevant to economic activity, in modern Egypt as in other countries. Before independence, there was a somewhat neat ethno-sectarian division of labor in the economy. Whereas the vast majority of Egyptians (Muslims as well as Copts) were predominantly employed in agriculture (59 percent), just 10 percent worked in industry and transportation, 6 percent in commerce and finance, and 5 percent in services. Foreigners were distributed quite differently, with 24 percent in industry, 22 percent in commerce, and 20 percent in finance.[34] Foreigners or residents who belonged to ethnic and religious minorities—namely, Jews, Greeks, Italians, Armenians, and Christian Levantines—dominated the biggest and most modern economic units.[35] Their educational levels were generally higher than others and they enjoyed cultural and economic ties to Europe, consular protection, and other privileges under the capitulations system. In these ways, they were often not seen, nor did they always see themselves, as fully "Egyptian," even if they had deep roots in the country. Little wonder, then, that Egyptian nationalism vowed to "Egyptianize" the modern economy, especially with the final elimination of the capitulations and the mixed court systems in 1949. Egyptianization turned into the expropriation and subsequent nationalization of foreign-owned assets in the aftermath of the 1956 war over the Suez Canal and amid rising nationalist sentiments among Egyptians after the creation of Israel. These foreign-owned assets became the nucleus of Egypt's huge public sector in 1961 after the regime expanded its nationalization efforts to large Egyptian private firms as well (See chapter 7 for a more detailed portrayal of the evolution of Egypt's political economy). Overall, Egyptian independence resulted in a decline in the presence of non-Egyptian and non-Muslim minority groups, leading eventually to the clear definition of the Egyptian nation as made of a Muslim majority and a Christian Coptic minority.

With the advent of *infitah* in the 1970s, habitus became much more prominent in shaping emerging markets and the resurgent private sector. Expectedly, religion played a significant role in this process as well. Indeed, one major example of the way that religion could facilitate exchange and draw official attention were "Islamic investment companies" (*sharikat tawzif al-amwal*), which were a direct product of the Islamic revival. The rise of religion led many pious Egyptians to seek new banking and investment options that were not based on interest on deposits and loans. Such interest was deemed by many pious Muslims (as well as authoritative scholars) as usury. Following the first and second oil booms of 1973 and 1979, the large inflows of workers' remittances from the oil-rich Gulf countries expanded this base of religiously conservative savers. Moreover, it intensified the competition within the financial sector over finding the right service and institutional arrangements that could capture these private savings.

As some sought out new instruments for their savings, private actors stepped forward in the late 1970s to found "Islamic" investment companies. By 1985, the number had reached 180.[36] These companies practically functioned as banks by receiving deposits. They were largely unregulated, as they did not fall under the supervision of the Central Bank of Egypt. They did claim to be operating in accordance with Islamic financial requirements (barring many forms of interest, for instance), though their exact operations were unclear. With a reputation for stability and trustworthiness, they attracted investments even from those who were not necessarily devout themselves. As Islamic investment companies mushroomed, state-owned and private banks responded by opening Islamic branches that offered noninterest-based services.

But after their rapid rise, some Islamic investment companies began to run into trouble. By the late 1980s, many were already facing huge financial problems, and some were no longer capable of paying back their depositors. Moreover, they were perceived as adversarial to the regime due to their actual or perceived links to the Islamist opposition. The regime had therefore come to view them as a potential threat.

The state took advantage of some institutions' financial precarity to strictly enforce Law 146 of 1988, which prohibited the collection of deposits by any nonbanking institution. Appealing to calls for the Islamization of public life, these companies developed a reputation for probity and piety that had allowed them to secure a clientele for over a decade. It is hard to know where the experiment would have led had the state not intervened so heavy-handedly to bring it to an end.

Another example of the merger between religion and the economy is the set of Brotherhood-affiliated business activities that emerged and expanded after the 1980s. The Muslim Brotherhood was not only active in the social and political realms; there was also a network of businesspeople and merchants that gave the Brotherhood an economic presence and helped with its functioning and financing. The Brotherhood's organization created a set of tight networks comprised of members and their families who were closely linked through intermarriage, business partnerships, and employment in companies owned and run by other members. With active membership a little short of a million strong (estimates set in the mid-2000s), members had to donate 7 percent of their monthly income to the organization. Given its illegal character, the Brotherhood never made information about its financial position or operations public.

As early as the *infitah*, which coincided with the reestablishment of the Muslim Brotherhood as an organization (and also the emergence of networks associated with it), a number of Brotherhood-related businesspeople started operating in Egypt. Since the 1980s, the Muslim Brotherhood itself invested in a number of trade- and service-based activities despite the impending risk of expropriation by the authorities. By the 1990s, the Mubarak regime claimed that the Brotherhood had developed an economic infrastructure of companies that were formally owned by leading figures in the organization. (Since the organization itself had no legal existence, it could not legally own assets in its own name. That made it difficult to determine whether an enterprise was personally owned by a Muslim Brotherhood member or simply registered in that person's name but effectively overseen by the movement. Such ambiguity helped the movement operate, but it also exposed the personal business activities of wealthy members to official scrutiny.) In 1992, the government expropriated several companies and personal assets that were allegedly tied to the Brotherhood. This came to be known as the Salsabeel case, after the name of the company owned by Khayrat al-Shater and Hassan Malik, the two allegedly in charge of running the Brotherhood's business ventures. The Brotherhood's alleged assets, legally belonging to rich members, were frozen and/or expropriated in 2006, following the organization's strong performance in the parliamentary elections of 2005. Once again, al-Shater and Malik were arrested, tried, and sentenced to prison for financing an illegal organization.[37] Instances like this showed that the Brotherhood's politics were never separate from its economics. They also demonstrated the Brotherhood's multifaceted character by showing it to be a sociopolitical organization, a religious association whose members pay *zakat* and charity to an internal hierarchy, and an incubator of for-profit market activities, especially in trade and services.

Religionized Consumption

Religious norms and customs usually generate an economy of their own, where goods and services meet specific demands for observing holidays, consuming halal or Kosher food, selling prayer rugs or rosaries, and providing travel and accommodation services for pilgrimages to Mecca, Rome, or Jerusalem. These are typically markets involving religious products and services; they may be, and often are, for profit. However, the role of religion and religiosity in market making goes beyond marketing religion (that is, selling religious products on the market). It also means religionizing markets by working to give a religious character to the consumption of ordinary goods and services.

Patrick Haenni's work on "Islam of the market"[38] has portrayed rather vividly how Islamized consumption through branding becomes an act of identity formation and confirmation. The consumption of products like Zamzam and Mecca Cola (the name of the first soft drink refers to a spring in the holy city of Mecca; the second refers to the city itself), veiled Barbie-like dolls, mobile phones apps that indicate *qibla* (helping the pious to face Mecca while performing prayer), among many other products, were used as acts of resistance to American imperialism and Western cultural hegemony, and as a public demonstration of one's commitment to religious and ideological causes. Egypt has been a rather wide market for such religionized consumption, especially in the 1990s and 2000s. This included Islamic weddings, shar`ia bathing suits, Islamized fashion, Islamized mobile phones voicing the call to prayers, Islamic media channels, and Islamized shopping centers, a famous example of which is the al-Tawhid wa-l-Nur department stores that sell basically everything and whose name means "Monotheism and Light."

None of these phenomena were separate from the broader social and political developments that stemmed from the increased Islamization of the public sphere from the 1970s on. This created a market characterized by certain consumption patterns and willing customers, and it also generated the incentives for bearers of the Islamic project to treat the market as a space for their struggle for cultural and social (and not just political) hegemony.

CONCLUSION

This chapter has tackled the question of religion in twentieth- and twenty-first-century Egypt. It showed empirically that religion remained relevant to political, social, and economic life despite the rising tide of modernization. Politically, Islam grew relevant after independence. State authorities sought to build their legitimacy by developing an official interpretation of Islam. This entailed the increasing bureaucratization of religious life, the incorporation of al-Azhar, the regulation of official relations with the Coptic Church, and the development of authoritative tools to monitor and police the religious sphere. As a whole, however, religious belief and practice remained independent of full state control. Religious organizations harbored some of the most significant rivals to the ruling regimes since the mid-1970s, ranging from the Muslim Brotherhood all the way to more radical and militant groups engaging in armed rebellion or attacks on Egyptian government targets. How Islam is to be articulated with public authority has been an issue of contention for the past decades, and there is no sign of this being resolved anytime soon.

The chapter has also shown that the significance of religion and religiosity was by no means confined to politics; rather, it encompassed a great deal of social life as well. The Islamic revival from the 1970s onwards involved deep social and cultural changes that aimed at remaking public life in Egypt according to stricter interpretations of Islam. Religion became increasingly important in defining social interaction and gender roles, as well as forms of social solidarity in a context of economic austerity and rising inequality. Not all manifestations of the revival took on a political or anti-regime character, however, as some of these forces found their way into state institutions or were coopted by rulers.

One additional aspect that this chapter has aimed to bring into scope was the economy. Bearing in mind how socially embedded economic activities have been in Egypt—as the next chapter will show—the growth in religiosity had economic implications as well. Public piety and increasing religious self-identification impacted the patterns of accumulation and consumption in Egypt from the 1970s onwards. They have also enabled the rise of certain market actors and facilitated some market transactions. This will serve as a good introduction to part 3, which focuses on Egypt's political economy.

PART III
The Egyptian Economy

In this section, we will tell a story that is both familiar and unfamiliar.

The liberalization of a socialist economy—or one with a strong commitment to state ownership, generous welfare benefits, and equity—is a very familiar story in many countries and regions of the world. Observers sometimes talk of "neoliberalism" when referring to a global trend toward states that are less intrusive in the economy, scale back on services they provide, and rely more heavily on markets. This is not merely a phenomenon of the developing world: developed economies in Western Europe and North America experienced a period of deregulation, decreased welfare commitment, and, in some countries, privatization. But if it is familiar globally, the trend was particularly marked in some developing countries for a variety of reasons: the urgings of international financial institutions and Western governments, the exhaustion of state-led industrialization efforts, and the model of a group of apparently successful "newly industrialized countries," which first appeared in East Asia and then elsewhere.

It is in comparison to such countries—and others that sought to emulate their experiences—that informs our analysis in this section.

What is striking about Egypt is not that its leaders spoke of various liberalizing economic reforms from the 1970s onwards, but rather the results—and some significant particularities. What draws our attention is that for all the talk of liberalization—and the many actual steps that were taken in that direction—the result was not a liberal economy based on free market exchange, private ownership, and low levels of state intervention.

We turn to this puzzle in chapter 7, arguing that the Egyptian economy saw considerable market making and privatization, reflected in private-sector expansion in output, employment, and investment throughout the past four decades. The rise in privately controlled economic space, however, did not mirror the neoclassical economic conceptions of a free market in which anonymous profit maximizers interact at an arm's length in the presence of robust market-upholding state institutions. But neither did it result in mere "crony capitalism," a term used to describe a system in which the market is an arena for the politically well-connected to enrich themselves. Instead, we develop the concept of a "habitus economy" where personal ties and social networks among economic actors are important even for parts of the economy where the politically powerful do not tread.

And there is a particular economic actor—the Egyptian military—that also seems a bit unusual. Though not unique to Egypt, the military's prominent role in the economy strikes most international observers, and yet it has sometimes proved difficult to analyze. Indeed, while almost all discussions of the Egyptian economy today mention the military, there is disagreement on how to understand current and past realities. What has been the military's economic role? How should we understand the form it has taken? What effects has it had? We try to answer these questions in chapter 8.

Chapter Seven

MARKET MAKING WITHOUT DEVELOPMENT

THE PROBLEM

How can a strong policy of economic liberalization be followed for years and not result in a liberal economy? Why hasn't an increasingly private-sector-dominated economy led to the generation of inclusive development? And what political repercussions have these failures had on state-society relations?

After nearly two decades of state-led development and public-sector hegemony, President Anwar al-Sadat launched the open-door policy, known as *infitah*, in 1974. Egypt was among the first Arab countries to adopt measures of economic liberalization, including encouraging foreign investment and private-sector development, deregulation, and privatization or divestiture of state-owned enterprises. Such policies were followed by successive rounds of trade liberalization in the 1990s and 2000s. Economic liberalization, however, did not produce a free market economy in the end. Why did this happen? And what has it produced instead?

After almost four decades of this transformation, Egypt no longer had a state-controlled economy. Even though the state remained a relevant actor in many important sectors, such as public utilities, infrastructure, and extractive industries, private-sector enterprises came to control the majority of output, employment, and investment as early as the 1980s.

Private-sector domination did not necessarily mean, however, the triumph of the free market. Neoclassical economists, the mainstream economic orthodoxy today, view a free market as one in which there is rule of law and clear and enforced property rights.[1] Strong property registration systems and reliable, impartial, and efficient judiciaries to enforce agreements are seen as crucial to enable economic actors, regardless of who they are, to seek to maximize their profits by engaging in transactions driven by prices. Rules-based institutions ensure that economic exchange is driven by the price efficiencies, rather than domination, coercion, privilege, or family connections.

Of course, a totally free market meeting that ideal image is unlikely, even in the most mature of capitalist democracies. But in Egypt, talk of economic liberalization took place while the economy remained markedly far from the ideal. In Egypt, private property rights and contracts remained weakly enforced amid rampant corruption and poorly upheld rule of law. So, it became difficult to locate Egypt's economy in the 1990s and 2000s on the spectrum between command and market-based systems.

There is much skepticism about Egypt's private sector. Perhaps because one understands its role only when one examines closely what is happening on the ground, Egypt's private sector has been systematically and adamantly dismissed by commentators and critics on the right as well as on the left. Despite the prevalence of the private sector in almost all aspects of output, employment, and investment, there has been a general denial of the existence of a market economy altogether, no matter how imperfect or how socially or politically embedded it may be.

Nobody denies that there is a private sector, but many observers do not pay much attention to it, seeing it as lacking in economic significance. They do so for two very different reasons. On the one hand, some political scientists view economic relations as a mere extension of power relations through state capture, cronyism, predation, and rent seeking where public authority has been used to serve the private interests of a few.[2] In other words, the private sector is real but it does not produce authentic economic actors; instead it is a by-product of politics. At the other extreme, many sociologists and anthropologists have been equally dismissive of the notion that the Egyptian private sector has a genuine "economic" or market character. Conversely, they perceive most economic relations as mere extensions of social relations driven by subsistence or social solidarity (i.e., self-employment, household producers, microenterprises, and necessity entrepreneurship that make up the bulk of the so-called Egyptian private sector).[3]

We wish to challenge these attitudes by carving a middle path. We agree that social relations and political power matter and affect the way markets operate—but they do not replace the market; rather, they shape it. With regard to the decades of liberalization in Egypt, we believe that changes have been significant but do not fit into the prevailing preconceived notions of what liberalizing reform looks like. In the introductory chapter, we briefly introduced the concept of a "habitus economy"; we now draw on that idea much more fully. We believe that markets matter, but that history and society—and not merely individual preferences—shape economic interactions.

Beginning in the 1970s, a "habitus market" emerged and took root in Egypt. Habitus is a concept that helps weld together the social and economic.[4] Instead of thinking of a separate "economy" where actors are understood in abstract and purely economic terms ("producer," "consumer," "investor"), this concept urges us to understand actors as existing in a dense web of social relations and suggests that these interactions deeply affect the ways such actors understand the world and behave in it. According to the French sociologist Pierre Bourdieu, "habitus is a logic in action" whereby social actors' positions and dispositions allow them to "construct the world and give it meaning."[5] Thus, when the forces of liberalization, deregulation, or privatization pick up force, (nascent) market actors react to the new opportunities, risks, and constraints from already existing social positions and dispositions (i.e., habitus). These social structures and constructions are what shape the process of market making in concrete contexts. Habitus markets hence can be defined as arenas for economic value production, distribution, exchange, and consumption that happen through social practices and dispositions. Habitus markets stand contrary to the neoclassical economic assertion of market making as a process whereby "notions such as rational action or preferences, which are in fact economically determined and socially shaped, [are treated] as ahistorical universals."[6]

The concept of habitus provides a unique window onto society. It combines the micro level (focusing on a ground-up view) with the macro level (focusing on the economy as a whole) in order to understand the social and political actors and processes at work in the wake of *infitah* and that shaped the contemporary economic order in Egypt. It depicts the mechanisms through which market making actually proceeds by looking at already existing social and political structures, practices, norms, and networks. It dispenses with the artificial distinction between formal and informal in favor of the exact modes of embeddedness in which economic transactions are conducted, especially in the absence of perfect public information and the reliable formal enforcement of agreements. Such mechanisms and processes are often overlooked by analysts who, understandably, focus their attention on the political sphere and the macro level of the Egyptian state and its regime, along with foreign conditionality and international linkages that influence state policies. But while these all matter—and will inform our understanding—prevalent approaches too often stop there, implicitly overstating the state's ability to shape social and economic outcomes in direct contradiction of the evident incapacity, incompetence, and incoherence that for long have characterized state action in Egypt and the Arab region more generally. We encountered the ways in which the state fell short of ruler ambitions or retreated in the political and social realms in parts 1 and 2. We now turn to the economic realm.

Egypt was by no means unique or exceptional in this regard. In fact, it shares numerous similarities with many "successful" contemporary capitalist transformations in East and Southeast Asia. Moreover, historically in the West, before the emergence of universal rule of law in the late nineteenth century, market exchange often depended on private rather than public institutions for property rights protection and contract enforcement. The influential social theorist Michel Foucault showed that the rule of law and protection of private property first emerged in an attempt to limit the risks of state predation rather than to have the state as a third-party enforcer of private agreements.[7] In brief, instead of being a precondition for free market capitalism, as neoliberals nowadays like to insist, formal market institutions emerged at a rather late stage in the modern evolution of markets.

Consequently, the relationship between markets and states and societies cannot be assumed in advance. Those with a more skeptical view of Egypt's private sector understand very well that society, politics, and history matter; however, they overstate the role of the social and political forces in the Egyptian economy. As we suggested above, they can focus on political power and social practices to such an extent that they fail to understand the importance of private actors and market exchanges, which they see instead as simple manifestations of those political connections and social practices they deem so important. Our concept of the habitus economy allows us to take political power and social practices seriously without reducing everything that takes place in the economic realm to noneconomic factors. We cannot ignore instances where the economic sphere (as an arena where price signals matter and where motives for profit making reign) does actually achieve relative autonomy from the social and the political spheres. We insist that there is historical variation here and that one cannot understand the motivations of a diverse group of social actors at any particular time without examining realities on the ground.

In technical terms, we refer to the relative autonomy of the economy when the allocation of resources on a market basis is grounded in three main components: the consideration of price signals, no matter how imperfect; the actors being driven by the motives of repetitive profit making through exchange (Weber's definition of capitalism); and the commodification of the factors of production, especially labor and capital (in the Marxist tradition, this was an essential component of capitalism). All three have existed in Egypt for some economic actors or have governed economic transactions at different times. And it is that variation over past decades we wish to explore.

Socially embedded actors produced for exchange and were bent on repetitive profit making using their social and cultural capital. They did not fall for over-socialization, whereby such relations and norms would completely substitute for market exchange or profit making as a motive. Such practices and actors coexisted with rampant rent seeking and cronyism as well as subsistence-driven microenterprises that engulfed most of Egypt's self-employed and necessity-driven entrepreneurs. Egypt is without a doubt a big country possessing a great diversity of actors, motives, and institutional arrangements governing the economic sphere. Yet this should not lead to the wholesale dismissal of the existence of an entrepreneurial population and genuine market relations, no matter how imperfect they may have been because of weak formal institutions and information asymmetry. After all, free markets can be quite idealistic, if not quite mythical, in a way that "is not relevant for developing economies and perhaps not for any economy."[8] This fact should not lead either to the conflation of the "private sector" with subsistence-driven and household economic activities, as some self-congratulating neoliberals have done.

In advanced market democracies, formal institutions uphold property rights and enforce contracts while making public crucial economic information at a low cost for market actors. In less developed and typically transforming contexts, these formal institutions are usually weak, if not largely dysfunctional. Yet market exchange, in the sense of being driven by price signals and involving business between anonymous persons and entities, still exists. In the case of Egypt, what emerged on the ground was a situation in which social relations and structures (e.g., family and clan, friendship, neighborhood ties, ethno-sectarian communities, people of the same geographic origin, etc.), values, norms, and practices (e.g., trust and reciprocity) performed market functions. Access to means of production like labor, capital, and technology, as well as access to markets, have been deeply embedded in broader political and social relations. Market exchange was both enabled, conditioned, and restrained by such relations in the absence of functioning formal institutions of property rights and rule of law. After all, there was an infrastructure for the emergence of a domestic market that resulted from nation-state building efforts dating from the early nineteenth century onward. Egypt had a national currency, uncontested control over almost all of its inhabited territory, and relatively developed transportation and communications networks inherited from colonial times. This created the physical conditions for the forces of demand and supply.

We are making this argument for Egypt, but we believe it would likely travel elsewhere. That might not be immediately apparent, since many writings on the economies of the global South rely on the concept of "crony capitalism" that can lead us not only to overlook instances and sectors where the economy does achieve some autonomy, but to understand the phenomenon as inconducive to development (and even pathological). There was nothing essentially nondevelopmental about the type of habitus market that evolved in Egypt. We claim habitus had a market-creating or -enabling effect in many instances through myriad mechanisms. What happened in Egypt was not so different from what took place in other parts of the global South during the same period, including in China and other East Asian "success stories" where varieties of habitus markets generated growth and global competitiveness. Those successes have led to the image of the "developmental state" in which states take on the task of assisting and guiding market-based development. In Egypt, conversely, what went missing was the complementarity between the state and habitus—or, in other words, the right mix of formal and informal institutions that could have empowered and allowed the capitalization of the broad base of the private sector. Whereas these institutional complementarities existed in more successful habitus market settings (the cases, especially in East Asia, that gave birth to the developmental state model), it failed to materialize in Egypt.

MODERN TIMES AND INDEPENDENCE

In modern times, Egypt was integrated into the European division of labor in the nineteenth century as a producer of agricultural commodities. By the time of World War I, high-quality cotton accounted for almost 90 percent of the country's total exports.[9] Economically, Egypt remained an agrarian country all the way to the 1960s. A majority resided in the countryside. Most of the active population worked in agriculture, which was dominated by a class of landowners that owned most of the land under high rates of land concentration. Attempts at diversifying the economy by developing industries and services started as early as the 1920s.

Following the nationalist uprising of 1919, segments of the Egyptian bourgeoisie started investing in light industries, especially textiles, in the hopes of exporting higher value-added cotton products. This was the era when an Egyptian bourgeoisie emerged next to a more established foreign bourgeoisie that was almost completely made up of ethnic and religious minority groups of Greek, Jewish, Italian, and Levantine origin. One defining feature of the latter group's business operations was their enjoyment of capitulations that granted them consular protection, exempted them from paying taxes in Egypt, and allowed them to sidestep Ottoman (or later, Egyptian) laws. However, beyond their legal status, these businesses operated within a rich web of community and family relations that defined their habitus in the sense of providing the social and political relations in which they were embedded and through which they could access the means of production and market outlets.[10] This habitus was not shared with the broader "Egyptian" and predominantly Muslim, population in a way that would prove detrimental to the development of a strong indigenous private sector after independence.[11] In other words, after independence, the Egyptian state had not inherited any institutional linkages that might have tied it to the broader base of the private sector.

This weakened the state's capacity to regulate and capitalize the private sector it had come to oversee.

Following the military takeover of 1952, Egypt's economy witnessed a shift along with its changing politics. The Egyptianization of the economy intensified. The trend itself started in 1949 with the abolition of the capitulations according to the Montreux Convention, signed in 1937. A company law was passed in 1949 requiring a gradual increase in the representation of Egyptians on the board, management, and labor force of any private company. This accelerated and intensified in the 1950s.

National independence was fully gained with the end of extraterritorial status for foreigners in 1949 and the final withdrawal of foreign military forces in the aftermath of the 1956 Suez Crisis. Following these developments, the state assumed a predominant role in the management of the economy.

The new regime quickly made use of its greater freedom of maneuver. Almost immediately after the 1952 coup, the military issued a land reform law targeting the class of large landowners. This proved to be the first in a series of land reform laws, the last of which was passed in 1961, that virtually decapitated the old landowning class and removed this formerly dominant group as a threat. It was henceforth incapable of imposing any internal limitations on the new military-dominated postindependence state.

And it was through the Suez Crisis of 1956 that a massive wave of foreign asset sequestration took place. These seizures targeted primarily French, British, and Jewish firms in retaliation for the attack of French, British, and Israeli forces. These enterprises, which constituted a significant share of big business units in key manufacturing, trade, banking, and insurance sectors, came to make up Egypt's public sector. In 1961, a definite socialist turn followed with the nationalization of virtually all large private enterprises, including those owned by Egyptians.

Throughout the 1960s, Egypt had all the features of a command economy, a term that refers to extensive state ownership of the means of production and bureaucratic control over the allocation of resources according to a centrally set plan. The public sector dominated almost all industrial and service enterprises, including in banking, tourism, construction, and insurance. The public-sector workforce expanded tenfold, with employment granted to university graduates in the government bureaucracy.[12] A Soviet-style five-year plan was adopted in 1960.

Egypt's state-led development was based on a model of import substitution industrialization (ISI). This was not the first time such a development strategy had been adopted in Egypt. In fact, there was an early phase of ISI in the 1920s led by a private sector professing economic nationalism.

We saw in part 2 the effects of this policy on Egyptian society and politics. The resumption of ISI in the 1950s and 1960s aimed at greater industrialization, extending into sectors like petrochemicals, electricity, iron and steel, and automobiles. But it was now dominated by public-sector companies that displaced virtually all private big business through the sweeping nationalizations of the early 1960s. By the mid-1960s, the state was the owner of all strategic industries and in general all medium and heavy industries, including all major textile, sugar-refining, and food-processing plants, and all major construction companies. John Waterbury has remarked that "few developing countries, other than those that are professedly Marxist, ever cut so deeply into their private sectors as Egypt."[13]

However, unlike Marxist-Leninist command economies, Egypt's private sector was not completely removed. On the one hand, agriculture remained strictly privately owned as land reform only meant the redistribution of land from landlords to landless and small peasants; the beneficiaries of land reform found themselves regulated (especially through membership in cooperatives, as we have seen), but private property was still the rule in the countryside. The private sector also persisted in urban areas, but it was confined to small-scale trade and highly informal, generally tiny and artisanal services and light manufacturing in workshops.[14] In fact, retail trade, personal services, and agriculture remained strongholds of private-sector activity, even during the heydays of state socialism. After almost fifteen years of state-led development, the private sector still supplied 56.18 percent of total output compared to 43.8 percent for the public sector.[15] This created a relatively large pool of private capital to the extent that the Sadat regime would target their mobilization via the 1977 investment law amendments, which extended the same incentives, exclusive to foreign investors under Law 43 of 1974, to Egyptians.

Import substitution started to run out of steam during the second five-year plan (1965–1970). With industry geared toward manufacturing for a protected domestic market rather than exports, the economy started to suffer from shortages in foreign currency needed to import technology and capital goods. According to scholars, Egypt had exhausted the easy phase of ISI and was facing challenges to deepen its industrialization drive. The model was, however, crippled not just by economics, but by geopolitics as well. The 1967 military defeat against Israel dealt a lethal blow to the Nasserist development model as the state's resources were steered from development to national security. Growth rates plummeted, plans for industrial upgrading and deepening were put on hold, and for six long years (1967–1973) almost all of the country's financial and human resources were directed to the war effort against Israeli occupation.

THEN CAME *INFITAH*

Following the 1973 war with Israel, Egypt joined a diplomatic process designed to remove it militarily from the conflict. While this brought the country face-to-face with its economic problems, this was also a time when some neighboring Arab states were witnessing a tremendous influx of oil revenues and the Cold War appeared to be easing. This made it seem an opportune time to consider a change of economic course. In October 1974, Nasser's successor, Anwar al-Sadat, launched the open-door policy. Economics and diplomacy now seemed to point in the same direction: the regime attempted to address immediate economic and fiscal crises and to send a clear signal that it was realigning its foreign policy with the Western bloc—a transition that would culminate in the peace treaty with Israel in 1979. The new policy turn was composed of partial import liberalization and the passing of private investment laws aimed at attracting private investment, mainly foreign, and a bit later Egyptian. This was in addition to the adoption of stabilization packages with the International Monetary Fund (IMF) in order to fix the country's fiscal and balance of payments problems.

After a brief, and initially strong, recovery thanks to massive inflows of capital from oil-rich Arab countries and Western donors, the government signed its first austerity package with the IMF in 1976. This was designed to signal that the Egyptian state would use aid for productive purposes, construct an environment more attractive for investors, and dial back its socialism in favor of more liberal economic policies. Among other measures, the package called for the raising of prices on some basic foodstuffs, which led to the eruption of popular protest and riots in January 1977, ultimately forcing Sadat to back down.

MARKET MAKING WITHOUT DEVELOPMENT

Following Sadat's assassination in October 1981, his successor, Hosni Mubarak, was reluctant to push for further liberalization throughout the 1980s. He could afford stalling by making use of Egypt's access to oil rents following the 1979 oil shock, including foreign aid from the West, workers' remittances from the Gulf countries and Libya, and the Suez Canal fees. The oil glut of 1986, however, denied the government access to critically needed revenues and forced the regime to negotiate a stabilization package with the IMF in 1987. But the regime lost its nerve even before the ink was dry out of fear of political turmoil, especially in the wake of the 1986 munity of the Central Security Forces. By 1989, Egypt was technically bankrupt, with the government unable to make payments on its external debt, totaling a massive $45 billion.[16]

But Egypt's participation in the liberation of Kuwait in 1991 led its creditors to take a friendlier attitude. In the early 1990s, a new IMF stabilization package was signed, coupled with a very generous debt-relief program.[17] Budget deficits were slashed, inflation rates brought down, and hard budget constraints with state-owned enterprises (SOEs) instilled. Meanwhile, a structural adjustment program was agreed with the World Bank with the aim of a gradual privatization of SOEs and the removal of biases against the private sector. Even though privatization of SOEs progressed rather slowly throughout the 1990s (until it picked in 2004), the private sector witnessed continuous and even accelerated expansion through the same period. This happened thanks to the deregulation and opening to private firms—both domestic and foreign—of many sectors where previously only SOEs had been allowed to operate.

The new policies had profound effects. In its great variety of sizes, legal statuses, and organizational forms, the Egyptian private sector has held the dominant share in output, employment, and investment since the 1980s. According to the World Bank, the private sector controlled 75 percent of Egypt's non-hydrocarbon GDP and around two-thirds of the total output. Private-sector enterprises successfully expanded their shares in key sectors.[18] For example, privately owned enterprises pushed their share in the manufacturing sector from 58 percent in 1991 to 79 percent in 1995–96, and by 2001 it was 85 percent through 2010. In construction, the share of the private sector grew from 71 percent in 1991 to 88.4 and 89.1 percent in 2006 and 2010, respectively. Its share in tourism, including restaurants and hotels, was 85 percent in the early 1990s and 99 percent in 2010. The private sector has always been dominant in the retail and wholesale trade.[19]

In the same vein, the private sector's share exceeded that of the public sector in gross capital formation as a percentage of GDP, which is an indicator of investment.[20]

According to the World Bank definition, gross capital formation refers to the increase in fixed assets of an economy and can include land improvement, the purchase of machinery, plants, and equipment, the construction of transport infrastructure and facilities, and increases in inventories of goods used for production. The share of the private sector in gross capital formation rose from 7 percent during the 1990s to 10.3 percent during the 2000s, whereas the public sector's share declined from an average of 14.7 percent in the first period to 8.7 percent in the second. The role of the Egyptian private sector became even more apparent given the limited role foreign direct investments (FDIs) played in non-extractive sectors. The ratio of net FDIs to GDP averaged 1 percent in the period between 1989 and 2004. The exception that proves the rule was the period between 2005 and 2009, when the ratio increased to 5 percent of GDP.[21] Moreover, around half of net FDIs have been concentrated in extractive industries with minimal presence in or linkages with important sectors like agriculture, tourism, and manufacturing.[22]

Market making and privatization were felt most in the realm of labor. According to Ragui Assad, the share of the public sector (including the huge civil service) in total employment contracted from 39 to 30 percent between 1998 and 2006, passing the burden of employment onto the greatly variegated private sector.[23] The relative and absolute expansion of private-sector employment went hand in hand with two other important phenomena: the *proletarianization* of significant segments of the working-age population, as the only option left for newcomers was joining in as wageworkers, and the *informalization* of labor relations, meaning that most wage jobs in the private sector were not regulated by formal laws and regulations and were not covered by any social security scheme.

Both phenomena demonstrated how deep market making had gone by either absorbing more and more Egyptians in unregulated and informal labor markets, where they may earn a living by selling their labor power, or by introducing them as self-employed individuals seeking income through market exchange of usually low-productivity, menial, and manual services. In other words, the private sector provided jobs, but most of those were poorly paid with few opportunities for training or upward movement. The kind of institutional channels that could have linked the private sector to state organizations and given access to desperately needed physical and financial capital were simply weak. As a result, the period from 1998 to 2006 witnessed a very high growth (7.8 percent per annum) of wage labor in private-sector enterprises, not to count the employers and the self-employed who are private by definition. Most of these wage jobs were informal and two-thirds of them occurred in private small businesses and microenterprises (employing less than ten workers).[24] By 2012, the overall share of the private sector, including wage laborers, the self-employed, and employers, stood at 63.55 percent versus 23.06 percent of state employees, with the rest as nonwage laborers.

Egypt had changed. A private-sector-dominated market economy did in fact emerge. However, it was not the neoclassical version of the market based on well-enforced private property rights, cheap and reliable public information, functional rule of law, and robust contract enforcement. It was, rather, more of a habitus market. Social and political relations, in which entrepreneurs were embedded inside their enterprises as well as in their interaction with other market actors and the state bureaucracy, managed to lower the cost of doing business transactions by circulating private information, creating mechanisms for enforcement of contracts, and norms to limit the risks of opportunism and defection.

So, if Egypt had existed as a socialist command economy but had not completely entered the free market, where was it?

A HABITUS MARKET

The term "habitus market" refers to a socially embedded economic order where preexisting social relations, structures, and cultural norms and constructions shape, enable, and restrain market transactions. They combine certain market elements, like price signals and repetitive profit motivation, with features of social and political embeddedness, such as family and friend networks or clan-like affinities, that are used successfully for market operations. For example, family structures are used to accumulate start-up capital and to collectively manage productive entities using family trust and solidarity in order to settle disputes and exchange information. Another example would be passing managerial and technical skills from one generation to another based on family and friendship. By the same token, social relations within extended families or clan-like networks, usually having to do with a similar geographic origin or a common ethno-sectarian identity, serve as mediums for the transmission of reliable private information about markets.

Of course, economists are aware that individuals are part of families, have friends, and are members of social groups. But they tend to view such ties as secondary—or, if they play a large role, as potentially distorting. We agree that their effects vary and may sometimes undermine economic performance. But we seek to integrate them into our analysis without assuming their effects in advance. In fact, they can sometimes facilitate economic activity, especially in the absence of formal institutions that secure the free flow of information and provide reliable protection for property rights and contract enforcement.

Overall, social and political relations (which by definition are driven not by price signals but rather by compassion, solidarity, or power) play a significant role in the access to the means of production, information, and market outlets. These relations internalize some market and state functions, capitalizing on trust, private information, and informal mechanisms of enforcement and, hence, compensating, partly or fully, for weak formal institutions. In turn, final products and services are then traded on the market using price signals, no matter how imperfect they may be.

In habitus markets, being socially embedded does not necessarily replace market exchange as anthropologist Karl Polanyi once supposed in his seminal work *The Great Transformation*, in which he portrayed market making in eighteenth-century England as based on the disembedding of production and distribution from social relations.[25] In his original theory, which has influenced much subsequent thinking, Polanyi portrayed market making as progressive disembedding of the economy from social relations and norms. Socially embedded transactions were replaced by market transactions, which are, by contrast, far more anonymous and oriented toward profit making. We suggest a different interpretation of Polanyi in today's global South. As revealed in many cases from around the world, social relations and networks, long with norms and structures such as extended and nuclear family structures and clan, ethnic, and sectarian groups, can be constitutive of markets.[26] Many economies in the global South demonstrate that social embeddedness may, and does, actually enable market making by providing, no matter how imperfectly, norms and mechanisms for contract enforcement and information circulation. In Pierre Bourdieu's words, "one strikes to substitute a personal relationship for an impersonal [one] by mobilizing guarantors and witnesses, whose role is to dissolve the relation between buyer and seller in a network of intermediaries."[27]

Habitus markets were forged in Egypt by multiple, and many times not so coherent, forces. They were not created as a conscious policy of the regime, but emerged because of some long-term political, economic, and social trends: protracted fiscal crises beginning in the 1970s; state policies on liberalization and deregulation; conditioning of international assistance on market-based reforms and reduced government expenditures; population growth; waves of urbanization due to the rural exodus;[28] travel abroad by male workers, leading to an inflow of remittances from those finding jobs in oil-rich countries after the 1973 oil boom; and the increased domestic consumption resulting from these inflows.[29] In a similar vein, the contraction in the public sector also contributed to the opening of potential space for market exchange. SOEs witnessed a consistent decline in their share of output, their ability to invest and provide employment opportunities, and their access to foreign currency and newer technology. The adoption of the structural adjustment program Law 203 of 1991 set the scene for the restructuring, privatization, and divestiture of SOEs. Even though the program advanced quite slowly through the 1990s, and only accelerated under the business-oriented Ahmed Nazif cabinet (2004–2011), the share of SOEs declined considerably, opening markets for newcomers from the private sector. With massive urbanization, the retreat in the share of agriculture in total employment, and the shrinking role of the public sector, Egyptians became increasingly dependent on the market, either as workers, in self-employment, or as merchants and business owners and managers. In the absence of evenly supplied property rights and equal access to permits, licenses, and public procurement, the state allowed well-connected cronies favored access to assets, market shares, and unnatural profits.

This story has been thoroughly documented in the scholarship on Egypt's political economy. But what some have missed is how many private businesses survived, and even thrived, without connections to politically powerful people,[30] albeit in suboptimal circumstances. These private establishments accumulated capital on different scales without suffering from systematic state predation. They either managed to do business informally or could adapt to corruption and informal payment requirements.[31] Cronyism existed, but some private-sector enterprises managed to forge connections with others without always going through state bodies, having friends in high places, or having regulators be told by their bosses to look the other way.[32]

The most obvious case is the role that nuclear and extended families played in accumulating capital, establishing and managing businesses, and conducting economic transactions. This was a strong feature of Egypt's private sector prior to the phase of state-led development. Following *infitah*, "family connection and wealth made a strong comeback."[33] Not only was this the case with big businesses; the same practices could be found among smaller units as well. For instance, strong clan and clan-like loyalties found primarily among rural migrants from Upper Egypt enabled their members to exploit burgeoning market niches. A good example is clan-like business organizations in sectors like cargo transportation. In Egypt, transportation is a high-risk business because of concerns about monitoring and disciplining drivers commuting with valuable cargo. Clan-like business organizations, especially among extended families descending from Upper Egypt, could find operable solutions for monitoring and transaction-cost problems depending on high-trust and social sanctioning mechanisms. This enabled them to grow and accumulate larger fleets while doing business with multinationals and large business conglomerates.[34]

More contemporaneously, habitus markets can explain the cases of developing economies that managed to generate high rates of growth and show strong competitiveness without possessing a priori universal rule of law or well-enforced private property rights. In a sense, almost all markets in the global South are habitus markets—they just happen to come in national and local varieties based on the specific social and political structures and constructions in charge of shaping fledging market orders. Prime examples would be post-1978 China, postindependence India, and Vietnam since the 1990s. As a matter of fact, it would make sense to expect the rise of state institutions that protect and enforce private property rights after, rather than before, the rise of sizable and powerful constituencies that hold private property and wish to protect it from potential state predation as well as the risks of opportunism. After all, capitalism comes in a variety of forms. It may assume a myriad of institutional arrangements depending on the extant modes of coordination that may be formally or informally institutionalized, or a mix of the two, as long as a bare minimum of price signals exist and as long as the actors produce for exchange with the intention of repetitive profit making.

Ultimately, habitus markets did provide a solution, at least partly, to the market coordination problem between the demand and supply forces in the absence of reliable and affordable public information and the universal rule of law. By coordination, we mean rules, norms, and practices that could govern business transactions and enable production for exchange. It established private, socialized mechanisms for information generation and circulation, as well as norms and mechanisms for agreement enforcement and mitigating the cost of doing business, referred to above as transaction cost. This contributed to the economy's capacity to create employment, generate growth, and allocate resources relatively efficiently. It may also explain the passing of the bulk of GDP into the private sector. However, most of the market transactions and private-sector capital accumulation and employment relations were not regulated by the state. This made it impossible to perform another form of coordination that we call "development coordination" characteristic of the developmental state model. In such a case, the state enacts policies and builds institutions to guide private actors to higher value-added activities, open new economic sectors, create competitive advantages, and make labor available for exploitation to big businesses (and cheap labor that exists abundantly in Egypt). The final outcome of the failure to build a developmental state along these lines was market making without much development.

PASSIVE PROPERTY RIGHTS ENFORCEMENT

Another decisive factor in the emergence of habitus markets was state inaction rather than action in the area of property rights protection. In a liberal model, a state exists in part to ensure that private property is protected and contracts are enforced—this is to allow private actors to engage in economic activity. But in Egypt, private-sector actors could not count on such a reality. As mentioned earlier, the state played a minor role as a third-party enforcer of contracts and upholder of property rights between transacting market actors: it simply lacked some of the administrative capacity and the courts were too clogged with cases for it to do so. However, the Egyptian state, since the launch of *infitah*, has instilled what can be labeled as passive private property protection by refraining from systematic and widespread state predation where incumbents would use their authority to expropriate private assets and incomes. Since *infitah*, there have been a limited number of cases where egregious predatory acts of expropriation took place against private market actors, especially big ones. Almost all this happened against actors considered politically adversarial to the regime rather than a generalized practice against private market actors. Prime examples of this were the expropriation of Muslim Brotherhood–related businesses and assets in 2006 and in the aftermath of the 2013 coup. Other than that, the state has refrained from any serious reversal of earlier guarantees against nationalization and sequestration that were given by the Sadat regime during the apex of *infitah*.

Restrained or politically guided predation can be explained by many factors, including ever-present international financial institutions (the IMF and the World Bank) since the 1970s in providing funding, policy advice, and conditionality. But there has also been a domestic element that has to do with a long and uninterrupted history of small private property even during the heyday of Nasserist state-led development that never extended its policies downstream to microenterprises and small businesses or to whole sectors like retail trade and construction, where the private sector remained dominant despite the state socialism of the 1960s.[35]

Combined, these factors allowed for the emergence and even the thriving of various socially embedded market actors and, hence, the creation of a habitus market order. That space was by no means confined to politically connected businesses or state cronies and captors. In fact, considerable tracts of Egypt's private sector were too invisible and small (or kept that way), which made them largely unregulated by state action. But even many of those who grew fairly large did not necessarily have organic relations with the state, especially in sectors like retail and wholesale trade and small-scale construction. To add even more complexity to the picture, rent seeking and cronyism did not always come at the expense of the market as preferential access to productive assets like land, credit, and subsidies allowed many cronies to grow entrepreneurial motives over time and to engage in market exchange, as will be shown briefly.

By the 1990s, Egyptians became accustomed to seeing enormous parts of the economy dominated by specific families. Most of the families that came to dominate the economic scene by the 1990s—such as the Sawiris (construction, tourism, and telecommunications), Elsewedy (electric cables), Mansour (tobacco, cars, and food), Ghabbour (cars), and Elaraby (electronics) families—did not emerge from the public sector or any security or military body. They were neither organically nor permanently affiliated with the ruling presidential families. Instead, some were relatively large capital holders (financial as well as social and cultural) from the pre-1952 period. Others came from the retail trade and construction sectors, which survived the state socialism of the 1960s. Historically, the families whose capital dated from the pre-1952 period were the traditional capitalist stripe that resurfaced after the *infitah*. Samiya Sa'id Imam considered many of these as outsiders—in contradistinction to the insiders emanating from the public sector—who capitalized on their connections within the state bureaucracy to start their own businesses.[36]

The burgeoning private sector of the 1970s and 1980s even had business elements that belonged to the Islamist camp and were seen occasionally as adversarial to the ruling regime—for instance, businessmen affiliated to the Muslim Brotherhood–established enterprises in a number of trade- and service-based activities since the 1980s, despite the impending risk of expropriation by the authorities.[37] This is a strong illustration of the existence of sources of private accumulation independent of state rent.

The success of such actors, then, did not always come because they were cronies of powerful figures. Many of the leading businessmen never joined the National Democratic Party (NDP), played an explicit political role, or partnered with security and military agencies; this was the case, for example, with the Elaraby and Elsewedy families throughout most of the 1980s and 1990s. Moreover, some business families, like the Mansours, became politically connected only after they joined the ranks of large enterprises. In some cases, too, those who were engaged in cronyism decided their fortunes would grow faster if they went beyond exploiting political connections to plunge into more free-wheeling market exchange. These instances proved that cronyism could feed into market making rather than hampering it. Looking at many contemporary and historical cases, ranging from the robber barons in the nineteenth-century United States to oligarchs in post-Soviet Russia, we see that this is hardly exceptional.[38] According to

Mushtaq H. Khan and Kwame Sundaram Jomo, "since transfers can be the basis of primitive accumulation, they can play an essential role in the transition to capitalism."[39] Cronyism serves here as a form of habitus whereby political connections govern access to inputs and market outlets.

We can illustrate this phenomenon in the Egyptian private sector by way of a few examples.

Mohamed Fareed Khamis, the owner and manager of Oriental Weavers, has always been viewed as someone close to the Mubarak regime. He was a loyal NDP member since the late 1970s and during the mid-1990s served as the first chairman of the Federation of Chambers of Industry to be drawn from the ranks of the private sector. Perhaps born a crony, he made the transition to a market-oriented entrepreneur. Regardless of the exact origins of his wealth and his continued relations with the Mubarak regime, the entrepreneurial aspect of his business endeavors met with great success. Khamis invested heavily in his vertically integrated business group, which he managed to expand, both within Egypt and abroad, through a strong export orientation. The elements of repetitive profit making and capital accumulation should be decisive in separating a person such as Khamis from mere rent seekers or looters, despite his political connections.

The same may apply to others, like Mohamed Abu al-Enein, the owner and manager of Ceramica Cleopatra, which grew visibly in the 1990s and especially in the 2000s. Abu al-Enein was a devout NDP member who served in several parliaments under Mubarak, and his efforts to finance the regime's presidential as well as parliamentary campaigns are well-known. His factory was also a beneficiary of the generous fuel subsidies of the 2000s, of which around a quarter went to energy-intensive industries. This enabled Cleopatra to expand its exports abroad. Despite operating in a distorted market, Abu al-Enein has been closer to an entrepreneur than a parasite milking state contracts.

In a habitus market order, not all the market-making forces emanated from above. Socially embedded practices and relations along family, clan, and neighborhood lines enabled the emergence from below of market actors in spaces permitted by deregulation, state fiscal crises, flows of remittances, and restrained predation. Embeddedness allowed capital accumulation through informal mechanisms within family structures and friendship networks. Mutual trust created and circulated private information and also supplied mechanisms of enforcement in the absence of formal rule of law. The construction and housing sector stands out as an example.

The informal urban boom through the past decades in Egypt has caused small and medium-size construction enterprises to thrive. They supplied over two-thirds of Egypt's total housing units and filled the gap for relatively cheap apartments left by larger public and private developers preferring to address the demands of higher income brackets. According to Galila El Kadi, this informal housing market served up to 70 percent of the rural migrants (estimated at 350,000 annually) flocking into the Greater Cairo Area in the 1970s.[40]

MARKET COORDINATION BUT NOT DEVELOPMENT COORDINATION

Habitus markets and the political and social relations that upheld them enabled some market coordination between the forces of supply and demand in the absence of well-functioning formal institutions and public information. Scholars have noted that not all capitalist economies are identical; there are other ways to facilitate market economies than the operation of a liberal state. Some speak of "varieties of capitalism," exploring a range of institutional arrangements (be they formal, informal, or mixes of both) and mechanisms through which information is circulated and in which agreements are enforced in a way that enables access to the means of production and market outlets for exchange.[41] For instance, in a liberal market setting, prices, supported by free public information and robust contract enforcement, serve the coordination function. By contrast, in a coordinated market economy, like those of Scandinavia and Germany, coordination happens through non-market mechanisms like corporatist institutions and business alliances.

In habitus markets, social and political embeddedness provided such institutional arrangements and mechanisms. They enabled exchange on final and factor markets. They were, however, not enough for coordinating development in terms of upgrading the Egyptian economy's structure into higher value-added products, higher productivity, and more competitiveness on both the world and domestic markets (against imports).

But the pattern we have discovered in Egypt—of a private sector that expanded impressively through a habitus economy that supported market development without always relying on political connections and cronyism—suggests that the state did not play the developmental role lauded elsewhere. The weakness of state leadership means that neither private-sector growth nor public policy could do much to remedy any of the country's major structural challenges, either with regards to its position in the global division of labor (i.e., the composition and volume of exports and imports) or social development (i.e., standards of living and the quantity and quality of jobs created in the economy).[42] Despite the generation of growth, Egypt's deep inequalities and the marginalization of much of the population remained.

This outcome has been a result of the institutional arrangements linking the state to the broad private sector. With the exception of the few large businesses at the top that actually did maintain strong (even crony) ties with the state, the broad base of private small businesses and microenterprises operated in the informal sector. For the vast majority of these tiny private-sector actors, market relations penetrated where the state was least present. This is in contrast to the traditional focus on top-down processes whereby state decisions around privatizing SOEs, deregulating markets, and liberalizing foreign trade and capital movement were seen as the sole market-making avenues. Economists, statisticians, and sociologists captured these forces from below under the broad label of economic informality. The vast majority of privately owned productive units have always operated informally. In 1998, 83.5 percent of all private small businesses and microenterprises were informal, compared to 82.2 percent in 1988.[43] In 2006, this had increased to 85 percent.[44] Even when these enterprises were legally registered (and thus moving, according to some definitions, from informal to formal), most of their business transactions were not recorded by any state body. Hence, their exchange with other businesses, hiring of workers, and accumulation of capital happened through networks devoid of state influence and based on non-state-enforced norms and mechanisms.

Formality, defined as doing things according to state laws and regulations, has been largely confined to direct transactions between private businesses and the state (i.e., the state is a party to such transactions rather than standing outside or regulating them). Whenever the state was an immediate party to a transaction with some economic or societal actor, things were done according to formal rules (sometimes supplemented by informal ones, to be sure). But for the broad base of the private sector, most transactions were mainly socially embedded, small in size, and informal in character. This meant that the state has seldom served as a third-party enforcer of private business agreements.

Conversely, in Egypt—as in the great majority of countries in the global South—most of the assets used for production or that were subject to exchange have not been registered.[45] The vast majority of the adult population does not use the formal banking sector, including almost all small businesses and microenterprises. Most private-sector wageworkers are informally hired. The state has shown at best a half-hearted interest in formalizing the broad base of the private sector, usually with an eye on expanding its tax revenue base, an objective that was viewed, unsurprisingly, as reprehensible by these small businesses and microenterprises.

Despite the long history of the Egyptian state, informality, in that broad sense, can be seen as linked to the general weakness of state capacity when it comes to regulating society.[46] If economic informality is defined in terms of total transactions that are conducted without being registered or regulated by any state rule or agency, it becomes clear that the Egyptian state has historically had limited capacities vis-à-vis the mass of market actors. Mai Hassan and Friedrich Schneider estimated the extent of informality in Egypt to be around 32 percent of the official GDP in 2013, which they considered massive. This was down from 50 percent in the mid-1970s, when *infitah* was first launched.[47] Having an authoritarian regime does not necessarily produce a strong state in the sense of being able to regulate social and economic exchange and to extract and redistribute resources; we have seen the shortcomings and retreat of the state in previous chapters.

Of course, the state is still present even if it is weak. For all the non-state character of much of Egypt's private sector, some big private enterprises are still deeply embedded politically in the regime and even intermeshed with the Egyptian state. Some enterprises are simply too big to hide even from a weak state and hence have to do things by the book (or at least to appear to be doing so while relying heavily on informal relations to grease the wheels). This also applies to crony businessmen whose access to assets, market share, and information is owed largely to dense and informal ties with state officials or bureaucrats. This is the part of the private sector that the state has been most acquainted with, formally and informally. We are reluctant to equate them with the entire private sector, but they do exist.

Those interested in the developmental state focus on cases in which state institutions cultivate favorites in the private sector in return for cooperation with state monitoring and regulation. Political connections here are used not simply to help the private sector make money but also to allow state officials to guide it in accordance with their developmental strategies. This is the symbiosis that Alice Amsden brilliantly formulated when she asserted that states may pick winners from among market actors and hence get prices wrong as long as they get institutions right.[48] Peter Evans held the institutional formula for coordinating economic upgrading to be embedded autonomy.[49] In order to do this, a state needs an autonomous, professionalized, and merit-based bureaucracy capable of identifying and pursuing some notion of the public good while maintaining dense ties with the private sector so as to collect and process information and monitor the implementation of its policies.

Egypt has not had a developmental state—far from it. That should not surprise us; developmental states have been the exception historically rather than the rule in the global South, where most states are only able to realize the ideal. In that regard, we should note that coordination between the state and big business in Egypt has achieved successes in certain areas. State support, in the form of subsidies, protectionism, or other forms of rent, was not always consumed by unproductive rent seeking, predation, and wastage. This uneven pattern, with pockets of developmentalism, is very common. The poor performance of various state departments and ministries is typical of states in the global South.

A good example in Egypt of this spotty record would be the tourism sector. State agencies provided heavily subsidized desert land plots on the coast of the Red Sea and in the Sinai to private investors. This form of rent seeking seemed to pay off. According to David Sims, "government figures show that, in effect, 'sun, sand and sea' has come to dominate the country's tourist industry, attracting over 81 percent of all tourist visitors to Egypt in 2012. As early as 2003, it was reported that 59 percent of tourists and 72 percent of tourist nights were found in South Sinai and Red Sea."[50] The tourism sector witnessed a secular increase in the number of hotel rooms, which jumped from 52,000 in 1992 to 144,000 in 2005, especially on the Red Sea coast and in the Sinai.[51] This paralleled leaps in the number of tourists from 2.87 million in 1995 to 5.12 million in 2000 and further to 8.24 and 14.05

million in 2005 and 2010, despite the adverse effects resulting from frequent terrorist threats.[52]

Despite being characterized by rent seeking and cronyism, another area where state-business coordination has been successful is in manufactured exports. This was especially the case under the Nazif cabinet (2004–2011), also known as the "businessmen's government." Politically connected exporters in manufacturing enjoyed generous subsidies and direct access to political power through informal networks with the Ministry of Industry and Trade. Informal ties between the owners of large private businesses and the Ministry of Industry and Trade (itself headed by Rachid Mohamed Rachid, a business tycoon) were formally institutionalized into sectoral exporting councils. These councils were staffed by business leaders handpicked by the minister's office, usually based on their weight in exports of certain goods. They also had, rather expectedly, strong social and political ties with the minister. Overall, there was a remarkable increase in manufactured exports during that time, with an impressive annual growth rate of 24.5 percent between 2001 and 2010, compared to 5 percent per annum in the interval between 1990 and 2000.[53]

It may be true that the total weight of manufactured exports did not change much during the two periods, hovering as it did around 37 or 38 percent of total exports. However, this happened alongside an expansion in energy-based exports, with the production of natural gas in 2006 and the increase in oil prices in 2007 and 2008. Hence, the preservation of the relative weight of manufactured goods during that period indicates that these exports were growing at a rate as high as gas and oil, which is unprecedented since *infitah*. Indeed, fuel exports during the 2001–2010 period grew at an annual average rate of 22.47 percent, compared to 24.5 percent for manufactured exports.[54]

A deeper problem with the wish for a developmental state is that it focuses most of its attention on big business and its relationship with the state. But in Egypt—though the country is hardly alone in this respect—much of the important activity and dynamism was, as we have seen, in smaller-scale and informal enterprises—a sector that is significant enough globally to earn its own acronym, SSE (small-scale enterprises). The developmental state, even when it works well (and it did not in Egypt), overlooks or excludes these enterprises.

SSEs are excluded not because they are politically unconnected or otherwise unable to take advantage of cronyism. To be sure, cronyism and rent seeking are issues, and they raise concerns about competition between large politically connected firms and their unconnected competitors, who are often as large but are denied the same access to rents. But the same problems rarely occur when we look at the masses of small businesses and microenterprises, nor do they explain their failure to scale up into the ranks of small and medium-size enterprises. Here, competition with big business is minimal. Rather, smaller establishments often operate in sectors or in market segments that are irrelevant for big businesses. Moreover, their scaling up and capitalization may even prove beneficial for large enterprises if they are to become cheap suppliers, subcontractors, or outsourced firms.

Neither the search for developmental states nor neoclassical institutionalism can actually explain the relatively successful market-based development that has occurred in China, Southeast Asia, and Turkey since the 1980s and 1990s. In none of these cases was there a fully-fledged developmental state like the one that existed in post–World War II Japan or in South Korea during the 1960s and 1970s. Nor was there robust protection of private property or contract enforcement, which are held by neoclassical institutionalism as the sine qua non for market-based capitalism. Conversely, in these "success stories" the decisive factor was not state–big business connectedness, but rather the state's ability to regulate (formally and informally) the broader base of market actors, be they small businesses and microenterprises or wage laborers.

WHAT WENT MISSING?

For the first time in Egypt's contemporary history, market-making forces from the 1970s through to the 2000s pulled into the orbit of market exchange millions of workers and hundreds of thousands of the self-employed and owners of small businesses and microenterprises. The redefinition of Egypt's mode of insertion into the global division of labor and the establishment of a capitalist model that could be inclusive and relatively developmental both depended on the upgrading of competitive and efficient labor-intensive industries and services. These would have enabled Egypt's big bourgeoisie, and the state sponsoring it, to exploit the one "factor of production" most abundant in Egypt, which is cheap labor and the small

MARKET MAKING WITHOUT DEVELOPMENT

businesses and microenterprises that absorbed most of them and occupied labor-intensive sectors.[55] Exploitation here refers to both the neoclassical sense of having to do with comparative advantage and factors of production and the Marxist sense of extracting the surplus value out of labor.

None of this happened on any large scale. Even though market making made labor widely available and cheap (young Egyptians poured into the labor force looking for jobs), equipping workers for more than very low-wage jobs required serious state investment in education and human resources more generally. But the state fell far short in this area due to chronic fiscal problems and the lack of institutional links with the vast majority of small economic actors. Efforts to coordinate development faced problems that had to do with the inability of the Egyptian state to penetrate the economy at large, especially the broad base of labor and small businesses and microenterprises, with the aim of making them available for exploitation by big businesses. Indeed, the share of wages in total GDP has been steadily declining across the past four decades. The ratio of wages to total GDP decreased from 48.5 percent in the late 1980s to 28.6 in 1995 and further decreased to 20 percent in 2007.[56] Labor in the private sector in Egypt is cheap and informal, so the balance of power sharply swings in favor of employers. According to the World Bank, vulnerable employment has been on the rise since the 1990s.

If labor was cheap, this did not lead to a competitive and robust economy closely inserted into the global division of labor. Unlike China, Southeast Asia, or even Turkey, proletarianization in Egypt did not serve the successful specialization in labor-intensive industries or services that are competitive enough to replace imports or to conquer export markets. The relative decline in wages, combined with more precariousness and informalization, just led to more misery.

Why was the Egyptian state unable to raise the skill levels of Egyptian workers or direct their energies into industries where cheap labor might make for internationally competitive industries? A key restraint on the Egyptian state's ability to play such a role amid the capitalist transformation was state finances. The creation of a cheap yet skilled labor force required public investment in human resources—namely, education, vocational training, and health care. The proletarianization that happened to millions of young Egyptian men and (to a lesser extent) women occurred in small businesses and microenterprises with low access to physical or financial capital as well as to technology. These units started tiny and remained so, with no credible chances of scaling up, in what Lois Stevenson called "the missing middle syndrome." The missing middle refers to the virtual absence of small and medium-size enterprises after decades of private-sector development. Rather, there were only either large businesses or microenterprises. On the top, there stood a few very large enterprises—primarily Egyptian—which held the greatest share of output and investment.[57] By contrast, according to estimates from the Central Agency for Public Mobilization and Statistics, the bottom was made up of more than two million microenterprises employing fewer than five workers (with some employing only their proprietors), and performing low-capital, low-technology, low-skill, and low-productivity activities.[58]

Relatively successful cases of state–big business coordination happened almost exclusively in capital- and energy-intensive sectors employing few Egyptians. The state has never had the resources to coordinate an upgrading of labor-intensive (and thus employment-generating) sectors with the aim of pulling major entrepreneurs into the building of these sectors. This is a result of the state's limited institutional capacities in the broader private sector. On the one hand, the state could not raise tax revenues from the private sector, to which the bulk of output and investment had passed, as shown above. On the other, given dwindling revenues, public expenditure was almost totally consumed by recurrent expenses, resulting in minimal investment in human resources.

Total state revenue as a percentage of GDP witnessed a steady decline throughout the 1990s, and it has hardly recovered twenty years later. In Egypt, average state revenue as a percentage of GDP was 30.8 percent in 1990, but this declined to 26.4 percent between 2005 and 2010. The stagnation in tax revenue has been due to the weak administrative and political capacities to collect taxes from property and capital holders.[59]

Whereas successive waves of deregulation, privatization, and liberalization managed to transfer the bulk of output and value added to the private sector, the state hardly augmented its capacity to collect taxes. Corporate taxes held a humble share in total tax revenue. Capital, industrial, and commercial gain taxes averaged around 5 percent of total tax revenue between 1990 and 2010.[60] Indirect taxes—namely, sales taxes and customs—stood for around two-thirds of tax revenue. The share of property taxes averaged less than 3 percent during the same period.

Instead of investment in human capital or cultivation of an expert technocratic bureaucracy able to guide the private sector, the role that the Egyptian state actually ended up playing during the capitalist transformation was dedicating resources to cushion the impact of liberalization and privatization on its base of state employees, primarily in the civil service and less so for the small SOE sector that survived privatization and divestiture. With dwindling tax revenues, almost 80 percent of state expenditure were recurrent, made up of wages and subsidies in addition to debt service, that was itself a result of the budget deficit. Direct investment averaged a meager 11.15 percent in the interval between 1990 and 2010.[61] This may help explain why the state had very little input in investing in human development, disabling it from catering to the national as well as sectoral interests of the burgeoning capitalist order. In such a context, no incentives existed for the erection of institutions that could have regulated the broader base of the private sector. Market making happened in a manner devoid of state intervention, regulation, or oversight. Whereas habitus enabled many private establishments to survive and a few to thrive, it did not in itself ensure long-term development due to the weak linkages with the state in a manner that led to perpetual undercapitalization for most private-sector establishments.

IMPLICATIONS FOR STATE-SOCIETY RELATIONS

This chapter holds that market making in Egypt was neither fully nor exclusively of the making of state actors or those allied to them (e.g., cronies and captors) or their external patrons (including multinational corporations and international financial institutions like the IMF). Many of the features of the private sector and habitus market sprang out of weak regulatory capacities (i.e., informality) or from altogether incremental nonpolitical factors, such as urbanization, migration abroad, and remittances. The key issue here is that the state has never wielded adequate institutional capacity to regulate, penetrate, or coordinate developmental interventions with the majority of private market actors. However, this was by no means a given. It was, rather, an outcome of political processes through which state incumbents got linked to various segments of market actors in a manner that offered neither the incentives nor the resources to bear the cost of building the "right developmental institutions."

What political repercussions did decades of market making without development have? We do not think all political outcomes (such as the 2011 uprising or the rise and fall of the Muslim Brotherhood) can be explained by reference to economics, but we do think there is a connection between economics and politics. And one clear theme in this analysis is the weakness—and sometimes the absence—of a clear political vision to redefine the role of the state in the service of the market by creating institutions that could deliver lower transaction costs, increased productivity, and competition with market actors. The Egyptian state failed to coordinate economic upgrading with private-sector actors. The size, structure, and scope of the intervention of state institutions have not undergone any meaningful transformation in order to perform coordination tasks with the broader private sector made up predominantly of socially embedded small businesses and microenterprises. The weakness that we traced in earlier chapters was deeply connected to the economic trajectory we have explored here.

The state was neither absent nor irrelevant, just weak. Overall, and throughout most of Egypt's transformation, the state did keep a considerable element of autonomy from private market actors. It was sometimes responsive to international actors (investors, multinationals, and international financial institutions). However, its actions and capabilities were confined to certain economic enclaves that were served by pockets of efficiency in the state bureaucracy. But, in general, no comprehensive restructuring of state agencies or filtering through regulations and laws took place. Most public resources flowed to state-dependent constituencies, increasingly made up of civil servants and their dependents (reaching 5.4 million strong in the 2006 census), with the selling away of SOEs diminishing that sector and its base of workers.

Even this was not done well thanks to the state's protracted fiscal crisis and the inability to raise tax revenues from the private sector, resulting in a large, bloated, and underpaid civil service. Not only was the bureaucracy incompetent and costly to deal with for businesses (and ordinary citizens), but it also became a major source of social unrest during Mubarak's last decade. High inflation rates and declining real wages pushed these "white collars" to join the blue-collar workers in SOEs that were protesting against similar grievances, to which they added the threat of privatization. Overall, civil servants made up one-third of all socioeconomic protests between 2006 and 2011, with another one-third by workers in SOEs.[62] It was within these ranks that the first independent trade union emerged in 2009, amongst the real estate tax collectors.

On the other side, Egyptian big business did wield considerable influence. Yet these informal ties, which involved considerable conflict of interest and lack of accountability, meant these businesses were "interested in politics rather than policy."[63] Businesses often employed their size, weight in critical sectors, and voice to cultivate individual and informal connections with bureaucrats and politicians. This hardly functioned as a robust mechanism for economic coordination in macroeconomic issues or in collectively negotiating with labor. In fact, it proved to be a major political liability, as corruption, state capture, and conflict of interest became contentious issues that fueled the opposition to the state's distance from business, serving as a continuous provocation for workers in the public sector.

The failure of the Egyptian state to service the broad base of the private sector severely hampered the development of a solid a middle bourgeoisie (i.e., owners/managers of small and medium-size businesses) that may have been politically supportive of further economic liberalization. A middle bourgeoisie could have functioned as an alternative social constituency against the losers from the liberalization drive—including labor, students, and public-sector employees—who constituted the core constituencies of the postindependence state. Conversely, the Mubarak regime became increasingly dependent on a few large capital holders to face numerous and increasingly dissatisfied and disenfranchised groups. This is different from other developing nations like Turkey, Taiwan, China, and Malaysia, where economic liberalization created a broad base of small and medium-sized enterprises with a potential to grow and to compete in national and exporting markets and that provided implicit and explicit support for ruling incumbents.

As mentioned earlier, economic structures are related to political events in mysterious ways. As much as this missing middle bourgeoisie may explain why market making never became a political project to guide state action or to inform the redefinition of the role of public authority vis-à-vis the economy, ironically, it might have also precluded the attempts of the Brotherhood to forge a broad social alliance in the aftermath of the 2011 revolution. Unlike the Justice and Development Party in Turkey, the Brotherhood did not have a robust constituency of market actors on which they could have counted for political support in their pursuit of more market-oriented reforms or in their fight to the death with the many actors within the military and civilian bureaucracies (see chapter 3 in this volume).

Eventually, the weak link between market making and politics made it possible for the state actors that took over after 2013 to disengage from private-sector actors altogether. It was against this political-economic legacy that the military aggressively broke into the economy in the name of national security, development, and megaprojects. Ever since, a new merger between power and wealth has been in the making. But this time, state capture is happening through state actors and is assuming both formal guises, where the military itself is the owner and manager of productive assets, and informal ones, through gray areas and officers' networks. This pulls the current formula of state-driven development away from any Asian developmental model, given the weak connectedness with, if not an ambivalence toward, the private sector.

Yet there have not been (so far) major reversals on the front of economic liberalization or privatization. This is not likely to happen given the strongly perceived need to lure in foreign capital. No massive expropriation or sequestration has taken place either, with the exception of targeting actual and potential political rivals, overwhelmingly from the Islamist camp. However, this is an exact continuation of the old formula whereby the majority of market actors operate on an informal basis through private and socialized mechanisms of enforcement and networks of exchange of goods, capital, labor, and information. The result is one and the same as the pattern of the past half century—market making without development—continues and the state becomes more and more disengaged from private actors. The overall outcome is an ever more diminishing state capacity to coordinate economic upgrading with what remains to be a private-sector-dominated economy.

Chapter Eight

THE MILITARY'S CIVILIAN ECONOMY

This chapter is about an unusual economic actor: the Egyptian military. Militaries in developed and developing countries have been the subject of extensive scholarship since the inception of the modern discipline of political science. Militaries are powerful institutions that often embody the state's physical might against actual and potential external enemies. They protect the territorial integrity of the state and help socialize individuals into becoming patriotic citizens. In developing countries, militaries have assumed domestic functions critical to keeping nation states bound together, preserving certain political regimes in power, and even imposing or upholding certain economic policies and models of development. In Egypt, the military's economic role is especially significant. In itself, a strong economic role for the military is not unusual, but in Egypt this role has taken some distinctive forms and changed considerably over time. In particular, the Egyptian military not only consumes but produces, and military production goes beyond military equipment and supplies to encompass other activities; this brings it into extensive interaction with civilian sectors of the economy in some unusual ways.

WHAT IS UNUSUAL?

In pursuing their multiple external and domestic tasks, militaries become involved in economic activities in myriad ways in both developed and developing nations. The size and degree of a given military's penetration into the economy are, however, decided by its "control of politics and governance, and the nature of civil-military relations in a particular country."[1] For example, in democratic countries like the United States, a massive military-industrial complex has existed since World War II. However, the military has been consistently and unquestionably under democratic civilian control and generally does not play a direct political role. Similarly, China's communist system has kept the People's Liberation Army (PLA) under the firm grip of the Chinese Communist Party. However, the PLA was allowed to develop an expansive economy that had both military and civilian aspects in the 1980s and 1990s. In other developing nations, such as Pakistan, Indonesia, Thailand, Turkey, and Egypt, militaries have at times wielded political power superior to civilian elites. In these contexts, they enjoyed a hegemonic role in controlling the state apparatus and accessing public resources, allowing them to develop internal economies that depended on their political power and served its reproduction over time.

Some of the military's activities are intimately tied to defense, armament, and provisioning. But some go beyond these areas and take on a civilian character to the extent that militaries have taken possession of productive assets with the aim of supplying goods and services for exchange upon the market, often with profit making as the objective. This has happened to varying degrees over time in Egypt, and it is this phenomenon that draws our attention in this chapter. The military-civilian economy (or MCE) encompasses the production and/or distribution of goods and services designed for civilian uses and targets civilian consumers on a market basis with revenue generation as the drive. Such activity is not unique, but it is unusual. And it varies over time. Moreover, its effects are controversial.

This chapter will therefore address a series of questions about the MCE. What role does the military play in the national economy? How and why did the Egyptian military build an economic empire in the 1980s and 1990s even as the public sector was ceding more space to the private sector and the economy was undergoing liberalization and deregulation? Did this economic empire restrain or enable the military after the 2011 revolution to claim political power? And how did the existence of such activities shape its interests and self-perception as a corporate actor (i.e., as a state institution whose members enjoy a common identity and can hence act collectively)?

In answering these questions, we will place Egypt in comparison with other developing countries marked by similar experiences. In some of these cases, the military expanded into economic activities without necessarily impeding private-sector growth, like in Turkey, Indonesia, and China.[2] We will see whether this also applies to Egypt.

Data on military economies in the developing world is notoriously scarce. In addition to the lack of transparency and public information (often justified in the name of national security), some of the military's economy is privately owned by former generals and their families and associates. It thus can be very hard to determine where the MCE begins and ends and to classify particular enterprises as either military or private. We follow a useful analysis of Pakistan that had this to say about such ostensibly private activity: "In such cases the economic or political exploitation is not necessarily institutional, but individuals can use their connection with the regime or the powerful institutions to create personal wealth . . . and tend to use structured institutional support to gain personal benefits."[3]

In this chapter, we will try to make do with available information with the aim of portraying the extent of the MCE in Egypt, its political and economic structure, and its impact on the country's overall evolution before and after the 2011 uprising.

WHY IS THE MCE PROBLEMATIC?

Liberal political-economic analysis has treated the MCE from two perspectives. The first is economic and stresses the adverse impact such activities have (or could have) on free markets, as they raise the barriers to entry, crowd out private investors, and increase the extent of cronyism, corruption, and rent seeking. The second is more political, focusing on the undemocratic character of such arrangements and the lack of civilian supervision and accountability over critical state activities and public funds.[4] This second critique stresses the importance of democratic civilian control of militaries, which is often lacking in many developing countries where militaries assume explicit political and economic roles in the name of nation building, national security, and economic development. An autonomous MCE has been viewed as giving the military both the incentive and the ability to hinder democratization or to undermine democratic rule by contributing to their ability to stage coups or retain their autonomy from elected officials.

This chapter argues that the economic and political arguments are misstated. The MCE poses serious economic and political questions, but the Egyptian experience shows that these cannot always be reduced simply to the harm done to economic development and governance. The effects—and even the causes—of the MCE vary over time.

Studying the case of Egypt since the 1980s, the military has never dominated any economic sector in Egypt (at least until very recently). The growth of the MCE has not undermined the creation of a private-sector-dominated economy. The evidence that we have so far managed to collect does not support the view that the MCE has amounted to a revival of Nasserist state-led development. Moreover, it could have grown—and at times clearly did—in tandem with a bigger private sector, especially since the 1980s and 1990s.

To add more complexity to the picture, the MCE in Egypt in the 1980s and 1990s did not result from the institution's hegemonic political position. MCE expansion happened not because the military was dominant but because it had to adapt to its declining role following the conclusion of the 1979 peace accord with Israel. The demobilization and shrinking of the armed forces, along with chronic fiscal crises, caused consistent cuts in the budget allocations to the military.[5]

Stretching back to the 1970s, the MCE has evolved over decades. Its current form is not the result of some coherent long-term strategy on the part of the military or the regime, nor was its expansion and sectoral composition always intended. Rather, much of the scope, scale, and form of the MCE were shaped by changes in Egypt's foreign policy and development model. They were also affected by the dynamics governing the ruling regime, of which the military was often a powerful, but not always dominant, component. Therefore, the MCE as it stands today bears the scars of big economic and political shifts to which the military had to adapt. It also sometimes reflects multiple tactical and strategic rationales and actions by the top leadership since the 1970s, in addition to internal power dynamics, both formal and informal.

The military has been one of the cornerstones of the modern Egyptian state (see chapter 2). Following the overthrow of the monarchy in 1952, the military became the key constituent element of the new regime. However, despite its centrality in the post-1952 authoritarian order, the military remained an autonomous state institution that the regime often had to struggle with in order to control, appease, or co-opt. Under Nasser's presidency (1954–1970), the regime departed from its military roots through progressive civilianization. On the one hand, Nasser developed a personal leadership style after the 1956 Suez Crisis that bestowed power upon him independent of his military affiliation. On the other, the cabinet, top bureaucracy, and fledgling public sector showed a steady increase in the number of civilian officials, especially technocrats, despite the presence of military retirees. More importantly, Nasser opted for the creation of mass state party apparatuses (the National Union in 1957, to be succeeded by the Arab Socialist Union in 1961) that granted the regime social constituencies beyond the military. Nasser was also not in full control of the military, which was left almost unchecked to his onetime friend and later rival Field Marshal 'Abd al-Hakim 'Amer. The power struggle between the two ended in the country's tragic defeat in 1967, dealing a lethal blow to 'Amer's power.

Under Sadat and Mubarak, the military was one component of the ruling coalition rather than the most dominant actor. In fact, the institutionalization and consolidation of Egypt's authoritarian regimes since the 1967 defeat was based on the military's professionalization and its exclusion from a direct political role. The military nonetheless remained a very powerful component of these regimes. Both presidents were drawn from the institution, and they took pride in their affiliation with it. When facing mortal internal threats, neither was reluctant to call in the military in order to save the public order and in the process safeguard the ruling regime. This happened in 1977 when Sadat deployed the military to control the bread riots that erupted in reaction to his government's austerity measures. Mubarak also relied on the military to crush the 1986 mutiny by the paramilitary Central Security Forces, which were under the control of the Ministry of the Interior. However, these were exceptional and typically emergency circumstances. Otherwise, the military was a professionalized, corporate, strictly hierarchical, and highly institutionalized state body that identified with the state more than with any particular regime or president. This is what enabled the military to stand apart from the Mubarak regime in 2011 and to claim that it was a representative of the state rather than the regime, unlike the security forces or the National Democratic Party. It also showed enough autonomy to step in and depose Mubarak when necessary.

To sum up, one cannot understand the MCE apart from the broader dialectic of state-regime relations since 1952. The military was a fundamental pillar of the Egyptian state since before the country's full independence, and it continues to be so. It was also the founding force of Egypt's authoritarian regimes, which have never degenerated, however, into direct military rule. Conversely, the institutionalization of these successive regimes both allowed and reflected the military's autonomy and institutionalization. This dynamic might have changed since 2013. We address this question at length in chapter 9.

Alternatively, we argue that the most problematic element in the MCE in the Egyptian context has been political rather than economic. The MCE proved to be a hindrance to political transformation, especially after the 2011 revolution. Access to economic resources—generated autonomously of any other sector and unaccountable to any actor within the state or civil society—proved essential in enabling the military to ascend to power after 2011 and to abort any meaningful political transformation. Rather than use its position within the state to enrich its members, the military used money to secure for itself a more prominent political role. In fact, the military in Egypt did not move in 2011 and 2013 to defend its economic interests; these were actually quite safe, and the new civilian elites were ready to trade the military's economic empire for restrained political influence. For instance, the military's political and economic autonomy were constitutionalized in the constitution pushed through by the Muslim Brotherhood in 2012. The MCE did not need to be defended. The military's deep political concerns focused instead on public order, national security, and its long-term institutional autonomy from the new elected elites. The MCE allowed it to act upon these political interests rather than being itself the motive for action.

In what follows, we first give a brief account of the recent history of Egypt's MCE since the late 1970s. We then provide an estimate of how big the MCE is using the scanty yet relatively reliable data we have collected. The section that follows expands on our argument by focusing on the re-politicization of the Egyptian military after the 2011 uprising and the role the MCE played in allowing it to remilitarize the ruling regime, especially in the aftermath of the July 2013 takeover.

A BRIEF HISTORY OF EGYPT'S MCE

Egypt's MCE resulted from a worsening fiscal crisis lasting from the late 1970s through to the late 1980s, as well as the postwar demobilization that accompanied the 1979 peace treaty with Israel. Overall, the military's economic expansion happened at a time when the military was becoming politically less relevant, depoliticized with the hope of preserving its hard-won professionalization in the aftermath of the 1967 defeat, and then faced with a shift in its mission away from the possibility of imminent war with Israel. This sets Egypt apart from other cases in the developing world like Pakistan, where "the needs of the ... defense establishment are completely catered for by the government."[6] There was an initial need to compensate for the Egyptian military's dwindling share in public expenditures, which pushed it to look for alternative sources of revenue. Because of the fiscal crisis of the mid-1980s, the state attempted to relieve itself of the burden of financing the military by enabling it to directly fend for itself. The idea was to allow the military to make use of the assets it controlled, to claim shares in expanding domestic markets, and even to seek partnerships with both Arab and global investors in the process.

The military had run its own defense industries since the 1950s and 1960s. The trend toward diversifying into civilian sectors began, however, in the late 1970s with the creation of the military-run and -owned National Service Projects Organization (NSPO). The NSPO was established by Presidential Decree no. 32 of 1979 under the Ministry of Defense's purview. The NSPO decree offers the institutional and legal framework for partnerships between the military and global and Arab capital and allows the securing of independent funding sources. According to the NSPO's official website, its mission is to achieve the financial independence of the armed forces so as to minimize or alleviate the state's fiscal burden while also providing surplus goods that exceed the military's needs to local markets, in addition to supporting the state' economic-development projects. Currently, the NSPO reportedly owns and runs twenty-six companies operating in a wide array of economic sectors, including construction, agriculture, food production, and cement, in addition to directly managing hotels, security services, and petrol stations.

Throughout the 1980s, the construction of an economic empire secured political autonomy and prestige for the military and mitigated the impact of fiscal contraction. However, this economic empire assumed a life of its own when it became a means of asserting influence for the institution and its all-powerful minister of defense, 'Abd al-Halim Abu Ghazala, who had a vested interest in underscoring the military's peacetime contributions to national development and industrialization. However, the military still maintained a rather large (by Egyptian standards) military-industrial complex thanks to rising Iraqi demand for arms during that country's long war with Iran (1980–1988). Egypt was also engaged in a missile-development project with Argentina and Iraq, which resulted in Abu Ghazala being forced out of office in the late 1980s, at least in part because of American pressure.[7] This, however, had little impact on the expansion of the MCE.

The military's financial autonomy was simultaneously bolstered by the initiation of U.S. aid in 1979, which, since 1982, has guaranteed an annual contribution of around $1.2 billion worth of weaponry and other forms of assistance to the Egyptian military.

The end of the Iraq-Iran War in 1988, the removal of Abu Ghazala, and Mubarak's growing weariness with the military's attempts at regaining influence, all contributed to limiting the military's defense industry base. This opened the way for the conversion of military factories and agencies into the production and distribution of civilian products in the 1990s. Not only the NSPO but also military factories owned by the Ministry of Military Production (created in the 1950s) witnessed an increasing reorientation toward civilian products in the 1980s and especially the 1990s. This also applied to the Arab Organization for Industrialization (AOI), which was originally created in 1978 as a joint Arab defense-industry complex. It briefly became an exclusively Egyptian body after the withdrawal of other Arab countries following Egypt's 1979 peace treaty with Israel. According to Abul-Magd, nine of the AOI factories were converted to civilian production.[8] At the same time, the Engineering Authority of the Armed Forces became increasingly involved in infrastructure projects.[9]

The 1990s witnessed a reinforcement of the earlier trend. In 1990, Egypt adopted a stabilization package with the International Monetary Fund according to which austerity measures were introduced with the aim of slashing the budget deficit and bringing down inflation. Data from the World Bank indicate a dramatic decline in the military's expenditure as a percentage of GDP after 1979 (figure 8.1). These figures include central government allocations, foreign military aid, and the pensions and wages of military personnel and civilian employees.[10] As mentioned earlier, it appears that the military has simply responded to the downswing in state financing by ramping up its civilian economic activity since the 1980s.

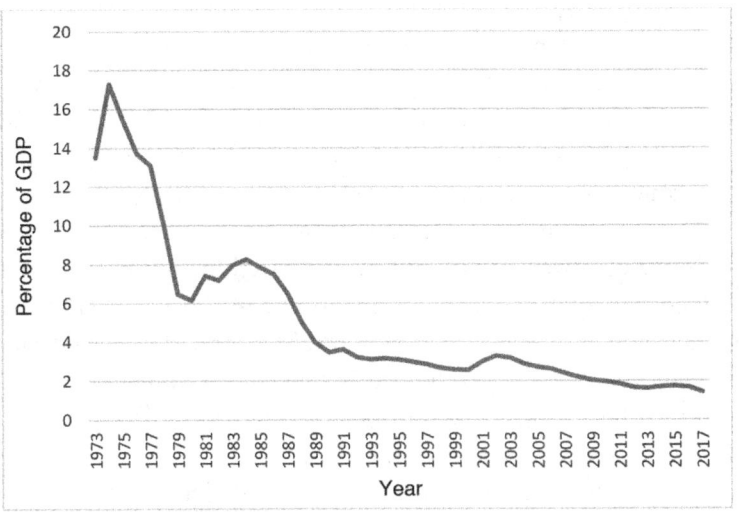

FIGURE 8.1. Military expenditure as a percentage of GDP, 1973–2017. *Source*: "Military Expenditure (% of GDP)—Egypt, Arab Rep.," World Bank, accessed December 20, 2018, https://data.worldbank.org/indicator/MS.MIL.XPND.GD.ZS?locations=EG.

THE MCE AND DESERT LAND

The military's engagement with the civilian economy was by no means confined to producing and distributing goods and services for civilian use. It also involved the management and regulation of publicly owned assets. This applied especially to desert land, which constitutes around 96 percent of Egypt's total surface area and represents a critical front for urban development as Cairo and the Mediterranean coastline have expanded. Land use is connected to a host of economic sectors, most notably construction industries and real estate services. Control over desert land proved to be of consequence for the military's access to resources, both for the institution as a whole and for the benefit of individual personnel. The military drew on its control of land by converting its broad regulatory mandate into different forms of investment premiums, rent from developers and consumers, and direct access to plots of land at below-market rates for military members.[11]

From the late 1940s on, the deserts to the west and east of the Nile Valley, including the Sinai, served as national frontiers or battlegrounds for the

Egyptian state. Frequent military confrontations with Israel—which took place in 1948, 1956, 1967, and 1973—provided the context in which the central government in Cairo regulated its relations with desert areas. Decades of military management and control have left a strong imprint on the regulatory and legal framework up to the present, with military and national security concerns, including border control, putting administrative and legal restraints on the use of desert land for economic purposes.

Ever since the 1970s, the military has enjoyed the ultimate say over all desert land slated for development. Not only was this a matter of making economic gains for the institution as a whole or for certain groups or individuals within it, but it also soon became tied to the military's search for a political role after the 1979 peace treaty with Israel. While the military's economic role is sometimes difficult to document in detail, Robert Springborg has shown how tight control of desert land helped the military recast itself in the 1980s as a vehicle for national self-sufficiency, development, and the employment of redundant military personnel.[12]

Indeed, the vast desert lands to both the west and east of the Nile Valley hold potential opportunities for future urban expansion and investment in agriculture, tourism, energy generation, and manufacturing. State policy determines access to land and its price, as well as subsequent access to financing for private enterprises, given that banks have high collateral requirements, usually in the form of land or buildings, for extending credit to private investors.[13] Moreover, houses are a crucial form of investment for the Egyptian middle and upper-middle classes, who prefer to put their savings into real estate units in light of chronically high inflation rates and the underdevelopment of financial markets.

By holding tight to its mandate over land, the military undermined the overall coherence of the state's land-use policies. This also created friction within the state, personified in the 1980s by the tensions between the all-powerful Field Marshal Abu Ghazala and civilian agencies in charge of building new towns and overseeing land reclamation. Mubarak was never capable of definitively resolving this tension, as guaranteeing military control over desert land was part of a bigger political settlement, originally struck under Sadat, that sought to give the military an increased economic sway in return for a contraction of its political role.[14] This was a reminder of the dialectical nature of state-regime relations, which governed the interaction between the Mubarak regime and the military as a state institution looking for influence, prestige, and resources. The tension over the use of land continued to hinder the regime's economic strategies and resurfaced strongly in Mubarak's last years (2004–2011) when politically connected private developers scrambled for desert land.[15]

Under the current legal framework, no plot of land can be allocated for economic use without prior approval from the minister of defense. By the same token, the minister determines which desert land is to be used for military or strategic ends, rendering the land thus designated unavailable to other public agencies or for private use.[16] In the same vein, only the minister has the legal right to alter the use of lands earmarked for strategic or military purposes. He is thus the ultimate authority over the use of desert land. As Abdel-Fattah Barayez explains, "the military is also entitled to compensation from the state treasury in cases wherein land used for military ends gets allocated for economic purposes, with their prior approval of course. The military's approval is also required for the allocation of lands in coastal areas—defined legally as borders—which typically attract high-value tourism investment, such as on the North Coast and the Red Sea."[17]

Presidential Decree no. 531 of 1981 also allowed the military to auction off land originally used for military purposes and to collect any proceeds for the construction of alternative military sites and facilities. This arrangement provided a formal channel for the military to convert its regulatory mandate over public lands into economic returns. In 1982, Presidential Decree Number 223 established the Armed Forces Land Projects Organization (AFLPO), whose mission was managing the sale of military-owned lands and using the revenue to build alternative facilities.

Moreover, the military regulates investment in the Sinai Peninsula through the Sinai Development Authority. Under Law Number 14 of 2012 on comprehensive development of the Sinai, the president of the republic appoints the head of that body based on an initial nomination by the minister of defense. Crucially, the law grants the Sinai Development Authority all regulatory power pertaining to land allocation on the peninsula for various investment purposes.

In addition to the military's institutional control over desert land allocation, it has also kept an almost institutionalized, albeit informal, presence in state civilian agencies in charge of desert land planning and development. Three of the four civilian land-management authorities in this area—those dealing with agriculture and land reclamation, tourism, and industry—have been almost continuously headed by retired generals. The fourth, the New Urban Communities Agency, in charge of housing and urban development, has been headed by the minister of housing since its creation in 1979. However, within the ministry itself, the planning department as well as the Land Survey Authority have usually been heavily staffed by retired military personnel.[18] "Military engineers flooded the Ministry of Housing and its various authorities responsible for distributing state land or building affordable housing.... Ex–air force pilots controlled the sector of civil aviation, all the way from the seat of the minister to the heads of relevant authorities and holding companies.... Ex-navy rear admirals and admirals swept positions as heads of ports as well as government authorities of maritime navigation and safety and chaired relevant state-owned companies."[19]

SECURING MARKET SHARE, NOT DOMINANCE

Thus far, we have seen how the military spread into different sectors of the civilian economy, either through expansion into productive activities or through the generation of rents using its regulatory mandates. However, contrary to popular thinking, the army's share in Egypt's overall economy is far from dominant.[20] The little hard data we have suggests that it is present in many sectors but does not occupy a dominant position in any. Indeed, it does not have any presence in a range of crucial economic sectors, such as banking and financial services. In fact, there is little evidence that the private sector has been crowded out by the military, at least not until recently, with the possible exception of government contracts for new megaprojects in the post–June 2013 period (an important topic we will examine more fully below). There are tentative signs, however, that this has been changing in the past couple of years with the unchecked and seemingly predatory expansion of the MCE at the expense of private enterprises, at least in some sectors such as the media, construction, and cement. If that is true, it would mark a transformation away from the model that has prevailed since the 1980s rather than a continuation or a natural culmination of it.

In fact, since the 1980s the MCE has grown hand in hand with the private sector's expanding share of the national economy. By the early 1990s, the private sector (in its great diversity, as shown in chapter 7) accounted for over 70 percent of the non-hydrocarbon economy in Egypt.[21] Among private-sector leaders stood an impressive class of family-owned conglomerates (often but not always politically connected) that operated in multiple sectors and dominated much of the Egyptian economy. The private sector has increased its share at the expense of a dwindling state-owned sector in trade, manufacturing, tourism and hospitality, transportation, and communication, industries where growth rates have been most pronounced. The fact that this private-sector expansion occurred as the military expanded its role in civilian economic activity suggests some coexistence was possible and that the notion of "crowding out" warrants greater empirical scrutiny.

In May 2015, the NSPO issued its first official statement disclosing the volume of production activities in firms it owns and runs. The statement was issued with the aim of demonstrating the agency's contribution to the state's "comprehensive development" plan. The NSPO's production and distribution statistics are a rare source of information on the rough market shares of its subsidiary companies in key economic sectors. Even though the NSPO is just one component of the MCE, it is the organization under which exclusively nondefense activities fall. Its subsidiaries cover sectors as diverse as agriculture, cement, iron and steel, and fertilizers, to name just a few. It is hence representative of the MCE, even though not in any exhaustive manner.

Based on the data in table 8.1, we can say that the Egyptian military has indeed developed a parallel civilian economy. However, the share of military-owned companies (i.e., the formal military economy) is not particularly significant in any of these sectors, forming anywhere from a low of 0.18 percent to a high of 3.9 percent of GDP. The military has been virtually absent from, or has retained only a tiny share in, a number of key economic sectors that grew considerably since the 1990s. In a sense, the MCE grew within a sociopolitical habitus shaped largely by the military's position in the ruling coalition and an evolving set of opportunities and restraints that set different institutional arrangements for the MCE.

NSPO statistics show 100,000 *feddans* (a *feddan* is a unit for measuring land and is very close in size to an acre) reclaimed in Sharq al-'Owainat in the Western Desert, where most military-owned farms are located. In 2013, these plots yielded around 78,000 tons of wheat, 156 tons of olive oil, 25,000 tons of dairy products, 2,000 tons of red meat, 60,000 tons of fodder, and about thirty million eggs. This produce was primarily used to supply a

TABLE 8.1
NSPO-Owned Companies' Economic Share in Selected Economic Sectors (2015)

Sector	NSPO-owned companies*	Total national production[†]	Share of NSPO-owned companies in total national production (%)[‖]
Cultivated surface area (thousand *feddans*)	100	8,619	1.16
Wheat (tons)	78,000	8,500,000	0.92
Oil olive (tons)	156	4,000[‡]	3.9
Dairy products (tons)	25,000	5,849,000	0.43
Red meats (tons)	2,000	990,000	0.2
Cattle heads (thousands)	16,000	9,100	0.18
Eggs (millions)	30	9,000	0.33
Fodder (tons)	60,000	—	—
Cement (tons)	3,000,000	50,000,000	6
Fertilizers (tons)	150,000	18,000,000	0.83
Mineral water (million bottles)	37	—[§]	3

* Data pertaining to the produce of NSPO companies are based on the military announcement published in *al-Yawm Al-Sabi'*, May 15, 2015, https://www.youm7.com/story/2015/5/29/%D8%A7%D9%84%D9%82%D9%88%D8%A7%D8%AA-%D8%A7%D9%84%D9%85%D8%B3%D9%84%D8%AD%D8%A9-%D8%AA%D8%AF%D8%B9%D9%85-%D8%AE%D8%B7%D8%A9-%D8%A7%D9%84%D8%AF%D9%88%D9%84%D8%A9-%D9%81%D9%89-%D8%A7%D9%84%D8%AA%D9%86%D9%85%D9%8A%D8%A9-%D8%A7%D9%84%D8%B4%D8%A7%D9%85%D9%84%D8%A9-%D8%AC%D9%87%D8%A7%D8%B2-%D8%A7%D9%84%D8%AE%D8%AF%D9%85%D8%A9%D8%A9\.

[†] Total production figures in 2012–2013, according to the Central Authority for Public Mobilization and Statistics, "Matrix of Social Accounts for the Egyptian Economy" [in Arabic], http://www.msrintranet.capmas.gov.eg/.

[‡] Data about olive oil production are from the Economic Affairs and Promotion Unit of the International Olive Council, "Country Profile: Egypt," https://www.internationaloliveoil.org/wp-content/uploads/2019/11/ENGLISH_POLICY_-EGYPT-2012_OK.pdf.

[§] Data about mineral water production are taken from Euromonitor International, "Bottled Water in Egypt," 2015.

[‖] Data is based on the authors' calculations.

number of NSPO-owned firms that compete in the civilian sector, including the military-owned mineral water brand Safi, which produces around thirty-seven million bottles a year. Because there are low barriers to entry in the market for consumption goods, it remains difficult for any enterprise or actor—including the military—to dominate. In the case of mineral water, the multinational Nestlé holds the greatest market share, at 26 percent, with Safi coming in at a distant third with 3 percent.

A similar dynamic obtains in agriculture. Nearly all cultivable land in the Nile Valley and Delta has always been privately owned; this was the case even before the Nasser era and it has hardly changed in following decades. Moreover, most desert land reclamation since the 1970s has been pursued by the private sector, including a class of large private producers and exporters.[22] Even though the military's limited role in that sector has traditionally boosted its popular support thanks to subsidized handouts to the poor on national and religious holidays, its share in total cultivable land is rather limited.

In addition to perishable goods, the NSPO owns both the al-'Arish Cement Company and the al-Nasr Company, which produce 2.5 to 3 million tons of cement and about 150,000 tons of cement fertilizers, respectively, each year. Most studies underline the presence of military-affiliated enterprises in these sectors yet refrain from showing their relative weight, especially compared to the private sector. For instance, in the case of cement, 97 percent of total annual production is attributed to privately owned enterprises—mostly multinationals—along with publicly owned firms in which the military plays no role. Similarly, the bulk of fertilizer production has remained in the hands of the private sector since publicly owned companies were sold off in 2008 and 2009.[23]

The same is true of significant service sectors such as tourism and construction. In June 2015, the minister of defense issued a decree, published in *al-Waqa'i' al-Misriyya*, the annex to the official gazette, listing all the real estate units owned by the military in those sectors. The decree declared all of these buildings and the land on which they were built exempt from taxation. This includes facilities used for different social and economic purposes, such as hotels, sporting clubs, parks, and schools. The decree makes no mention of other plots of land that are vacant. There is no reason to suspect the comprehensiveness or accuracy of the lists contained in the decree, as it was meant to be an exhaustive list of sites addressed to the tax authorities for full exemption.

Tables 8.1 and 8.2 suggest the MCE's rather humble share in the hospitality and tourism sector. Found in remote, non-touristed areas across Egypt, most of the military-owned facilities primarily serve Ministry of Defense personnel and their families. In the North Coast region, a popular area for domestic tourism, the military owns only 4 of the 128 tourist villages and hotels.[24] The remainder fall under the ownership of the private sector—which expanded its investment in tourism considerably over the last decade—or of cooperatives established by employees in ministries, public universities, professional syndicates, or the New Urban Communities Agency.[25]

The military's share of the construction sector has been historically large, especially in utilities and infrastructure. However, this has gone hand in

TABLE 8.2
Military-Owned Facilities by Use

Unit	Number
Parks under military administration	17
Tourist villages	8
Cinemas and theaters	18
Resorts for civil and military workers at the Ministry of Defense*	12
Press houses	2
Service complexes	13
Sports and social clubs	73
Schools and institutes	5
Gardens	7
Bakeries and slaughterhouses	6
Shops and outlets	24
Hotels	17
Military facilities	24

Source: Based on authors' calculations.
* Ministry of Defense decree issued in *al-Waqa'i'al-Misriyya*, no. 127 (June 3, 2015).

hand with the expansion of the private sector. Indeed, according to the Central Bank of Egypt, publicly owned firms held 11.51 percent market share, with the private sector holding 88.84 percent. Most of the supply of housing has been constructed by small and medium-size enterprises, often in an informal manner (i.e., without permits) on agricultural land adjacent to Egypt's main urban agglomerations.[26]

The 1980s and 1990s witnessed the rise of a class of private urban developers that often maintained strong personal ties with the Mubarak regime via membership in the then state party (the National Democratic Party) and through informal networks with the presidential family. These tycoons enjoyed privileged access to desert land in new urban communities. Their emergence and expansion in the 1990s, and especially through the 2000s under the business-oriented cabinet led by Prime Minister Ahmad Nazif (2004–2011), demonstrated with clarity that the military's influence was far from hegemonic during those decades. Even though it developed a significant share in the market, and it still retained regulatory control over desert land use and generated rent from it, it was just one member, albeit a powerful one, of the ruling coalition under Mubarak. This allowed the emergence of a division of labor between the burgeoning large private sector and the MCE. The civilianized character of the authoritarian regime under Mubarak allowed counterweights and created mechanisms for arbitration and rent sharing. The market making that followed *infitah* and especially the adoption of structural adjustment programs in 1990 and 1991 also accommodated military plans (and the plans of military personnel) for revenue generation. Abul-Magd refers to this last group as "military entrepreneurs" in reference to retired army personnel and their families and cronies who were bent on exploring opportunities made available by their institutional influence for their own private means, leading to a growing class of neoliberal officers who were nevertheless "far from being believers in the free market."[27]

Given the political and economic contexts of the 1980s and 1990s, the MCE has barely been integrated into Egypt's financial sector. This was a by-product of two factors. The first is the financial autonomy that the military enjoyed; after all, the main motive behind its expansion in the first place was to compensate for lower public allocations. This reduced the incentive for reaching out for bank credit. The second factor is the institution's lack of political hegemony, with the military comprising one powerful member among others within the ruling coalition under Mubarak. These two factors seemed to have contributed to the lack of financial sophistication of the MCE, which remained almost strictly in nonfinancial sectors, cut off from the banking system as well as from capital markets and the stock market.

It has been remarkably different in other countries in the global South, such as in Pakistan and post-1980 Turkey, where the military expanded its civilian economy while enjoying full political dominance. In the former case, the Pakistani military, since the time of Zia ul Haq's coup in 1978, has developed its own civilian economy while claiming large shares in the state budget. Moreover, in addition to having a bank of its own that received deposits from the general public, the Pakistani military had semiprivate funds that were publicly traded in the stock market.[28] Similarly, in Turkey, the MCE enjoyed a high level of integration into the financial sector. Taking the form of a pension fund for the military's personnel, the Ordu Yardimlasma Kuruma (or Army Solidarity Organization) developed in the 1980s and 1990s into one of Turkey's largest holding companies that made use of its legally "private" status to integrate itself into the broader economy and financial sector.

This appears not to have been the case in Egypt. Central Bank annual reports from 2002 to 2016 reveal that the Treasury has become the largest borrower from the banking sector, but these loans are not related to military activities. Rather, the government competes with the private sector in securing loans to finance its ever-widening budget deficit. In an economy that chiefly depends on a banking-based system, the military's tiny share of bank loans suggests that it does not enjoy a dominant position in the economy. Even if military-owned companies could do without resorting to the banking sector through some form of self-financing or earning-retention program, this itself would indicate that its firms do not require the extensive capital that only large banks can provide in the form of loans.[29]

DEVELOPMENTS SINCE 2011

We have shown how the MCE in Egypt has developed hand in hand with a multiplicity of private-sector actors since the late 1970s. The military followed a strategy of diversifying into unrelated sectors without necessarily holding a dominant position in any. This, however, was commensurate with the military's position within the ruling coalition under Sadat and Mubarak as a powerful member of a broader ruling coalition of state and business actors. This institutional habitus would prove crucial for determining the pace, scale, and scope of MCE expansion after 2011, not just for the whole organization but for its personnel and the networks they belong to. Even with the dramatic change in the political situation after 2011, the mission, structure, and corporate identity of the military defined the institution's reaction and repositioning within the state and vis-à-vis society.

Now, we seek to address whether the MCE has grown along these same lines after 2011, especially after the 2013 takeover, when the military emerged as the single most powerful state actor.

Did the uprising and the post-2013 system have any effect on the MCE? Remarkably, while the MCE might have seemed politically exposed in the upheaval after 2011, it has actually expanded in scope and influence.

The overall political situation dramatically changed following the 2011 revolution that brought down the Mubarak regime (see chapter 9). An unintended consequence of the uprising was the expansion of the political power that the military has enjoyed since 1967. In fact, the uprising managed to destroy the Mubarak regime by pushing him out of office and forcing him to abort the plan to pass power to his son, disbanding the National Democratic Party along with the two parliament houses it dominated, and suspending the 1971 Constitution. It also crippled the security forces. More importantly, it deeply disrupted the informal, often corrupt, networks on which the regime had depended to coordinate action between the state bureaucracy and the business community. The only surviving member of the old coalition happened to be the military, to which power passed as the manager of the post-Mubarak transition between February 2011 and July 2012.

Following the brief and quite unstable reign of the Brotherhood-backed president Mohamed Morsi, the military made an even stronger comeback. As of mid-2013, and especially after al-Sisi's formal ascent to power as president in July 2014, it became obvious that the military has become the one state actor in charge of remaking Egypt's political regime. Egypt has only witnessed such a dynamic in the early 1950s, before the consolidation of power under Nasser's presidency by 1956.

The altered composition of Egypt's ruling coalition as of 2013 had almost immediate implications for the MCE. The military expanded its access to economic resources and opportunities. This served different economic and political ends. On the one hand, the military, through the NSPO, the Engineering Authority, Ministry of Military Production, the AOI, and the AFLPO, among other bodies, became invested in carrying out the regime's economic plans. This was particularly the case in national megaprojects like the digging of the "New" Suez Canal, the New Administrative Capital, and a myriad of other infrastructure projects, ranging from the construction of roads and airports to desert land reclamation, energy plant construction, and social housing programs. On the other hand, the new political environment increased the MCE's access to public resources and state-owned assets—namely, desert land for urban development purposes. The context was also ripe for the creation of the institutional framework (as well as the informal ties necessary) for partnerships between MCE agencies and between private domestic and foreign capital.

Once again, these plans unfolded primarily in the real estate and construction sectors, especially around the New Administrative Capital project—an ambitious plan launched by President al-Sisi himself to build a new city in the desert east of Cairo to house state bodies. In 2015, Presidential Decree Number 446 allowed the AFLPO to establish economic enterprises that it may fully own or run in partnership with national or foreign private-sector companies. This is a new development that may pave the way for the direct involvement of the AFLPO in construction and service projects in the near future, either solely or with private partners. The amendment provides the legal framework for military business engagement in areas where the army already owns plots of land, like the Suez Canal Zone and the New Administrative Capital.

Based on anecdotal evidence, the MCE has expanded in the past several years. However, it is not yet clear whether this expansion will lead to a qualitative or a quantitative shift in the structure and magnitude of the MCE, or even its overall share in the national economy. It seems that the MCE is preserving its old strategy of diversifying into more economic sectors, most recently cement, telecommunications, automobile importation, pharmaceuticals, and iron and steel production. What is changing, however, is the MCE's stronger appetite for dominating rather than just participating economically by capturing a share. This is especially the case in the media sector, where the crowding out, if not shutting out, of private producers and owners of satellite channel has happened consistently since 2014. It also seems to be taking place, albeit on a relatively smaller scale, in the construction of luxury and high-income compounds and villas in the desert outskirts of Cairo.[30] Recent developments suggest that the military is indeed becoming the most dominant actor on all fronts, ranging from land-use planning, allocation, and development.

But this is not a general phenomenon across all sectors—the MCE is not displacing or crowding out private-sector developers, for instance. As a matter of fact, new areas of partnership have emerged with a number of large businesses from the Mubarak era that were attracted into investing in MCE-dominated projects like the New Administrative Capital.[31] The problem, rather, seems to be that these private businesses, either those that are inherited from the Mubarak era or new market entrants, are reduced to the status of mere junior partners. Overall, they enjoy little control of the terms of engagement with the military-dominated processes of land planning and allocation, not to mention broader economic policy making. Moreover, there have been multiple attempts at establishing partnerships with foreign investors from the UAE and China, though these have not always been successful.

It might be too early to pass judgement of whether Egypt's economy is undergoing a major transformation toward military domination. Perhaps the most significant repercussions of the expansion of the MCE are political rather than economic, so it is to politics that we now turn.

THE MCE AND THE RE-POLITICIZATION OF THE MILITARY AFTER 2011

We have questioned the liberal economic argument that the MCE necessarily undermines the market economy. As demonstrated above, the MCE in Egypt has coexisted with private-sector expansion, the attraction of foreign direct investment, and more trade and capital account liberalization since the late 1970s. The Egyptian case is hardly an anomaly for it has been replicated in different forms almost at the same time in China, Turkey, Indonesia, and Vietnam, where private-sector development, liberalization, and economic globalization all coexisted with militaries trying to gain shares in these expanding markets. In Egypt, the military established its own patronage and crony networks, using its privileged access to state power in order to secure assets and market shares. However, this was barely different from how the big private sector operated, often through dense ties with the state in the absence of robust rule of law and contract enforcement.

But what about the political realm? In the same vein, the MCE does not seem to be a barrier to democracy, as many might think. There is little evidence that an increasing stake in the civilian economy invites coups and hinders or undermines the transition to democracy. We argue that it was not (as might be assumed) simply the push of military economic interests or business ambitions that led to the military's growing and imposing economic role.[32] More significant was the pull of a civilian economy that provided the resources for the re-politicization of the military as well as the remilitarization of the regime in Egypt. Since 2011, the collapse of public order and threats to state authority reawakened the military's political mission. There was also the concern with Egypt's geopolitical status, especially with preserving the peace treaty with Israel and relations with the members of the Gulf Cooperation Council (GCC). Saudi Arabia and the United Arab Emirates harbored fears that Egypt may be drifting away from its earlier commitment to Gulf security in the face of perceived threats by Iran. There were also concerns about the potential dangers posed by an internationalized Muslim Brotherhood organization that could destabilize GCC monarchies.

In that context, economics were a secondary concern. In fact, Muhammad Morsi, the Brotherhood-backed candidate who won the 2012 presidential elections, entertained demands by the military for institutional and financial autonomy. The 2012 Constitution, written under Brotherhood leadership, provided guarantees on both issues. The military's economic empire was mentioned in the Constitution, safeguarded formally from oversight by elected executive officers, including the president, the legislature, and any public auditing institution. The military budget was to be expressed in one single figure without any breakdown, and even that was to be exclusively "debated" by the National Security Council in the parliament. No mention whatsoever was made of the army's civilian economy, which is naturally off budget.

The 2012 Constitution also provided full autonomy to the military by reserving the right to appoint and depose the minister of defense to the Supreme Council of the Armed Forces, who is ratified by the president. Other national security questions, including the declaration of war, were conditioned upon a prior approval from the Supreme Council as well.

Moreover, the subsequent expansion in military economic activities was primarily political, increasing the military's access to resources to support an effectively bankrupt state it came to dominate. For example, in 2011, the vice minister of defense for financial affairs revealed that the military deposited $2 billion into the Central Bank of Egypt in an attempt to boost the country's dwindling foreign reserves.[33] Another political motive behind economic expansion was securing access to more resources as a means of securing loyalty and internal cohesion.[34]

Even though not ideal, having an MCE should not necessarily preclude a country's chances for democratization. The experiences of post-2002 Tukey and post-Suharto Indonesia actually suggest the exact opposite. In both cases, civilian elites interested in establishing procedural democracy and averting the risk of coups or military interference tolerated and even institutionalized a bigger MCE. It was thought that this would work as a trade-off with protected revenues and rents and financial and institutional autonomy serving to de-motivate the military from assuming a political role, hence allowing democratic introduction and consolidation or even gaining time for civilian elected elites. In both cases, these militaries had a long institutional tradition as parent-guardians of their nation-states following independence.[35] The strategy seemed to work, at least somewhat.

In Indonesia, the military retained much of its civilian economic empire inherited from the Suharto dictatorship.[36] Despite rampant corruption and rent seeking, civilian elites did not attempt to tamper with the military's economic interests. The end result provided Indonesia's democracy some stability and consolidation and a de facto guarantee against military coups despite the lack of genuine civilian control.[37]

In Turkey, the military has historically been the political actor par excellence since independence in 1923, and it remained so despite the introduction of electoral democracy in 1946. It staged three coups—in 1960, 1970, and 1980—that toppled civilian governments, changed constitutions, and reconfigured political life, and a semi-coup in 1997 that forced the prime minister out of office. Following the coming to power of the Justice and Development Party (JDP), the MCE was tolerated. This did not hamper the economic prospects of Turkey's class of (often politically connected) large businesses or the establishment of a new class of small and medium-size enterprises allied to the JDP. Despite the increasing economic stakes and the Turkish military's history of interventionism, the JDP managed to keep it from direct involvement in politics from 2002 through mid-2016, when a failed coup was attempted but rather easily aborted in two days. The attempted coup demonstrated that Turkish civilian elites did not really enjoy full control over the military. Yet, the trade-off between political intervention and economic interest gave them time to consolidate their power, penetrate the civilian bureaucracy and the judiciary, and introduce constitutional changes reinforcing such penetration. The JDP, and more precisely Erdogan, emerged as a winner in the end. Despite an attempt by some factions within the military to reverse Erdogan and the JDP's hold on power, it proved to be too little, too late.

It appears that this strategy was pursued consciously in post-2011 Egypt. During its brief period in power, the Brotherhood seemed to offer the military whatever it demanded economically and institutionally as long as this would avert the risk of a coup or at least allow newly elected Morsi some time to tighten his grip over power. This may explain why the 2012 Constitution simply adopted all the clauses and articles proposed by the military's representatives in the Constituent Assembly, while almost all non-Islamist actors refused to partake in the deliberative body. Concessions and guarantees were, however, not enough to keep the military out. Exactly a year after Morsi's inauguration, the military stepped in in the wake of massive popular demonstrations, deposing Morsi on July 3, 2013.

Why did the Brotherhood fail while civilian leaders in Turkey and Indonesia succeeded? The Egyptian military's decision to intervene politically could be explained by a variety of factors beyond mere economic interests, real though those were.[38] The MCE was shielded constitutionally and was not under threat by any means. To be sure, there was a lack of long-term mutual trust between the Brotherhood and the military.[39] However, the deeper concern was political, with the Brotherhood's potential penetration of the military causing the latter to worry that it would lose autonomy vis-à-vis the new ruling faction. Added to this was the suspicion the military and other security agencies harbored toward the Brotherhood, an international religious organization with dubious ties to Hamas in Gaza and other armed Islamist radicals throughout the region, and especially with the insurgency in the Sinai.

Beyond these motives, having direct and autonomous access to economic resources proved crucial in enabling the military to stage the 2013 takeover. This went hand in hand with other enabling factors like regional support from the oil-rich regimes (particularly the United Arab Emirates and Saudi Arabia) and the deep divisions among political elites, in addition to the massive mobilization against and for the Brotherhood, which threatened to lead to civil strife and the breakdown of public order.

CONCLUSION

The Egyptian case reveals that the MCE is best understood in a very broad historical context. Militaries are seldom merely self-serving and profit-oriented actors. Their access to economic resources, rents, and market shares all depend on their access to state power. This is decided by the historical evolution of the state and its different components. The bigger the role the military plays at critical junctures dealing with external threats or preserving national integrity and public order, the greater its ability to access economic resources.

A quick comparison here helps illustrate the distinctive Egyptian path—and how past patterns can guide subsequent developments. In China, the military also plays a significant economic role. The PLA has extended its tentacles into various sectors of the economy since the late 1970s. The military tried to make up for its budget cuts by conquering shares in China's burgeoning domestic and external markets.[40] This led it to invest in a great variety of civilian manufacturing, agricultural, and service sectors beyond any obvious national security or defense logic. However, this failed to offset decades of institutional practice whereby the military was firmly put under the control of the Communist Party. By the late 1990s, the party was powerful enough to push the military out of many sectors, forcing it to divest its companies and confine its operations to those directly related to national security and defense, hence reconfiguring the relationship between the military and civilian sectors in China.

Egyptian history offers no comparable example of such dominant political leadership. With a firmer footing in the country's political establishment, the Egyptian military was not as easy to dislodge. Accessing economic resources aided the military's ability to reproduce earlier patterns of interaction with other state agencies and societal actors, which in turn served to shore up the military's political influence and support further intervention. As explained by Siddiqa in the case of Pakistan, "although the military's internal economy is not necessarily the main cause of its political ambitions, the various financial advantages sought by the senior officers have a cumulative effect in enhancing their interest in staying at the helm of affairs."[41] Doubtless, having an economy of its own creates incentives for the military to intervene against perceived or actual threats as well as to search for more rents. However, challenging the military economy in developing countries has seldom been a priority for forces pushing for democracy.

In countries like Egypt where postindependence state formation relied heavily on an active political role for the military, establishing and keeping an autonomous political arena from military intervention has often been the priority rather than compromising the military's financial and institutional autonomy. There may be strong normative reasons to question the military's economic role, but we should examine the effects of such involvement, not assume them.

Chapter Nine

THE UPRISING OF 2011 AND THE NEW REGIME

In 2011, Egyptians and their rulers were taken by surprise by a mass uprising that brought down Egypt's longest-serving president, Hosni Mubarak. Suddenly, Egyptian politics, dull and predictable for decades, entered a tumultuous phase. Egyptians, and those who followed the dramatic events in the country closely, often reacted strongly and emotionally. For some, the uprising marked an outbreak of hope, freedom, and possibility followed by bitter division, polarization, and harsh disappointment. For others, especially but not exclusively those who came to rule the country after 2013, what Egypt faced in the years after 2011 was growing chaos, division, and disintegration; state institutions lost capacity, will, and popular respect—and those things had to be restored to protect the society.

We do not write out of despair or relief but in an effort to understand. After a chaotic post-uprising political process that saw multiple competitive elections, a new authoritarian regime emerged rather than a democratic one. How did social actors that had been contained and coerced for so long suddenly shift the balance of forces and remove Mubarak? How did a new authoritarian regime arise?

In this concluding chapter we will begin by summarizing what we have learned in the preceding chapters. We will then use those lessons to probe the series of rapid developments—the sequence of mobilization, uprising, regime change, polarization, contention, conflict, and renewed authoritarianism—that produced a period of unprecedented uncertainty, social turmoil, and political contestation before a clear regime was reestablished.

WHAT WE HAVE LEARNED ABOUT EGYPT

We believe we have assembled the tools to explain Egyptian politics over the past decade. In part 1, we analyzed how (and which) strong state institutions arose as part of a state-building effort that could be traced back to the nineteenth century (with roots in earlier institutions and practices). The state's presence in society continued to grow well into the twentieth century, reaching a peak with Egypt's socialist period in the two decades after 1952, after which a slow, uneven, and partial withdrawal of state control became evident. And we explored not only the state as a whole but also how regimes used the state apparatus to secure their position, pursue their (shifting) policy goals, and control society. We also saw the limitations of those efforts, with tentative and uneven liberalization in evidence off and on since the 1970s, expressed in the ability of some state institutions to gain autonomy.

Part 2 explored how Egyptian society became organized—in ways that showed increasing strength on the part of civil society and even some signs of independence and ability to protest, but also in ways that led to polarization and division. This was not a linear process, however. In the years after 1952, the regime created broad corporatist arrangements that monopolized interest representation, controlled social demands, and repressed potential opponents. This system showed signs of stress by the late 1960s and began to decay in the 1970s. The regime adjusted to the decay of corporatism by co-opting the top echelon of corporatist organizations, a process that was successful over the short term and inhibited collective action by various social groups, but which in turn created its own strains as it triggered conflict between the leadership and social bases of these organizations. In some cases, this even encouraged those bases to occasionally try to act on their own (with wildcat strikes, for instance). And in the 1990s, as the state jettisoned or scaled back many of its social welfare commitments, civil society organizations proliferated. The multiparty system that had emerged was complemented by the combination of an increasingly organized society and a more open political environment, which in turn allowed many actors to push political boundaries and circumvent legal restrictions.

But Egyptian civil society, while more active, remained fragmented and even polarized. Efforts to build coalitions and reach across ideological divisions were not totally fruitless—they helped fuel activism before the 2011 uprising and were on display in the uprising itself. But in the years after 2011, the legacy of polarization returned with a vengeance. In part 2 we also saw that religion in general, and Islam in particular, constitutes an integral part of state, society, and even economy in Egypt. We also saw that religion is a contested field, with strong state institutions, popular oppositional movements, and faith-based civil society organizations all operating simultaneously, sometimes in complementarity but also in competing ways.

In part 3, we looked at the same sets of issues from an economic perspective, witnessing the economic changes that attended a decrease in state control and management that paradoxically did not produce liberalization.

It is this set of ingredients that allow us to explain the events of recent years.

WHAT NEEDS TO BE EXPLAINED AND HOW?

Upheavals often surprise even those participating in them, but the mass Egyptian uprising of 2011 seemed especially surprising—and in the following years, the country seemed to veer rapidly and unpredictably in several different directions.[1] For most of the period covered in this book, Egyptian politics seemed to change very slowly. Indeed, in almost six decades, Egypt had only three presidents; its leaders constantly tinkered with the structure of the system and introduced new policies, but change seemed incremental and gradual when it did occur; and its longest-serving president, Hosni Mubarak, seemed to regard continuity and stability as critical virtues.

Mubarak did not speak for all Egyptians, however, and, as we have seen in previous chapters, an increasing number of social actors found their voices and used them to call for change. In 2011, a large group of those actors came together under the slogan "The People Want the Fall of the Regime." And they got it. Egypt entered a period of transition in which it was clear what various movements were rejecting. But the political and social forces spearheading the uprisings were deeply divided about what they were transitioning to. The massive mobilization that welded together political and socioeconomic demands in order to overthrow Mubarak was remarkable, but the movements' victories were neither straightforward nor durable. Over two years' worth of contention, elections, demonstrations, and polarization mounted—and finally ushered in a new authoritarian system, one that was less friendly to political pluralism than the old one had been.

Political scientists like to explain outcomes. But the word "outcome" suggests a finality that does not exist in the real world. Politics will never end, so the "outcome" that scholars like to explain is often what strikes them as dramatic or unexpected at a particular time. That means that writers on Egypt—as with other countries undergoing rapid and confusing change—often shift in what they seek to understand. In 2011, it was the uprising. In 2012 and 2013, it was regime type (and especially possibilities for democratization). After 2013, it was regime type of a different sort (enhanced authoritarianism). In this chapter, we will explore this series of events with an eye to explaining all three: the uprising of 2011, the short interlude of Brotherhood rule and the possibility of democratic transition, and the reinstatement of authoritarianism after Morsi was dislodged. In so doing, we seek an understanding of Egyptian politics that can help us see all three "outcomes" rather than just one. We are striving to tell a story not merely of popular uprising, or of disappointed hopes and failure, or of authoritarianism, but one in which three seemingly different "outcomes" occur simultaneously or in rapid sequence in a highly volatile and uncertain context.

Periods of intense uncertainty—such as those following the collapse of a long-standing authoritarian regime—offer actors an unpredictable environment in which they must base their decisions on rapidly changing and unclear circumstances. In the next two sections of this chapter, we explore how some coordinating efforts, ultimately ephemeral, among Egypt's disparate and polarized opposition led to the removal of Mubarak and brought a wide range of actors to the negotiation table to change the rules of the political game. In the third, we examine the political tumult that followed Mubarak's removal, the electoral rise of Islamists, and the role of state structures in trimming the Islamists' sails. The fourth section investigates the Brotherhood's short tenure in office and its encounter with the state apparatuses. Finally, we close by analyzing how the state reassembled itself and its structures banded together to dislodge the Brotherhood and then overpower other social actors, paving the way for the installation of a new authoritarian regime.

EGYPT IN 2010–2011: REGIME CRISIS AND MASS MOBILIZATION

In order to present our understanding of the uprising itself, we return to the analysis of the Egyptian regime developed in part 1, the rising mobilization described in part 2, and the economic concerns explored in part 3.

Egypt's political order was upended in a national uprising in 2011—one that surprised its leaders, to be sure, but still built unmistakably on trends and repertoires we analyzed earlier, especially in chapter 5. From 2004 through 2011, the regime seemed impervious to its critics but still staggered from crisis to crisis. Laborers broke free of their own co-opted unions and developed new tactics to contest and pressure the regime. Political and social opposition groups started to translate their criticisms into concrete political programs and demands for systematic change and to pursue them through a range of new tools, from demonstration to satire. Opposition coalesced around resistance to an unspoken (but increasingly suspected) regime plan to have Mubarak's son succeed him.

The rise in social and political protest cannot be viewed separately from the sharp turns in economic policy that the regime took in the last decade of Mubarak's rule, especially the intensification of its liberalization and privatization drives. A series of economic reforms won Egypt some plaudits from international observers but hit different groups in Egypt in quite disparate ways. For instance, Egypt's national currency was significantly devalued in 2003 in order to make its exports more attractive to world markets—but this also unleashed high inflation that harmed the standard of living of workers and civil servants, among other middle-class groups.

A new cabinet of technocrats and businessmen-turned-politicians was formed in 2004 to pursue economic liberalization, including a strong push for the privatization and divestiture of state-owned enterprises. Unionized workers in state-owned enterprises feared that this would threaten the privileges they had enjoyed since Egypt's socialist period.

But it was not merely the content of these policies that provoked concern; it was also a pattern of implementation that led to charges of conflict of interest and widespread corruption. A significant portion of state assets, be they in the form of privatized enterprises or state-owned land allocated for investment, went to businesspeople who were already dominant market actors. As indicated in our presentation of Egypt's habitus economy (see chapter 7), even though state-business intimacy contributed to strong economic performance and allowed some coordination when it came to promoting exports and tourism and attracting foreign investment, the ties between the private sector and parts of the regime proved to be politically problematic on two fronts. On the one hand, these business actors were increasingly tied to the rise of Gamal Mubarak and his plans for succeeding his aging father, sharply (and publicly) linking policy, economic performance, and questions of current and future political power. On the other hand, the gains that resulted from Egypt's strong economic performance were not widely distributed. Once again, as explained in chapter 7, a clear majority of Egyptians were kept away from contributing meaningfully to the creation and distribution of economic value.

The effect was that controversial economic measures, corruption, authoritarianism, and the regime's succession plans all began to be associated in many Egyptians' minds, and in this way, grievances became linked together and generalized. This gave a boost to a slowly building social and political protest movement that had emerged in the early 2000s, which in turn translated into a rising tide of labor strikes, attempts at building independent unions, and increasingly bold and public discourse among the intelligentsia calling openly for Mubarak's removal. It was in this context that organized opposition (the al-Mahalla workers' strikes in 2007 and 2008; the Kifaya movement since 2004) began to emerge, with activists attempting to move beyond talk to mobilization and action.

These separate protests remained somewhat disjointed. In 2011, however, a large swath of Egyptian activists representing a range of political and religious views swung behind the call for a "Day of Rage" on January 25, 2011. Operating in the immediate aftermath of a popular uprising in Tunisia, organizers hoped for a large turnout, but the response surprised even the most optimistic activists as tens of thousands responded to the call. Gathering in public squares throughout the country—most notably in Cairo's Tahrir Square—they clamored for "Bread, Freedom, Social Justice, and Human Dignity." The security forces attempted to disperse crowds with tear gas and divert those seeking to join them, and generally alternated between discrediting the demonstrations and denying their existence.

Organizers responded by stepping up their campaign by calling for a "Friday of Anger." And they escalated their demands to include Mubarak's resignation. Opposition groups that had been too cautious to participate on January 25 (most notably the Muslim Brotherhood) threw in their lot with the demonstrators. Groups normally seen as apolitical—such as "Ultras," fans of Egypt's various soccer teams, upset by the way they had been treated by the police—began to see the demonstrations as an opportunity to press their grievances. Massive numbers of marchers snaked through Cairo's streets on January 28, 2011, chanting, "The People Want the Fall of the Regime." And while Cairo's demonstrations understandably attracted the most attention because of their size and location, many cities throughout the country saw similar gatherings.

January 28 marked a turning point as various parts of the state apparatus scrambled to respond. The Ministry of Interior had lost control of public space and its periodic efforts to use force only sparked more outrage. State media alternated between pretending nothing was happening and blaming foreign agents in a manner that lost it whatever credibility it had with those sympathetic to the protestors. The military deployed but did not attempt to take on the police's coercive role, allowing demonstrators to hope that they could drive a wedge between the military and Mubarak.

The regime began to search for concessions that would assuage the demonstrators or deprive them of support. On February 1, Mubarak renounced any intention to run for another term after his current one expired later in the year. But the protests continued unabated. Realizing that the military seemed to be hesitating, demonstrators beckoned it into an alliance with the popular chant "The Army and the People Are One Hand." On February 11, the intelligence chief whom Mubarak had just appointed vice president announced that Mubarak had been forced to resign and that the military high command would govern the country on an interim basis.

While Mubarak was now gone, Egypt's political course was completely unclear. The leaders of the uprising—who now proclaimed it a "revolution"— felt that they had won a tremendous victory. Indeed, the uprising represented the most serious challenge to authoritarianism in the country since the installation of the Free Officers' regime in 1952. For the first time, Egyptian social actors, rather than the state, seemed to be driving politics. But for all the confusion, the state apparatus remained very much intact. Leaders of the military, the judiciary, the police, and other parts of the state—like al-Azhar, the media, and the bureaucracy—seemed uncertain how to respond. And if the old regime was discredited, very few positions had actually changed hands. The leaders of many state bodies did face calls for reform within their own ranks. But nobody had any clear idea how strong the revolutionary fervor was or how long it would last.

If state actors were uncertain, so was the opposition. Although the protests encouraged various forces from across the political spectrum and among different socioeconomic strata to participate, no grand deal had been reached among the diverse camps on a united vision for Egypt after the departure of the head of the regime. It was not just the presidency the crowds brought down—parliament was disbanded and the Constitution suspended. But while much was swept away, it was not clear what would emerge. In some ways, the loose coalition that swung behind the uprising was paying the price of its quick success—in some other instances in which authoritarian regimes have been brought down by popular mobilization, various opposition groups succeeded only after hammering out joint programs and demands. In Czechoslovakia in November 1989, for example, a short-lived but effective "Civic Forum" unified dissident voices during the so-called Velvet Revolution and formed a mechanism to coordinate strategies and make decisions. Other societies (but not all) in the Soviet bloc followed a similar path in the late 1980s. But in Egypt, opposition forces remained fractious, incapable of translating their tactical victories in the street into a coordinated strategy to secure structural changes—or even of agreeing on what changes were needed. The pluralistic foundation of the revolt, which was hailed as its greatest strength, seemed to be the main obstacle to transforming an uprising against Mubarak into a genuine democratic accord. In particular, the failure of Islamists and their non-Islamist rivals to build a durable coalition ultimately enabled the military to take the reins of power and hold off demands for structural reform of the state.

A FRACTIOUS OPPOSITION AT THE NEGOTIATION TABLE AND ENDEAVORS OF INSTITUTIONAL RECONFIGURATION

In January and February 2011, the regime disintegrated and many of the institutions of state (described in part 1) appeared both challenged by the mobilization and uncertain about how to respond. We now move to considering how the various mobilized actors described in part 2 interacted while remaining mindful of how the economic developments described in part 3 did not simply spark popular demands but also deepened some of the divisions among various institutions and actors.

Soon after Mubarak's ouster, a wide schism between Islamists and their opponents appeared, with debates breaking out over political tactics, electoral processes, and competing platforms. Why did polarization set in so quickly? We will first examine the political struggle in order to see how groups and networks moved from an initially proactive stance to distinctively reactive positions, particularly as the Islamists showed their electoral prowess and some non-Islamists felt driven to embrace state structures, even those that remained deeply authoritarian in outlook. Second, we will shift our attention from the political conflict to the social and economic struggle and investigate how laborers and other social forces failed to harmonize their demands, undermining the uprising's calls for social justice and dissipating the revolutionary enthusiasm in a collection of erratic and sporadic events.

The Islamist/Non-Islamist Divide

The military high command (the Supreme Council of the Armed Forces, or SCAF) quickly offered a vague endorsement of the popular movement and promised a democratic future. Military leaders claimed to be exercising all authority in the people's name and called for the demonstrations to end. The SCAF appointed a committee to offer some constitutional amendments that would guide any transition process. The eight-member committee included some Islamist intellectuals and even a Brotherhood member. The process devised by this body seemed so rushed and limited that its work led to an immediate rupture in the coalition that had formed during the uprising. Islamists generally supported a quick transition and early elections; non-Islamists wanted deeper political changes, and few felt confident of their ability to translate their success in organizing demonstrations into the construction of viable electoral machines. The amendments were approved in a March referendum in which non-Islamists were defeated in their attempts to demand a different process.

The referendum and a series of decisions by the SCAF led to a clear sequence in which parliamentary elections would be held, the new parliament would select a committee to draft a new constitution, and presidential elections would follow, even while the new constitution was written. Until the new president was elected (and perhaps until the new constitution was finalized and approved in a referendum), the military would remain in control.

The split over the March referendum proved to have wide repercussions: it led non-Islamists to be suspicious of the process and Islamists to be confident of their electoral abilities (they had campaigned heavily for the amendments). Indeed, over the coming months, it sometimes seemed that Islamists and non-Islamists were contesting Egypt's future on different battlefields—the Islamists hoping to win at the ballot box and non-Islamists through demonstrations and mobilization. The SCAF stood above the struggle, making decisions that appeared to endorse a democratic transition while offering no real power to election winners. This led Islamists to regard the military as a tactical ally at times but one that might not be ready to share real power; it led non-Islamists to charge that the Muslim Brotherhood was colluding with the military to stop the revolution in its tracks. Later, some of those same figures would themselves seek to court the military's support.

To be sure, there were efforts to overcome these differences. The Muslim Brotherhood quickly formed its own political party, the Freedom and Justice Party (FJP). It reached out to non-Islamist groups to form an electoral alliance, but its potential partners were suspicious of the FJP and saw themselves as being offered the position of junior partners. Many non-Islamists worked to form their own bloc to contest elections. When this non-Islamist bloc suggested that all forces agree on a set of "supra-constitutional guarantees," the Islamists accused them of trying to impose their will by circumventing the electoral process. The SCAF seemed to back some of these supra-constitutional principles, leading the Islamists to make their own charges that their opponents were colluding with the military in order to limit the people's will.

Amid these deepening suspicions, Islamists and non-Islamists began calling for demonstrations with separate agendas. The Islamists, for instance, organized a massive demonstration against the supra-constitutional principles. When some of the more revolutionary non-Islamist groups launched their own effort to bring down military rule in the fall of 2011, Islamists stood aloof, suspecting that this was really an attempt to circumvent upcoming parliamentary elections.

Indeed, competition was not simply setting in between the two camps; it also occurred within them. Non-Islamists were divided over strategies and demands (with more radical groups calling for deep social and economic change and others focusing more on political reform). Islamists and non-Islamists argued among themselves about how to handle the old regime, its supporters, and key state institutions such as the military and the police.

And the Brotherhood suddenly found it was hardly the only Islamist political force. Salafi groups, too, made use of their strong social presence to create political parties. For example, the al-Da'wa al-Salafiyya (the Salafi Call) emerged out of the student movements and general religious revival of the 1970s but had generally avoided active political work before 2011. However, after witnessing the Brotherhood's success in the aftermath of the uprising, the movement's leaders decided to create their own political party, al-Nur. While non-Islamists often viewed the Brotherhood and the Salafis as two sides of the same coin, the leaders of the two movements saw each other as rivals. They had different ideological and religious orientations (with the Brotherhood religious but less insistent on any specific religious interpretation and the Salafis focusing much more on the literal meaning of religious texts and their day-to-day application). But they nonetheless seemed to be aiming to mobilize similar constituencies, especially after 2011. Brotherhood leaders believed that the old regime had let Salafis have a far freer hand when it came to organizing in poorer and working-class areas as a way to limit the Brotherhood's influence among these constituencies; for their part, Salafi leaders derided the Brotherhood as being more concerned with politics than with religion or serving the poor.[2]

In this deteriorating atmosphere, Egyptians were summoned to the polls for a series of elections and referenda. In parliamentary balloting, non-Islamists offered voters a smorgasbord of ideologies, parties, and individual candidates. Some new parties did well, but collectively Islamists dominated the new parliament. Because Salafis had been less active politically and were less visible among the elite, their electoral success after the uprising came as a surprise to everyone but them. Salafis captured about one-quarter of the seats in the parliamentary elections of 2011–2012. The Brotherhood, which won a bit less than half, thus found in the Salafis both a potential partner and a serious rival. Together, the two were able to dominate the drafting committee for the country's new post-uprising constitution.

The political transition process was not only conflictual; its dynamics led actors to refrain from reaching out to their rivals. The Islamists and non-Islamists (including liberals, leftists, secularists, and revolutionary youth) did not perceive themselves as part of a single pluralist project. Instead, they each claimed to represent the entire nation and accused the other groups of hijacking the revolution for narrow partisan benefits.

We have focused so far on the political struggle over Egypt's governing system. But one of the reasons that Egyptians referred to the events of 2011 as a revolution was that more fundamental changes seemed to be on the agenda. Indeed, in most Egyptian institutions there was strong internal pressure for reform—university faculty members wished to elect their deans; students wanted freedom in their elections; editors in state-owned media organizations found themselves criticized by younger journalists for corruption or for favoring the old regime; workers in state-owned enterprises and public agencies organized wildcat strikes; and more generally, older unions found themselves under pressure as members deserted them for newer structures that were supposed to be free of regime control.

The political fragmentation of the revolutionary coalition—to which we return below—was not the only reason for the dissipation of revolutionary enthusiasm. In spite of all the pressure on so many institutions, actual change was very limited. The Egyptian state apparatus and the various structures it used to dominate society were very much threatened in 2011, and there was widespread disarray. But few top personnel were dismissed or replaced. And in the period after the initial wave of protests, the state apparatus—its constituent parts and the state as a whole—gradually began to reassemble itself in 2012 and especially 2013. It likely could not have done so unless the uprising within so many Egyptian schools, offices, and factories had not already been blunted. Again, the Islamist/non-Islamist divide came into play, though it was not the only factor.

It is to that story that we now turn—or more precisely, to the labor sector, where we can trace it more clearly.

Fragmented Demands of Isolated Workers and Added Fissures in the Non-Islamist/Islamist Divide

The corporatist arrangements that we saw fraying in part 2 came under severe pressure after 2011. Workers' strikes played a pivotal role in the uprisings when workers circumvented the old (and corporatist) Egyptian Trade Union Federation (ETUF), with its legal monopoly on trade union organization, and formed the Egyptian Federation of Independent Trade Unions (EFITU). The EFITU was the first new institution to emerge after the uprising. It was preceded by a few independent sectoral unions that were formed in 2008 (for real estate tax collectors, teachers, and health technicians) as well as a grassroots NGO focused on labor issues that was established in 1990, the Center for Trade Union and Workers' Services. Labor mobilization did not lose momentum and continued at an unprecedented level during 2011 and early 2012. As we saw in chapter 5, workers established hundreds of independent enterprise-level unions.

But in the long run, the effect of the revolutionary pressure was to split the labor movement between the old structures that had legal protection, financial resources, and experience but remained estranged from their membership and the new and more active structures that lacked experience and resources. Egyptian labor leaders thus saw their efforts divided, in contrast to labor movements in some other post-authoritarian societies. In Tunisia, for example, the existing General Union of Tunisian Workers deserted the regime and swung in support of that country's uprising in 2010 and 2011. In Poland, an independent trade union (Solidarity) was formed in 1980 and gained important (often bitter) political experience before the momentous changes of 1989.

With the old structure still very much in place and co-opted by the old regime, Egypt did not follow the Tunisian path. Neither did the Polish path prove applicable. The independent Egyptian labor movement was too fresh and untested to take the lead when the unrest swept through the country. After the successful deposing of Mubarak, events outpaced the newly emerging leaders' ability to adapt their organizations. Financial and organizational problems prevented the nascent movement from developing a national leadership or political program. The existing legal frameworks preserved the structure of centralized decision making within the ETUF, making it difficult for workers to break with it without risking losing their access to the union funds that provided critical health or retirement benefits. Existing laws turned out to be full of traps. For instance, the new unions' ability to collect membership fees was restricted, while the law from Egypt's corporatist era that barred more than one union in a sector remained on the books.

Of course, legislative changes were possible. However, the newly elected (and soon to be disbanded) parliament had no clear legislative authority and was too inexperienced to set a clear legislative agenda. The emerging Islamist leadership seemed more comfortable with the old structures than the ones struggling to emerge. Nor did the labor activists have much support. It is true that 2011 and 2012 saw tremendous enthusiasm and activism. But, surprisingly, workers were unable to get much support from other political actors. Some in both the Islamist and non-Islamist camps were simply too socially and economically conservative and nervous about trade union activism, which they denounced as an effort to help only one sector of society. Many paid lip service to socioeconomic grievances but worried about any attempts to reverse Egypt's economic liberalization program. Their solution was to return to the stability and economic growth of the pre-2011 period rather than redistribute wealth.

Even many activists and movements who protested en masse throughout 2011 considered workers' social and economic grievances selfish "sectorial demands" (*fi'awia*)—as opposed to proper "national" demands[3]—that would compromise political order and undermine the democratic struggle.

Moreover, labor movements in Egypt lacked strong allies and interlocutors in the emerging institutions after Mubarak's departure. The Brotherhood-dominated parliament actually endorsed a proposal that permitted only one trade union per enterprise, a relic of Egypt's corporatist period, in a move that simply protected the ETUF and the existing leadership. The parliament also approved the SCAF's law (i.e., Military Decree no. 34—later Law 34) criminalizing sit-ins and labor strikes that "harm the economy and impede the work of public institutions." In some unions and professional syndicates, internal struggles also reflected the larger polarization between Islamists and non-Islamists. Rather than unify around economic demands or common interests, those who supported the Brotherhood or Salafi movements did not always trust their non-Islamist fellow workers or professionals, who often returned the favor. And, as always, there was still rivalries within each camp.

THE EGYPTIAN STATE WITHOUT A REGIME, AND TRIMMING ISLAMIST SAILS

We now focus more specifically on the state actors described in part 1 and how they worked to reassemble a coherent regime with the help of some of the social actors described in part 2 and the vehement opposition of others.

In 2011, the diffusion of protests overwhelmed the state apparatus. Important figures (for instance, some judges) had come to resent presidential intrusion into their affairs; others balked at the idea that Mubarak might pass the presidency on to his son as if the Egyptian state were the property of a single family. With the demonstrations of 2011, the military quickly concluded that Mubarak was a liability and therefore abandoned him and sought some autonomy from the presidency. State actors saw the regime crumble but wanted to preserve order. When it announced that Mubarak had stepped down and suspended the Constitution on February 11, 2011, the SCAF assumed the position of interim president and also the authority to issue interim constitutions, promulgate laws, and appoint and dismiss ministers. From both a practical and a legal standpoint, the SCAF *was* the regime until a new president was elected and a new constitutional order put in place. In a more practical sense, Egypt did not really have a clearly defined regime: various parts of the state apparatus continued to operate but it was not obvious who was in control of them. The military retained an oversight role. It was not clear, however, if that could be maintained under the combined pressure of popular mobilization and competitive elections.

During its sixteen months in power, the military leadership worked to demobilize the streets and restore stability and order. The SCAF engaged in substantial repression of popular forces and approved a draconian order banning strikes (Military Decree no. 34, referred to above). Military trials of civilians continued in secrecy and Mubarak's security and intelligence apparatuses remained intact. The military leaders invoked the rhetoric of nationalism and patriotism to stymie more radical demands. The generals also used state media to portray political activists as a fifth column comprised of troublemakers and the agents of foreign powers.

The military and the Brotherhood had some common interests. Having taken responsibility for maintaining order, the military prioritized a speedy restoration of normal governance. The Brotherhood saw itself as profiting from the recent elections and able to participate in governing for the first time in its history. Continued instability and mass mobilization served neither the army nor the Islamists. The Brotherhood's opponents deeply resented this and spoke of an alliance between the Brotherhood and the military. It is impossible to know what went on behind closed doors, but, in a sense, no explicit deal was necessary. While the Islamists and the generals sometimes shared some common tactical interests, they remained deeply distrustful about each other's long-term intentions.

And to be fair, all forces—except the revolutionary coalitions who turned against the military—deferred in toto to the military, allowing the generals to decide on a short-term road map in hopes that the constitutional processes and political dynamics they chose would in the end help to bring about a genuine democratic transition. The Brotherhood's leadership came to realize that its organizational assets and political experience would put it in a privileged position in any system allowing for voting, so the group decided to take on a strong political role, calling for early elections and a democratic transition. Non-Islamist forces, however, asked for military protection to prolong the transitional period, since a rapid transition would bring the Islamists to power.

The result, which saw the military remain in the driver's seat, looked different from other democratic transitions. Some Egyptian political actors were far more willing than others to make the transition to electoral politics. In Latin America in the 1980s, as authoritarianism broke down and democratic politics beckoned, the leaders of social movements made the leap from activism and political struggle to the electoral and parliamentary arenas in an attempt to domesticate contentious actors and access state power. In Egypt, the onset of electoral politics triggered uncertainty and conflict among political players rather than an agreement to settle differences according to democratic rules. As the opening of the 2011–2012 parliamentary elections drew nearer, the division among non-Islamists, revolutionary youth, and the Brotherhood escalated. At that time, the Brotherhood began to fear that elections might be canceled or that the constitution (to be written by an assembly chosen by the new parliament) would have its content dictated in advance by the military or elements from the old regime. Revolutionary youth worried that the latter were solidifying their grip on power and that Islamists were playing into their hands in the hope of joining an emerging regime. So, rather than form an alliance, groups fractured once again. In violent street protests against the military and security forces in November 2011, revolutionary youth groups, finding themselves on their own, charged the Islamists with betraying the revolution. For their part, the Islamists charged the demonstrators with disrupting the democratic process. The military and security forces turned back the challenge with force.

The deepening divisions among political actors highlights another distinctive element in Egyptian politics: the military remained the arbiter. In Latin America, the military often exited politics quickly and democratic elections were fairly free and definitive. In some cases (such as Chile or Brazil), it attempted to secure a continued but diminished role in return for accepting democratic outcomes. But the Egyptian military remained in control and it was never clear to the various groups vying for electoral supremacy what winning in a democratic context would mean. In 2011, the SCAF had delegated the day-to-day business of government to Mubarak-era officials even after Mubarak had been deposed. That seemed to continue even after parliamentary elections in late 2011 and early 2012. An attempt to exclude some regime officials from electoral eligibility was struck down by the courts. The parliament that was seated in early 2012 discovered that the interim constitution issued by the military did not allow it to legislate without the military's approval or to oversee the cabinet in any substantive way.

By early 2012, political actors began to realize that the SCAF seemed to hold all the cards until a new president was elected and a new constitution was written. And they began to change their behavior accordingly. For presidential elections, the Brotherhood had first indicated it would not field a candidate; it said it wanted to work with other political forces rather than win outright and spark a reaction. In 2012, however, the Brotherhood began to suspect that the military was trying to hem it in and that other political actors were trying to deny it the fruits of its electoral victories. So it entered not one candidate but two (in case one was disqualified). And indeed, a number of leading candidates (including the Brotherhood's first choice) were dropped from the ballot on a series of legal technicalities. The Brotherhood's second choice, Muhammad Morsi, made it to a runoff against a regime figure (and former general), leading many supporters of the uprising to despair that they were being shut out completely. The Brotherhood reached out to some by giving assurances it would rule consensually if it won—and Morsi did in fact squeak into office (with the electoral commission taking so much time to announce the winner that it sparked rumors that an attempt to falsify the results was underway).

Though Morsi had been elected, his authority, the willingness of state institutions to accept him, and the fate of the momentary détente between Islamists and non-Islamists were nonetheless all unclear. With its parliamentary and presidential victories, the Brotherhood seemed on the brink of governing. But in reality, the results proved a mixed blessing for the movement. First, they frightened rather than persuaded non-Islamists, who began to charge that the Brotherhood was simply consolidating its power and using democratic mechanisms to insert itself permanently.

Second, the Islamists' electoral successes provoked state bodies to seek ways to limit the Brotherhood's rise. The judiciary (especially the administrative courts and the constitutional court) hamstrung efforts to write a new constitution and disbanded the parliament; the military accepted Morsi's election as president but kept him at arm's length. These patterns—the alienation of non-Islamists and the resistance of the state apparatus—only grew more marked over time and ultimately proved fatal to the Brotherhood's hopes. The processes unleashed by the uprisings led to a period full of elections but not to stable democratic governance. We now turn to the collapse of these democratization efforts.

THE BROTHERHOOD'S SHORT TENURE IN OFFICE AND CONTINUED MILITARY-JUDICIAL TUTELAGE

Why did the revolutionary forces fail to form their own new regime?

In 2011, the Egyptian state remained intact but the regime's collapse had deprived it of clear leadership and coordination. While state institutions could sometimes seem paralyzed, they remained powerful—even if President Mubarak had resigned and his former party and networks of supporters had been disbanded and could no longer control and guide that state apparatus.

In the electoral process, Islamists looked to be consolidating a degree of political leadership. In the end, however, that process proved unsuccessful. State institutions resisted the Islamists in various ways and to different degrees, and the Islamists' opponents gradually rallied together. As a result, a new democratic regime did not emerge despite a plethora of elections.

As the Islamists gained a majority of parliamentary seats, they had a decisive voice in choosing delegates to the Constituent Assembly. The Brotherhood adopted an exclusionary approach, choosing a significant number of Islamists while largely excluding Copts, women, or non-Islamists. The joint Brotherhood-Salafi domination of the Constituent Assembly threatened marginalized non-Islamists, representatives of some key state bodies, and Christians churches, which pushed these groups to withdraw from the proceedings and denounce the constitution even before it was put before the public.

While Islamists controlled the parliament and the presidency, they found they could not dominate the state, important parts of which retained significant autonomy, which in turn quickly grew into opposition. By April 2012, judicial actors seemed threatened by the course that Egyptian politics was now taking, and by the rise of Islamist political forces specifically. An administrative court dissolved the first Constituent Assembly, accepting the argument that Islamists had packed it. In June, the Supreme Constitutional Court (SCC) dissolved the parliament on the grounds that the law on which it had been elected was unconstitutional (but perhaps also because some parliamentarians had begun working on laws that would remake the SCC). When Morsi was elected president at the end of June, he immediately clashed with the courts over a series of issues; some of his supporters reacted to the resulting legal defeats, real or anticipated, by demonstrating at some courts and actually forcing the SCC to curtail its operations. As the confrontation intensified over the coming months, Morsi's supporters began to draft legislation that would lower the retirement age for judges, effectively decapitating judicial bodies that worked so thoroughly on the grounds of seniority. In an unexpected move to control the judiciary, Morsi issued a constitutional declaration in November 2012 that placed him beyond the reach of the constitutional court's review. The declaration triggered deadly clashes between Brotherhood supporters and opponents, the latter protesting en masse in front of the presidential palace.

Under such pressure, the Brotherhood continued its collaboration with the military. But there were signs of deep and continuing mistrust. The ruling SCAF issued a supplementary constitutional decree in June 2012 (immediately before Morsi took office) that gave the head of SCAF the right to veto any clause drafted by the assembly if it conflicted with the "goals of the revolution or constitutional principles from Egypt's previous constitutions." If the assembly overturned the veto, the issue had to be referred to the SCC for deliberation. And if the assembly failed to finish drafting the constitution in time and the court ruling calling for its dissolution came into effect, the SCAF was legally empowered to appoint another assembly.

The implicit threat against the Brotherhood-dominated assembly never materialized—but that only deepened the alienation felt by non-Islamists. The assembly did finish drafting the 2012 Constitution, and indeed, the representatives of key state institutions, including the military and al-Azhar, never withdrew from the process. The final document was written by the Islamist-dominated assembly and did nothing to answer some people's demands that the military accept civilian oversight or that military courts be barred from trying civilians—indeed, it did just the opposite. The Constitution made explicit a potentially broad jurisdiction of military courts over civilians, and a National Security Council was to be involved in policy issues, budgets, and legislation on matters related to domestic and international security. Non-Islamist political forces saw the result as a Brotherhood constitution with concessions to the old political order that they had fought so hard to change.

The result was continuing political contestation. During the year in which an elected president served and a new constitution was in force, it was not always clear who was ruling Egypt; it was during this period that the term "deep state" came into circulation, especially among the president's supporters. The idea—as we saw in chapter 3—is that a shadowy group comprised of senior officials and members of various state institutions (generally in the military, security services, upper bureaucracy, and judiciary) makes major decisions despite formal constitutional procedures, even those pertaining to elections, parliamentary oversight, or the like.

It was certainly clear that the military as an institution was resistant to any kind of civilian oversight. It did acquiesce in some formal meetings in which President Morsi sat with the SCAF, ostensibly heading it; senior officers also acquiesced in the face of the president's move to push aside the defense minister and another senior general and move 'Abd al-Fattah al-Sisi into the position of general commander and minister of defense. But if Egypt had a constitutional order for some of this period, it became increasingly clear that the military leadership stood outside of it. Beginning with the clashes of November 2012 (and emphatically by June 2013), the military—as an institution—was explicitly and publicly speaking to political actors (including the elected president) as if it was the ultimate defender of the state and the society.

The Brotherhood seemed to count on its constitutional and electoral legitimacy to outweigh its opponents. But the Brotherhood made strategic miscalculations. In the second round of elections, held when the atmosphere of revolutionary euphoria was at its peak, Morsi won by a very narrow margin—51.7 percent to 48.3 percent— against his competitor, Ahmad Shafiq, who was perceived as a candidate of the old regime (having served as a longtime minister before becoming Mubarak's last prime minister). This close result should have signaled the deeply polarized nature of Egyptian society after 2011: when faced with a stark choice between representatives of the previous regime and the Brotherhood, nearly half of Egyptians were still in favor of the old guard.

When the exhilaration of revolution abated, the Brotherhood's insistence that it had legal legitimacy and majority support only heightened polarization and pushed its opponents to mobilize against it. The rhetoric from the various camps grew increasingly harsh and violence against Brotherhood offices, Christian churches, and some state targets brought an unfamiliar alarmist and polarized element to Egyptian political life. In this atmosphere, various state actors and political forces turned against the Morsi presidency, seeing it as the source of disorder, and ultimately overthrew it in 2013.

THE STATE REASSEMBLES ITSELF: CIVIC FOUNDATIONS OF DEMOCRATIC REVERSAL AND THE INSTALLATION OF A NEW REGIME

In the spring of 2013, most of the non-Islamist political forces that had been previously unable to coordinate their actions gradually began to coalesce around a strategy to oppose and bring down the Brotherhood and President Morsi. A major step was taken by a new movement, Tamarrud (Rebellion), which presented itself as the youthful voice of revolution; it accused the Brotherhood of dividing the nation and betraying the revolutionary forces. In May, it launched a petition demanding early presidential elections with the aim of collecting more signatures than the total number of votes for Morsi a year earlier. With most non-Islamist forces enthusiastically joining the effort, the requisite number of signatures were quickly gathered; the coalition then aimed for a massive nationwide demonstration on June 30.

In addition to broad support from non-Islamist social and political movements, parts of the state apparatus appeared to be cheering on the anti-Brotherhood effort—security services, state media, and many privately owned media outlets in particular. In public, the military assumed a neutral stance vis-à-vis Morsi and Tamarrud, refusing to back the presidency. It also warned of the threat of civil conflict and suggested it would intervene if needed. In the days leading up to June 30, the military deployed in public places, explaining it was doing so not "to protect the Morsi regime.... but rather to fulfil [the military's] patriotic duty to protect the Egyptian people... from any attack from armed militias."[4] The reference to armed groups was an implicit suggestion that the Brotherhood was mobilizing its supporters for combat.

The effect was to create a broad and disparate coalition. Tamarrud appealed to revolutionary youth; its petition campaign also appealed to much more conservative Egyptians who wished for a return to order and the status quo ante. They saw in the assurances of the military and the assistance of the Interior Ministry an offer of support and a chance for the restoration of state power and a return to the relative stability of the Mubarak era.[5]

Indeed, violence was rising in Egypt in the lead-up to the demonstrations. Brotherhood offices were attacked throughout the country; for its part, the Brotherhood, under the belief it still had mass support, began to call for counterdemonstrations. Egypt was now completely polarized and the threat of violence between the two camps seemed to be growing.

On June 30, massive anti-Morsi demonstrations were held under the protection of the security forces. Three days later, the minister of defense and commander in chief of the armed forces— 'Abd al-Fattah al-Sisi—gathered important state leaders around him (along with some civilian political leaders and activists) and announced that Morsi had been deposed and the Constitution suspended. The head of the SCC would serve as interim president while the country followed a "road map" for constitutional revision, reform, reconciliation, and parliamentary and presidential elections. With significant support from large parts of Egyptian society (but with most Islamists swinging sharply into opposition), the leaders of critical state institutions seemed to be coming together to reconstitute a new regime.

Manufacturing Mobilization to Demobilize Society and Repress Opponents

The new leaders—and al-Sisi in particular—called for continued popular mobilization to overcome any resistance and to support their claim that

Egypt was experiencing another revolution (or continuing the 2011 revolution) rather than a simple military coup. And they received the response they requested. In early 2011, there was a semblance of coherence among the political forces that gathered in Tahrir Square in support of democracy and socioeconomic change; now, some of those same forces were calling for draconian measures to repress the Brotherhood, while the Brotherhood, for its part, clung to power. Instead of pushing against the police as they had in 2011, demonstrators chanted, "The Police and the People are One Hand," substituting the 2011 mention of "the army" with "the police" while hearkening back to the military's decision to force Mubarak out two years earlier. Some of those demonstrating had supported the pre-2011 order (and had been denounced in 2011 as the "remnants" of the old regime), but others saw themselves as revolutionary forces who believed that the Brotherhood had hijacked the popular revolt to seize control for themselves.

On July 24, 2013, al-Sisi addressed the nation during a speech at a military parade and called for mass demonstrations to grant the Egyptian military and police a popular "mandate" to crack down on "terrorism." Millions heeded the call in the form of mass demonstrations, but they were not the only ones on the streets. Even before Morsi's removal, his supporters began organizing huge sit-ins in Cairo's Raba'a and al-Nahda Squares. On August 14, 2013, security and military forces raided the two camps and forcefully dispersed the sit-ins. The attacks were described by Human Rights Watch as "one of the world's largest killings of demonstrators in a single day in recent history, as a minimum of 817 people and more likely at least 1,000 died during the dispersal."[6] Even the official Human Rights Council agreed that hundreds were killed, though the security forces blamed Morsi supporters for the violence.

Islamist leaders and followers reacted by challenging the new regime on the streets with anti-coup demonstrations. Their insistence that the legitimate government had been overthrown led to a wave of violence, with Morsi supporters attacking police stations and Christian targets throughout the country. Sectarian rhetoric became increasingly shrill as violence against Copts swept the country. In normal times, Egypt's minorities face various forms of discrimination, of which the targeting of Copts is the most obvious example. After the unrest of 2013, this dynamic only intensified; according to Eshhad, an Egyptian human rights group, "between August 2013 and the third quarter of 2017, of the recorded incidents [of sectarian violence], 92 % of the victims targeted were identified as Christians."[7] A low-level insurgency in the Sinai Peninsula also intensified after August 2013, with radical groups there able to portray Egyptian government forces as oppressive and illegitimate.

In the face of escalating violence, the authorities declared the Brotherhood a terrorist organization and imprisoned thousands of its supporters. They also targeted a wide host of companies, NGOs, and charity funds that were allegedly tied to the Brotherhood and some of its leading members.

As had happened in February 2011, the military was now largely in control. While the interim president was the chief justice of the SCC, and a new constitution was written by a panel of judges, civilian officials, and political actors, it was clear that the military was overseeing the process, vetoing constitutional clauses that might diminish its authority (such as one that would have barred military trials of civilians), and ultimately endorsing the decision of its new head, al-Sisi, to run for the presidency.[8] In that sense, the military was more than the backbone and recruiting ground for the regime, as it had been in the 1950s and 1960s. It was now taking on the duty, as an institution, of reconstituting a new Egyptian regime.

The New Regime and the Post-2013 Turn to Repression

While it is difficult to explain the course of Egyptian politics in 2011 without acknowledging the incomplete but real separation of state and regime, various parts of the state apparatus—including the police and other security and intelligence forces, the judiciary, state media, and the official religious apparatus—all came together in 2013 to endorse regime change and try to build a new regime under military leadership. That process has succeeded to an extent: it has returned a military figure to the presidency and facilitated his attempt to control the entire state apparatus from the presidency.

In al-Sisi's first year, important civilian actors and movements were gradually pushed aside; protests and rallies by Islamists were harshly repressed and non-Islamist demonstrations barred; labor strikes and other forms of social protest were shut down; and the media and civil society more tightly controlled.

A new order was slowly constructed. The first step was a new constitution (or, technically, a comprehensive amendment of the one passed in 2012 that had only operated for six months). The document was not all that different from the one it replaced, but it gave protection to the military, the judiciary, and other state bodies. It was written largely by state officials, though important political leaders and intellectuals supportive of the 2013 overthrow of the Brotherhood were included as well. This was followed by presidential elections (with the presidency in the process of being restored as the central institution in the Egyptian state—it had been vacant from Mubarak's departure until Morsi's inauguration, after which it was held by a figure who could not exercise presidential authority fully).

With the backing of his fellow officers and most political forces (and with an anemic campaign for an alternative candidate harassed by official bodies), al-Sisi was elected president in May 2014 with an official vote share of nearly 95 percent. Following the presidential elections, parliamentary elections were held in November and December of 2015. The law for these elections was amended to weaken the role of political parties, thus enabling politically well-connected individuals, former security officials, and their allies to win seats. Critics charged that security agencies had vetted the candidates, encouraging some while hampering others. Whether fairly or not, most of the parliamentary seats were won by al-Sisi supporters.

More than one-tenth of the parliament elected in 2015 was controlled by former military, police, and intelligence officers. No political party held a majority that allowed it to organize the parliament, which was kept under the watchful eye of a regime-appointed speaker. Approximately 140 parliamentarians came from the private sector, but these are generally not holdovers from the old regime. In 2020, a new parliament was elected (and the regime brought in a new speaker), this time with a quickly assembled "Future of the Homeland Party" that had no clear unifying principle other than loyalty to the regime. Indeed, even many of the old networks connected to the abolished National Democratic Party of the Sadat and Mubarak eras are shut out since they represent strong (if not oppositional) interests. The new regime has not allowed Mubarak-era businesspeople to regain the kind of political influence they exercised before 2011. Even though they retain control of large assets, market shares, and the know-how deemed necessary for Egypt's economic recovery, businesspeople have not been encouraged to play any direct political role. This applies also to the areas of economic policy making over which they had gained much influence during the last decade of Mubarak's rule. Moreover, within the economic sphere, they have increasingly been reduced to the status of junior partners in military-affiliated agencies and companies, which have come to play a central role in national megaprojects.

The regime gradually reasserted the authority of state institutions and clamped down on politics in most forms, expanding the targets of repression beyond the Brotherhood to include any potential opponent who expressed criticism of the regime or its policies, even those who were initially supportive of the army's ousting of Morsi.

The regime constructed a new set of legal rules to restrict associational space and derail social activism. First, an October 2014 law granted the military the authority to protect public and state facilities for two years. It declared roads and bridges to be "strategic institutions"; anyone who trespassed on them—including in the form of political protests—was henceforth subject to "military tribunals."[9]

Second, in July 2014, the regime offered a proposal that would see the forced dissolution of all NGOs operating in Egypt and their subsequent reregistration with the Ministry of Social Solidarity within forty-five days. In the end, restrictive laws were passed in 2017 and then modified in 2019, with other tools (including those from an older 2002 law) used in the meantime. For instance, the regime attempted to use antiterror legislation to trim the branches of the Brotherhood's education network, charitable activities, and social service branches and to confiscate the assets of groups deemed a threat to public order.[10] And such steps could be used to harass other organizations that had no ties to Islamists or the Brotherhood.

Third, an August 2014 counterterrorism law defined terrorism as the "use of force or violence or threat" that aims to "disrupt general order" or "harm national unity." This broad language has been used to qualify any act of dissent as terrorism requiring prosecution by a specialized judicial panel. Opponents face stiff penalties and military courts are authorized to try civilians deemed threatening to national security.[11]

Fourth, in 2018, Egypt's parliament approved the "Anti-Cyber and Information Technology Crimes Law." The law could be used to penalize what had previously been considered lawful online expression and to close independent media outlets. Blocked websites include those of news outlets and human rights organizations.[12]

The system built after 2013 is not a recreation of that which existed in the 1950s and 1960s. Several critical differences means that the current system more closely resembles the conservative regimes common in central and southern Europe in the period between the two world wars or Latin America and southern Europe in the decades after 1945. First, the regime seems antipolitical. While the Egyptian regime of the 1950s and 1960s sponsored mass rallies, built a ruling political party, and propagated a strong nationalist and socialist ideology, the country's post-2013 regime bans protests, eschews parties, and pursues a nationalism that emphasizes duties and security rather than social justice, equality, and transformation. It also advocates a "national security" doctrine that places the nation above the individual and draws heavily on old notions of geopolitics once promoted by European nationalists.[13] Egypt's military and political leaders speak of threats against the nation, "fourth generation warfare," and of a "war on terror," thereby promoting a sense of crisis among citizens and the idea that Egypt needs its security bodies to eradicate not only the remnants of the Brotherhood but other foreign and domestic enemies.

Al-Sisi presents himself as the protector of the nation who can direct the organs of the state and guide citizens to do what is required of them. The post-2011 discourse of democratic values, freedom, and individual expression has given way to a stress on national security, which requires conformity with a single set of values and a strong leader and authoritative institutions. This official discourse has prioritized stabilty and the countering of various threats—effectively treating society as something to be protected rather than listened to. The result is a new regime that rests on a powerful but narrower ruling coalition comprised mainly of members of the security apparatus and the military.

The depoliticization of society made possible some bold policy moves without any need to reincarnate Nasser's class alliance; this includes the policies associated with a set of austerity measures taken in November 2016 to attract the assistance of the International Monetary Fund. Most remarkably, the Egyptian pound was floated at the time, resulting in the sudden loss of around 50 percent of its value.[14] While select groups of Egyptians did well (such as those paid in dollars or who exported goods), prices soared for all Egyptians and many saw their effective wages slashed. The post-2013 regime also has consistently worked to decrease public expenditures and liberalize fuel prices with the pronounced goal of correcting the country's macroeconomic indicators. These neoliberal measures earned the respect of some international investors and financial institutions, but they led to significant short-term hardships for many Egyptians. Moreover, they were combined with an expansion in the economic role of the military, as discussed at length in chapter 8. Many Egyptians have privately grumbled, but there has been no space to organize politically against these moves.

In addition to these economic and political changes, the new regime has emphasized conservative social values—like religion, family, and hierarchy—much more than youth and revolutionary change. Religion has been used to strengthen presidential and state authority, neutralize Islamists, and promote compliance with the regime's strategic orientation.

Regime Consolidation and a Restructured State

The post-2013 regime rests strongly on existing state institutions. Unlike the Free Officers who came to rule the country in the decades after 1952, al-Sisi spent much of his youth and all his adult life inside military institutions; lacking a political profile, he moved into a political leadership role after receiving the blessing of the senior military leadership rather than organizing secretly without their knowledge (as Nasser and his contemporaries had done). The senior leadership of other state institutions treated the Muslim Brotherhood, the Morsi presidency, and the turmoil of the post-2011 period as grave threats to the Egyptian state, and they have therefore largely supported al-Sisi's efforts.

The institution of the presidency has been shorn of some of the structures of civilian political support, such as a political party and experienced political advisers, that it had acquired in the pre-2011 period. Al-Sisi therefore took office heading a regime that appeared to be more of a consortium of state institutions than a recreation of the earlier regime. Yet in the years since 2013, the regime has evolved significantly to increase the prominence of the military and security institutions as well as slowly strengthen the presidency.

And this is reflected in the formal legal order—such as a step to immunize senior military commanders from being prosecuted over the deadly crackdown that followed Morsi's ouster. Moreover, the parliament has approved the expansion of military involvement in the economy and constitutional amendments asserting the supremacy of the presidential institution and criminalizing possible dissent.

But while the military has been protected, it has also been placed under the firmer control of the presidency. This has been done in part by key appointments and retirements, allowing the president to place supporters and allies in key positions. But subtle legal changes have been made as well, such as one empowering the president to "call upon senior army officers to serve in the military for life, even if they have already resigned their military posts and rejoined the civilian workforce." This effectively prevents potential contenders within the top brass from running for office and challenging al-Sisi, as Egyptian law "prohibits active or reserve military from holding office"—a constraint that the state used to bar a prominent general from running against al-Sisi in 2018.[15]

Indeed, when al-Sisi ran for reelection that year, he faced only one challenger, a marginal figure whose own party supported al-Sisi. All other viable candidates were pressured or harassed out of the race. The following year, the parliament passed a set of constitutional amendments and submitted them to a referendum (in which over 88 percent of voters ratified the new measures) strengthening presidential control over the judiciary, assigned the military the duty to "protect the constitution and democracy, and safeguard the basic components of the State and its civilian nature, and the people's gains, and individual rights and freedoms," and widened the jurisdiction of military courts.[16] It was not merely state institutions—the military and the presidency—that were strengthened; al-Sisi himself had his term extended and the restriction on his running for a third one removed.

The regime had evolved from a military-led one in 2013 to a presidential dictatorship rooted first in the military, second in the internal security apparatus, and third in its domination of all other state institutions. Political activity and any kind of public accountability was edged aside, with the result that the concentration of authority in the hands of a single person was difficult to debate, much less challenge.

CONCLUSION

Conflictual political dynamics in the transitional period between 2011 and 2013 reflected the will of several dominant actors who were fundamentally at odds with each other. During that period, as Egyptian politics witnessed enormous turmoil at the top (with the key elements of the old regime— the presidency, senior security officials, army officers, and top bureaucrats— competing as much as cooperating), state bodies sought to protect themselves, stay on the right side of a deeply uncertain and rapidly changing political situation, and preserve their own interests and autonomy. Most weathered internal challenges from younger or more junior members, but not without difficulty or some personnel changes at the top. The result was that the state apparatus continued its resistance to the Brotherhood, at times obliquely and at times directly. During the 2011–2013 period, the military acted as if it was part of the state, one that was willing to cooperate but not beholden or accountable to the ruling regime. Also, parts of the bureaucracy simply overturned presidential orders or refused to respond to presidential directives, and the judiciary operated as an opposition force within the state itself.

While structural factors such as the size of the military and its access to military resources, the deep state, and authoritarian legacies do have some explanatory merit when it comes to analyzing democratic deficits in Egypt, such a perspective tends to treat the dynamics following the 2011 protests and up till Morsi's removal as mere details that distract us from long-term factors. Certainly, the popular uprising disrupted existing structures of power and brought new actors to the forefront, including previously restricted political groups (e.g., Islamists). Social and political actors, for all their conflictual behavior between 2011 and 2013, brought fundamental shifts in conceptions of political legitimacy and state-society relations, the impact of which are still felt—and indeed could still manifest in new ways in the future. The course of events between 2011 and 2013 appear clearer in retrospect than they did at the time, and that should lead us to suspect that in such critical historical moments, outcomes are not predetermined. In the end, these events suggests that democratic outcomes depend in part on leaders who display and retain their commitment to and confidence in democratic procedures, regardless of the uncertainty that democracy brings through periodic competitive elections. Elite choices in Egypt, whatever their intentions (and they were mixed), effectively steered the country toward a new authoritarianism. The Brotherhood gambled that it could ally with the military and did not need non-Islamist support—and lost. Non-Islamists proved ill-prepared for elections and ultimately allied with the military—an alliance that led to them being deprived of their ability to pursue their political goals.

The point, however, is not that Egyptians acted unintelligently. Certain actors made choices in an uncertain environment that sparked fears among non-Islamists and rapidly polarized the Egyptian political scene in the post-uprising period. As we have seen in previous chapters, when Egyptians experience politics, either as bystanders or as active participants, they often encounter a myriad of religious groups, civil society actors, state institutions, political forces, and individual issues with whom they differ deeply. The inability to manage these differences proved fatal to the goals of the 2011 uprising, leading Egyptians to continue the debate over whether authoritarianism is the best remedy or whether a new path must eventually emerge.

NOTES

2. GOVERNING EGYPT: THE CONSTRUCTION OF THE MODERN EGYPTIAN STATE

1. Charles Tilly, "War Making and State Making as Organized Crime," in *Bringing the State Back In*, ed. Peter Evans, Dietrich Rueschemeyer, and Theda Skocpol (Cambridge: Cambridge University Press, 1985), 169–191.
2. There are many academic writings that help tell this story, or particular aspects of it. For a focus on the early nineteenth century, see Khaled Fahmy, *All the Pasha's Men: Mehmed Ali, His Army and the Making of Modern Egypt* (Cairo: American University in Cairo Press, 1997). For a study that focuses on agriculture and land ownership, see Kenneth M. Cuno, *The Pasha's Peasants: Land, Society, and Economy in Lower Egypt, 1740–1858* (Cambridge: Cambridge University Press, 1992). Both Fahmy and Cuno are alert to continuities with the past and with Egypt's Ottoman context, elements that are less prominent in many older accounts that understand the early nineteenth century as a sharp breaking point and Egypt as distinct and best understood in its own terms.
3. This period has also drawn tremendous scholarly attention. See, for example, Juan R. I. Cole, *Colonialism and Revolution in the Middle East: Social and Cultural Origins of Egypt's 'Urabi Movement* (Princeton, N.J.: Princeton University Press, 1992), and Raouf Abbas and Asem El-Dessouky, *The Large Landowning Class and the Peasantry in Egypt, 1837–1952* (Syracuse, N.Y.: Syracuse University Press, 2011).
4. For some of the very complicated ways nationality operated in Egypt, see Will Hanley, *Identifying with Nationality: Europeans, Ottomans, and Egyptians in Alexandria* (New York: Columbia University Press, 2017).

5. See Joel Gordon, *Nasser's Blessed Movement: Egypt's Free Officers and the July Revolution* (Oxford: Oxford University Press, 1992) for an account of the politics of this period.
6. John Waterbury, *The Egypt of Nasser and Sadat: The Political Economy of Two Regimes* (Princeton, N.J.: Princeton University Press, 1983).

3. BETWEEN STATE AND REGIME: THE EVOLUTION OF EGYPTIAN AUTHORITARIANISM

1. On the origins of the term, see Ryand Gingeras, "Last Rites for a 'Pure Bandit': Clandestine Service, Historiography and the Origins of the Turkish 'Deep State,'" *Past and Present*, no. 206 (February 2010): 151–174.
2. Juan Linz, "An Authoritarian Regime: Spain," in *Cleavages, Ideologies and Party Systems: Contributions to Comparative Political Sociology*, vol. 10, ed. Erik Allardt and Yrjo Littunen (Helsinki: Academic Bookstore, 1964): 1467–1531.
3. On attempts to organize Egyptian society, see Robert Bianchi, *Unruly Corporatism: Associational Life in Twentieth-Century Egypt* (New York: Oxford University Press, 1989).
4. On patronage in Egyptian politics, see Mohamed Fahmy Menza, *Patronage Politics in Egypt: The National Democratic Party and Muslim Brotherhood in Cairo* (London: Routledge, 2012).
5. Nathan J. Brown, *The Rule of Law in the Arab World: Courts in Egypt and the Gulf* (Cambridge: Cambridge University Press, 1997).
6. For an analysis of the role that new (and old) media played in the 2011 uprisings, see Marc Lynch, *The Arab Uprising: The Unfinished Revolutions of the New Middle East* (New York: Public Affairs, 2013).
7. On the military's political role and interaction with other forces, see Hazem Kandil, *Soldiers, Spies, and Statesmen: Egypt's Road to Revolt* (London: Verso, 2014).

4. THE RISE AND DECAY OF SOCIAL CONTROL—AND THE PERPETUATION OF AUTHORITARIANISM

1. When we refer to corporatism in this book, we will be exclusively referring to state corporatism, since that is the only variant that existed in Egypt. Many scholars have followed Philippe Schmitter in distinguishing between corporatism established by the state, generally imposed in an authoritarian fashion, and that which arises when social groups come together, enlist state support, and negotiate arrangements. For the full history of the term and an examination of these variants, see Philippe C. Schmitter, "Still the Century of Corporatism," *Review of Politics* 36, no. 1 (1974): 85–131.
2. Paul Simon Adams, "Corporatism in Latin America and Europe: Origins, Developments, and Challenges in Comparative Perspective," in *Authoritarianism and Corporatism in Latin America Revisited*, ed. H. J. Wiarda (Gainesville: University Press of Florida, 2004), 62.
3. Schmitter, "Still the Century of Corporatism," 93–94.

4. THE RISE AND DECAY OF SOCIAL CONTROL

4. Ruth Berins Collier and David Collier, "Inducements versus Constraints: Disaggregating 'Corporatism,'" *American Political Science Review* 73, no. 4 (1979): 969–970.
5. Alfred Stepan, *The State and Society: Peru in Comparative Perspective* (Princeton, N.J.: Princeton University Press, 1978), 82–83.
6. James Malloy, "Authoritarianism and Corporatism in Latin America: The Modal Pattern," in *Authoritarianism and Corporatism in Latin America*, ed. J. M. Malloy (Pittsburgh, Penn.: University of Pittsburgh Press, 1977), 3–22.
7. John Waterbury, *The Egypt of Nasser and Sadat* (Princeton, N.J.: Princeton University Press, 1983), 313–315.
8. Maha Abdelrahman, *Egypt's Long Revolution Protests* (London: Routledge, 2015), 130–131.
9. Evelyn Stevens, "Mexico's PRI: The Institutionalization of Corporatism?," in *Authoritarianism and Corporatism in Latin America*, ed. J. M. Malloy (Pittsburgh, Penn.: University of Pittsburgh Press, 1977), 227–257.
10. Before the Free Officers took power, the law of 1942—passed by the Wafdist government—organized trade union membership and authorized the MOSA to approve or close down labor organizations. Although the law allowed for pluralism in these organizations, it fragmented the movement, limited its membership, and imposed financial constraints by restricting involvement in profit-making enterprises.
11. Robert Mabro, *The Egyptian Economy, 1952–1972* (Oxford: Oxford University Press, 1974), 154–160; Robert Bianchi, *Unruly Corporatism: Associational Life in Twentieth-Century Egypt* (Oxford: Oxford University Press, 1989), 134–135.
12. Bianchi, *Unruly Corporatism*, 128–129.
13. The modified Law 35 of 1981 extended the confederation's authority over the new Workers' University, established to centralize union leaders' training programs, formerly ran by different rival state agencies.
14. Bianchi, *Unruly Corporatism*, 129–130, 141.
15. Only in the last days of Nasser's life was the Egyptian Confederation of Agricultural Cooperatives created.
16. Alan Richards, *Egypt's Agricultural Development, 1800–1980: Technical and Social Change* (Boulder, Colo.: Westview Press, 1982), 90.
17. Bianchi, *Unruly Corporatism*, 151–152.
18. For more details on syndicates under Nasser's regime, see May Kassem, *Egyptian Politics: The Dynamics of Authoritarian Rule* (Boulder, Colo.: Lynne Rienner, 2004); Robert Springborg, "Professional Syndicates in Egyptian Politics, 1952–1970," *International Journal of Middle East Studies* 9, no. 3 (1978): 275–295.
19. Clement Henry Moore, *Images of Development: Egyptian Engineers in Search of Industry* (Cambridge, Mass.: MIT Press, 1980), 58.
20. Stepan, *The State and Society*, 98.
21. Kassem, *Egyptian Politics*, 110.
22. Bianchi, *Unruly Corporatism*, 150–157.
23. Kassem, *Egyptian Politics*, 114. See also Springborg, "Professional Syndicates in Egyptian Politics."
24. For further details on the confrontational strategies adopted by some professional syndicates, as well as the rising power of Islamists in professional syndicates and

4. THE RISE AND DECAY OF SOCIAL CONTROL

efforts to combat their power in the 1990s, see Sara Ben-Nfissa, *The Relationship between the Egyptian State and NGOs Since the 19th Century* (Cairo: Al-Ahram Center for Political and Strategic Studies, 1994); Ibn Khaldon Center, *Al-mujtama` al-madani wal-tahawwul al-dimuqrati fi al-watan al-`arabi: Al-taqrir al-sanawi* [Civil society and democratic transition in the Arab region: The annual report] (Cairo: Ibn Khaldon Center, 1996).

5. CIVIL SOCIETY ORGANIZATIONS: LIMITED POLITICAL AGENDA AND MOUNTING RESISTANCE

1. Gabriel A. Almond and Sidney Verba, *The Civic Culture: Political Attitudes and Democracy in Five Nations* (Princeton, N.J.: Princeton University Press, 1963).
2. Maha Abdelrahman, *Civil Society Exposed: The Politics of NGOs in Egypt* (London: Tauris Academic Studies, 2004), reading 139, 140.
3. Ideologically, Islamists did not aim to eliminate class differences or deny the right of the rich to be rich as long as they fulfil their duties to the poor by giving zakat.
4. For further details on al-Jama`iyya al-shar`iyya and its political role, see Mohamed Menza, *Patronage Politics in Egypt: The National Democratic Party and Muslim Brotherhood in Cairo* (London: Routledge, 2012).
5. Ray Bush and David Seddon, "Editorial: North Africa in Africa," *Review of African Political Economy* 26, no. 82 (2007): 438.
6. The EOHR was registered at the MOSA in 2003.
7. Al-la'iha al-tanfiziyya li-qanun al-jam`iyyat w al-mu'assasat al-ahliyya raqam 84 li-sanat 2002 [The executive regulation of the Law on Non-governmental Associations and Organizations No. 84 of 2002], ch. 3, art. 48.17 (2002), https://manshurat.org/node/604.
8. Al-la'iha al-tanfiziyya li-qanun al-jam`iyyat w al-mu'assasat al-ahliyya raqam 84 li-sanat 2002 [The executive regulation of the Law on Non-governmental Associations and Organizations No. 84 of 2002], ch. 2, art. 24.11 (2002), https://manshurat.org/node/604.
9. Samer Soliman, "State and Industrial Capitalism in Egypt," *Cairo Papers in Social Science* 21, no. 2 (1998): 72–82.
10. Ramón Fogel, *Movimientos campesinos en el Paraguay* (Asunción: Centro Paraguayo de Estudios Sociológicos, 1986).
11. Carol Ann Drogus and Hannah Stewart-Gambino, *Activist Faith: Grassroots Women in Democratic Brazil and Chile* (University Park: Pennsylvania State University Press, 2005), 50, 60–62.
12. Maria Helena Alves, *State and Opposition in Military Brazil* (Austin: University of Texas Press, 1985), 174, 175.
13. Rabab El-Mahdi, "The Democracy Movement: Cycles of Protest," in *Egypt: The Moment of Change*, ed. Rahab El-Mahdi and Philip Marfleet (London: Zed Books, 2009), 87–102.
14. Maha Abdelrahman, "'With the Islamists?—Sometimes. With the State?—Never!' Cooperation Between the Left and Islamists in Egypt," *British Journal of Middle Eastern Studies* 36, no. 1 (2009): 43–45.

6. ISLAM AND RELIGION IN EGYPTIAN STATE, SOCIETY, AND ECONOMY

15. For further details on labor protests, see Rabab El-Mahdi, "Labor Protests in Egypt: Causes and Meanings," *Review of African Political Economy* 38, no. 129 (2011): 387–402; Joel Beinin, "Workers Protest in Egypt: Neoliberalism and Class Struggle in 21st Century," *Social Movement Studies* 8, no.4 (2009): 449–454.

6. ISLAM AND RELIGION IN EGYPTIAN STATE, SOCIETY, AND ECONOMY

1. "2016 Republican Party Platform," American Presidency Project, UC Santa Barbara, accessed September 18, 2020, https://www.presidency.ucsb.edu/documents/2016-republican-party-platform.
2. See Kenneth M. Cuno, *Modernizing Marriage: Family, Ideology, and Law in Nineteenth- and Early Twentieth-Century Egypt* (Syracuse, N.Y.: Syracuse University Press, 2015).
3. Gregory Starrett, *Putting Islam to Work: Education, Politics, and Religious Transformation in Egypt*, vol. 25 (Berkeley: University of California Press, 1998).
4. Fawaz A. Gerges, *Making the Arab World: Nasser, Qutb, and the Clash That Shaped the Middle East* (Princeton, N.J.: Princeton University Press, 2018).
5. For example, when the Wafd-dominated parliament passed legislation transferring control of religious schools and institutes from al-Azhar to the Ministry of Education in 1927, the king backed al-Azhar clerics who rejected the law and called for dissolution of the parliament.
6. For further details on the history of Salafisim, see Henri Lauzière, *The Making of Salafism: Islamic Reform in the Twentieth Century* (New York: Columbia University Press, 2015)
7. While the Jewish community was generally considered unitary from a legal point of view (with a small Karaite sect that had separate status) and had some joint institutions, it contained considerable diversity. Some of the Jews who a communal presence in Egypt came from other Arab countries (Palestine, Yemen, Syria, Tunisia, Morocco, Iraq) and were known as "Oriental Jews." Some other Jewish groups, known as Sephardim, had foreign origins (from Spain and Portugal, as well as Italian Jews who settled in Egypt). The Sephardim constituted the largest segment of Egyptian Jews and contributed most economic and communal leadership for the community for a long period. See Michael M. Laskier, "Egyptian Jewry under the Nasser Regime, 1956–70," *Middle Eastern Studies* 31, no. 3 (1995): 573–574.
8. See Joel Beinin, *The Dispersion of Egyptian Jewry: Culture, Politics, and the Formation of a Modern Diaspora* (Berkeley: University of California Press, 1998).
9. Laskier, "Egyptian Jewry," 573.
10. For further details on Zionist emissaries and Arab Jews, see Yehuda Shenhav, *The Arab Jews: A Postcolonial Reading of Nationalism, Religion, and Ethnicity* (Stanford, Calif.: Stanford University Press, 2006), chap. 7.
11. Gudrun Krämer, *The Jews in Modern Egypt, 1914–1952* (London: I. B. Tauris, 1989), 169.
12. Krämer, 139–145. Some of local Jews joined communist movements beginning in the late nineteenth century in an endeavor to participate in the political life of the country.
13. Krämer, 201.
14. Krämer, 202–203, 211.

15. Laskier, "Egyptian Jewry," 576.
16. Laskier, 582–583.
17. The Constitution of the Arab Republic of Egypt, 1971 (as Amended to 2007), accessed October 12, 2020, http://constitutionnet.org/sites/default/files/Egypt%20Constitution.pdf.
18. Vivian Ibrahim, *The Copts of Egypt: The Challenges of Modernisation and Identity* (London: I. B. Tauris, 2013), 101, 106, 115, 116; and Mariz Tadros, *Copts at the Crossroads: The Challenges of Building Inclusive Democracy in Egypt* (Cairo: American University in Cairo Press, 2013), 62–63. The mandate to oversee the *waqf* funds had long been a highly contested issue between the church and the Majlis, and the control over *waqf* property had been rotated between the Majlis on the one hand and the patriarch and the bishops on the other. See Ibrahim, *The Copts of Egypt*, 116–117, 122–123.
19. Paul Sedra, "Class Cleavages and Ethnic Conflict: Coptic Christian Communities in Modern Egyptian Politics," *Islam and Christian-Muslim Relations* 10, no. 2 (1999): 255.
20. The bylaw stipulated that the candidate must have been "ordained as a monk for at least 15 years" and adopted a draw system between candidates with the largest votes. See Tadros, *Copts at the Crossroads*, 63. For more details on the relationship between the church and the state, see Tarek el-Bishrim, *Al-dawla wa-l-kanisa* [The state and the church] (Cairo: al-Shuruq, 2011).
21. Ibrahim, *The Copts of Egypt*, 178.
22. Tadros, *Copts at the Crossroad*, 67.
23. Tadros, 72.
24. Tadros, 90.
25. Yasmine Saleh and Paul Taylor, "Egypt's Pope Says Islamist rulers neglect Copts," Reuters, April 26, 2013, https://www.reuters.com/article/us-egypt-pope/egypts-pope-says-islamist-rulers-neglect-copts-idUSBRE93P0B620130426.
26. Aaron Rock-Singer, *Practicing Islam in Egypt: Print Media and Islamic Revival* (Cambridge: Cambridge University Press, 2019).
27. For audio of the exchange, see "Liqa' tarikhi bayna al-Sadat and `Abd al-Mun`im Abu al-Futuh" [Historical encounter between Sadat and `Abd al-Mun`im Abu al-Futuh], Hesham Salah, February 17, 2018, YouTube video, 6:13, www.youtube.com/watch?v=wFvBndJDZpA.
28. Carrie Wickham, *Mobilizing Islam: Religion, Activism and Political Change in Egypt* (New York: Columbia Univerity Press, 2002), 116–118.
29. Michael Dodson, "Nicaragua: The Struggle for the Church," in *Religion and Political Conflict in Latin America*, ed. Daniel H. Levine (Chapel Hill: University of North Carolina Press, 1986).
30. Saba Mahmood, *Politics of Piety: The Islamic Revival and the Feminist Subject* (Princeton, N.J.: Princeton University Press, 2005), 47.
31. Mona Oraby, "Authorizing Religious Conversion in Administrative Courts: Law, Rights, and Secular Indeterminacy," *New Diversities* 17, no. 1 (2015): 64–75.
32. Wickham, *Mobilizing Islam*, 95–96.
33. Joseph E. Stiglitz, *Wither Socialism?* (Cambridge, Mass.: MIT Press, 1994), 85.
34. Charles Issawi, *Egypt: An Economic and Social Analysis* (New York: Oxford University Press, 1947), 163–164.

35. Najat Abdulhaq *Jewish and Greek Communities in Egypt: Entrepreneurship and Business before Nasser* (London: I. B. Tauris, 2016)
36. `Abd al-Satar al-Tawila, *Sharikat tawzif al-amwal wa-al-mustaqbal al-ghamid* [Capital investment companies and the uncertain future] (Cairo: Al-Sawi, 1988), 91.
37. Ahmad `Abd al-Hay, Khayri `Umar, `Abd al-Hafiz al-Sawi, and Wisam Fu'ad, *Al-mu`arada al-mustabaha* [Violated opposition] (Cairo: Sawasiyya Center for Human Rights, 2006).
38. Patrick Haenni, *L'islam de marché* (Paris: Editions du Seuil, 2005).

7. MARKET MAKING WITHOUT DEVELOPMENT

1. Douglas North, *Institutions and Their Consequences for Economic Performance: The Limits of Rationality* (Chicago: University of Chicago Press, 1990), 383–401.
2. See, for example, John Sfakianakis, "The Whales of the Nile: Networks, Businessmen, and Bureaucrats during the Era of Privatization in Egypt," in *Networks of Privilege in the Middle East: The Politics of Economic Reform Revisited*, ed. Steven Heydemann (New York: Palgrave Macmillan, 2004), 77–100; and Safinaz El Tarouty, *Businessmen, Clientelism, and Authoritarianism in Egypt* (New York: Palgrave Macmillan, 2015).
3. Diane Singerman and Homa Hoodfar, eds., *Development, Change and Gender in Cairo: A View from the Household* (Bloomington: Indiana University Press, 1996).
4. Pierre Bourdieu, "The Production of Belief: Contribution to An Economy of Symbolic Goods," trans. Richard Nice, *Media, Culture and Society* 2, no. 3 (July 1980): 261–293.
5. Pierre Bourdieu, *Pascalian Meditations* (Stanford, Calif.: Stanford University Press, 2000), 142.
6. Bourdieu, *Pascalian Meditations*, 159–160.
7. Michel Foucault, Arnold I. Davidson, and Graham Burchell, *The Birth of Biopolitics: Lectures at the Collège de France, 1978–1979* (New York: Palgrave Macmillan, 2008).
8. Mushtaq H. Khan and Kwame Sundaram Jomo, eds., *Rents, Rent-Seeking and Economic Development: Theory and Evidence in Asia* (Cambridge: Cambridge University Press, 2000), 140.
9. Charles Issawi, *Egypt: An Economic and Social Analysis* (Oxford: Oxford University Press, 1947), 112.
10. Najat Abdulhaq, *Jewish and Greek Communities in Egypt: Entrepreneurship and Business before Nasser* (London: I. B. Tauris, 2016).
11. See Robert L. Tignor, *Capitalism and Nationalism at the End of Empire: State and Business in Decolonizing Egypt, Nigeria, and Kenya, 1945–1963* (Princeton, N.J.: Princeton University Press, 2015); and Robert Vitalis, *When Capitalists Collide: Business Conflict and the End of Empire in Egypt* (Berkeley: University of California Press, 2018).
12. See John Waterbury, *The Egypt of Nasser and Sadat: The Political Economy of Two Regimes* (Princeton, N.J.: Princeton University Press, 2014); and Iliya Harik, "Continuity and Change in Local Development Policies in Egypt: From Nasser to Sadat," *International Journal of Middle East Studies* 16, no. 1 (1984): 43–66.

7. MARKET MAKING WITHOUT DEVELOPMENT

13. Waterbury, *The Egypt of Nasser and Sadat*, 76
14. Mahmoud 'Abd al-Fadil, *Al-iqtisad al-misri bayn al-takhtit al-markazi wa-l-infitah al-iqtisadi* [The Egyptian economy between central planning and open-door policy] (Cairo: Ma'had al-Inma' al-'Arabi, 1980), 207.
15. Waterbury, *The Egypt of Nasser and Sadat*, 160.
16. Khalid Ikram, *The Egyptian Economy, 1952–2000: Performance Policies and Issues* (London: Routledge, 2007), 150.
17. Alan Richards, "The Political Economy of Dilatory Reform: Egypt in the 1980s," *World Development* 19, no. 12 (1991): 1721–1730.
18. World Bank, *From Privilege to Competition: Unlocking Private-Led Growth in the Middle East and North Africa* (Washington, D.C.: International Bank for Reconstruction and Development/World Bank, 2009), 26.
19. Amr Adly, *Too Big to Fail: Egypt's Large Enterprises after the 2011 Uprising* (Washington, D.C.: Carnegie Endowment for International Peace, 2017).
20. According to the World Bank definition, gross capital formation refers to the increase in an economy's fixed assets and can include land improvement, the purchase of machinery, plants and equipment, the construction of transport infrastructure and facilities, and increases in inventories of goods used for production. See "Gross Capital Formation (% Of GDP)," World Bank, Data Catalog, accessed December 20, 2018, https://datacatalog.worldbank.org/gross-capital-formation-gdp-2.
21. "Foreign Direct Investment Net Inflows (BoP, Current US Dollars)—Egypt, Arab Rep.," World Bank, accessed December 20, 2018, https://data.worldbank.org/indicator/BX.KLT.DINV.CD.WD?locations=EG.
22. Shima Hanafy, "Sectoral FDI and Economic Growth: Evidence from Egyptian Governorates," MAGKS Joint Discussion Paper Series in Economics, no. 37, School of Business and Economics, Philipps-Universität Marburg, 2015.
23. Ragui Assad, ed., *Suq al-'amal al-misriyya fi al-alfiyya al-jadida* [The Egyptian labor market in the new millennium] (Cairo: Economic Research Forum and Al-Ahram Center, 2010), 34.
24. Assad, *Suq al-'amal al-misriyya*, 41.
25. Karl Polanyi, *The Great Transformation* (Boston: Beacon Press, 1957).
26. William G. Ouchi, "Markets, Bureaucracies, and Clans," *Administrative Science Quarterly* 25, no. 1 (1980): 129–141.
27. Bourdieu, "The Production of Belief," 20.
28. According to the World Bank, Egypt's urban population increased from 10.25 million in 1960 to 35.3 million in 2010. The percentage of urban dwellers within the total population jumped from 37.86 percent in 1960 to 43.85 percent in 1980 and stabilized around 43 percent through to 2017. The urban population is, however, expected to be significantly larger in absolute and relative terms than official figures suggest; its size is a matter of definition as well as counting. The Egyptian government depends on outdated maps from the 1940s to distinguish urban from rural areas. Consequently, many people listed as living in "rural" areas are in fact not. See "Urban Population (% of Total Population)—Egypt, Arab Rep.," World Bank, accessed September 19, 2020, https://data.worldbank.org/indicator/SP.URB.TOTL.IN.ZS?locations=EG.
29. According to the World Bank, Egypt received a massive $166.56 billion in remittances during the 1990–2012 period, which is a far greater sum than that received

7. MARKET MAKING WITHOUT DEVELOPMENT

by countries of similar population sizes, like Turkey for instance. Egypt received an average of $5 billion annually in workers' remittances between 1989 and 2012. Compare this to $935 million for Tunisia, $2.3 billion for Turkey, and $8.8 billion for China during the same period. See World Bank. "Personal Remittances, Received (Current US$)—Egypt, Arab Rep., Tunisia, Turkey, China," World Bank, accessed October 9, 2020, https://data.worldbank.org/indicator/BX.TRF.PWKR.CD.DT?locations=EG-TN-TR-CN.

30. Amr Adly, *Cleft Capitalism: The Social Origins of Failed Market Making in Egypt* (Stanford, Calif.: Stanford University Press, 2020), 226–230.
31. Amr Adly and Lina Khatib, *Reforming the Entrepreneurship Ecosystem in Post-revolutionary Egypt and Tunisia* (Stanford, Calif.: Center on Democracy, Development and the Rule of Law; Washington, D.C: Center for International Private Enterprise, 2014).
32. In fact, the opening of the market since the 1970s even allowed entrepreneurs that were by no means regime sympathizers to grow based on their external market linkages, provided that they played no active role against the ruling regime. This is how Muslim Brotherhood–related businesspeople (e.g., 'Abd al-'Azeem Loqma and 'Abd al-Rahman Se'oudi) were able to expand their businesses. The Brotherhood organization itself has invested in a number of trade- and service-based activities since the 1980s despite the impending risks of expropriation. Other examples include the old Wafd-related families (e.g., the Badrawis, the 'Abd al-Nours, and the Serag Al-Dins) who expanded their businesses despite the tension around the resurrection of the Wafd Party in 1970s and 1980s. While they may have been politically co-opted to an extent, it would have been far-fetched in this early stage to describe these families as regime cronies. By a similar token, Coptic business families, such as the Sawirises (construction, telecommunications, and tourism), the Ghabbours (automotive), Beshay (steel), the Berzys (textiles and then foodstuffs), Magued Sami's Wadi Degla Group (construction, housing, and sports clubs), and Sami Sa'd's Samcrete Engineers and Contractors, to name a few, were for the most part able to operate successfully despite having little opportunity to marry into the families of the predominantly Muslim bureaucratic elite.
33. Bent Hansen, *The Political Economy of Poverty, Equity, and Growth: Egypt and Turkey* (Oxford: Oxford University Press, 1991), 31.
34. Mohamed Gabr (corporate lawyer), personal interview with Adly, Cairo, September 19, 2017.
35. Galila El-Kadi, *Al-tahaddur al-'ashwa'i* [Random urbanization], trans. Menha El-Batrawi (Cairo: Al-markaz al-qawmi lil-tarjama, 2009), 133.
36. Samiya Sa'id Imam, *Man yamliku misr?! Dirasa tahliliyya li-l-usul al-ijtima'iyya li-nukhba al-infitah al-iqtisadi fi al-mujtama 'al-misri, 1974–1980* [Who owns Egypt? An analytical study of the social roots of the open-door economic elite in Egyptian society, 1974–1980] (Cairo: Dar al-Mustaqbal al-'arabi, 1986).
37. Amr Adly, "Between Social Populism and Pragmatic Conservatism," in *Egypt's Revolutions: Politics, Religion, and Social Movements*, ed. Bernard Rougier and Stéphane Lacroix (New York: Palgrave Macmillan, 2016), 61–78.
38. Anders Aslund, "Comparative Oligarchy: Russia, Ukraine and the United States," CASE Network Studies and Analyses 0296, CASE-Center for Social and Economic Research 2005.

7. MARKET MAKING WITHOUT DEVELOPMENT

39. Khan and Jomo, *Rents, Rent-Seeking, and Economic Development*, 126.
40. El-Kadi, *al-tahaddur al-`ashwa'i*, 90.
41. Peter Hall and David Soskice, eds., *Varieties of Capitalism: The Institutional Foundations of Comparative Advantage* (Oxford: Oxford University Press, 2001), 137–138.
42. Amr Adly, *State Reform and Development in the Middle East: Turkey and Egypt in the Post-liberalization Era* (London: Routledge, 2012).
43. Ministry of Foreign Trade (Egypt), *Profile of M/SMEs in Egypt* (Cairo: Ministry of Foreign Trade, 2003).
44. `Aliya' al-Mahdi and Ahmed Rashed, "Al-munakh al-mutaghayyer wa-tanmiyat al-mashru`at al-saghira wal-mutanahiyat al-sighar fi misr 2006" [The changing environment and the development of small and micro projects in Egypt 2006], in *Suq al-`amal al-misriyya fi-l-alfiyya al-jadida* [The Egyptian labor market in the new millennium], ed. Ragui Assad (Cairo: Economic Research Forum and al-Ahram Center, 2010).
45. Andreas Buehn and Friedrich Schneider, "Shadow Economies around the World: Novel Insights, Accepted Knowledge, and New Estimates," *International Tax and Public Finance* 19, no. 1 (2012): 139–171.
46. Nazih Ayubi, *Over-Stating the Arab State: Politics and Society in the Middle East* (London: I. B. Tauris, 1996); Joel S. Migdal, *Strong Societies and Weak States: State-Society Relations and State Capabilities in the Third World* (Princeton, N.J.: Princeton University Press, 1988).
47. Mai Hassan and Friedrich Schneider, "Modelling the Egyptian Shadow Economy: A Currency Demand and a MIMIC Model Approach," CESifo Working Paper Series 5727, 2016.
48. Alice H. Amsden, *The Rise of the Rest: Challenges to the West from Late-Industrializing Economies* (New York: Oxford University Press, 2001).
49. Peter B. Evans, *Embedded Autonomy: States and Industrial Transformation* (Princeton, N.J.: Princeton University Press, 2012).
50. David Sims, *Egypt's Desert Dreams: Development or Disaster?* (Cairo: American University in Cairo Press, 2015), 178.
51. World Bank, *Egypt Public Land Management Strategy*, vol. 2, *Background Notes on Access to Public Land by Investment Sector—Industry, Tourism, Agriculture, and Real Estate Development* (Washington, D.C.: World Bank, 2006), 38.
52. "International Tourism, Number of Arrivals—Egypt, Arab Rep.," World Bank, accessed February 10, 2010, https://data.worldbank.org/indicator/ST.INT.ARVL?locations=EG.
53. Adly, *State Reform*, 97.
54. "Egypt: Merchandize Exports by Product Group—Annual," World Trade Organization, accessed August 8, 2020, https://data.wto.org/?idSavedQuery=100ca753-8352-4441-9770-1f2bae2f17a5.
55. Assad, *Suq al-`amal al-misriyya*, 32.
56. Ahmad El-Naggar, *Al-inhiyar al-iqtisadi fi `asr mubarak* [Economic collapse in Mubarak's time] (Cairo: Dar Mirit, 2009), 49.
57. Lois Stevenson, *Private Sector and Enterprise Development: Fostering Growth in the Middle East and North Africa* (Ottawa: International Development Research Center, 2010), 81.

8. THE MILITARY'S CIVILIAN ECONOMY

58. Sanaa Abdel-Wahab, "Al-ihsa: 99.97% min al-munsha'at al-iqtisadiyya fi misr khassa" [Central Agency for Public Mobilization and Statistics: 99.97% of economic enterprises in Egypt are private], *Almasryalyoum*, October 21, 2014, https://www.almasryalyoum.com/news/details/551769.
59. "Central Bank of Egypt Time Series State Budget: Revenues (2006–2014)," Central Bank of Egypt, accessed September 20, 2018, https://www.cbe.org.eg/_layouts/15/WopiFrame.aspx?sourcedoc={D9FB8A71-BB7D-44D1-B554-DD2FBA49A126}&file=Revenues%20Annual.xlsx&action=default.
60. "Central Bank of Egypt Time Series State Budget."
61. "Central Bank of Egypt Time Series State Budget."
62. Fatima Ramadan and Amr Adly, *Low-Cost Authoritarianism: The Egyptian Regime and Labor Movement Since 2013* (Washington, D.C.: Carnegie Endowment for International Peace, 2015).
63. Ben R. Schneider, "Hierarchical Market Economies and Varieties of Capitalism in Latin America," *Journal of Latin American Studies* 41, no. 3 (2009): 557.

8. THE MILITARY'S CIVILIAN ECONOMY

1. Ayesha Siddiqa, *Military Inc.: Inside Pakistan's Military Economy* (London: Pluto Press, 2007), 30.
2. See, for instance, Jörn Brömmelhörster and Wolf-Christian Paes, eds., *The Military as an Economic Actor: Soldiers in Business* (London: Palgrave Macmillan, 2003); and Kristina Mani, "Militaries in Business: State-Making and Entrepreneurship in the Developing World," *Armed Forces & Society* 33, no. 4 (2007): 591–611.
3. Siddiqa, *Military Inc.*, 126–127.
4. See Harold Trinkunas, "Crafting Civilian Control in Argentina and Venezuela," in *Civil-Military Relations in Latin America: New Analytical Perspectives*, ed. David Pion-Berlin (Chapel Hill: University of North Carolina Press: 2001), 161–193; and David Pion-Berlin and Craig Arceneaux, "Decision-Makers or Decision-Takers? Military Missions and Civilian Control in Democratic South America," *Armed Forces & Society* 26, no. 3 (April 2000): 413–436.
5. Abdel-Fattah Barayez, "'This Land Is Their Land': Egypt's Military and the Economy," *Jadaliyya*, January 25, 2016, https://www.jadaliyya.com/Details/32898; Samer Soliman, *Al-nizam al-qawi wal-dawla al-da`ifa: Idarat al-azma al-maliyya wataghyir al-siyasi fi `ahd mubarak* [Strong regime and weak state: The management of financial crisis and political change under Mubarak] (Cairo: General Organization of Culture Palaces, 2005), 82.
6. Siddiqa, *Military Inc.*, 191.
7. For more details, see Robert Springborg, *Mubarak's Egypt: Fragmentation of the Political Order* (Boulder, Colo.: Westview Press, 1989); and Zeinab Abul-Magd, *Militarizing the Nation: The Army, Business, and Revolution in Egypt* (New York: Columbia University Press, 2017).
8. Abul-Magd, *Militarizing the Nation*, 14.
9. According to Abul-Magd, "the military business enterprises that exist today fall under the umbrellas of eight different conglomerates and organizations: (1) the

Ministry of Defense's ... National Service Projects Organization ... which was created with the peace treaty in 1979, began engaging in civilian production during the 1980s, and now owns eleven gigantic firms with subsidiaries; (2) the MoMP [Ministry of Military Production], which was created in 1950s and grew into a conglomerate of sixteen factories now involved in defense conversion; (3) the AOI, which was created in 1978 and has nine defense factories that have also been converted to civilian production; (4) the Engineering Authority of the Armed forces ... which functions as a gigantic parastatal contractor for government and military construction projects; (5) Maritime Industries and Services Organization ... which owns four companies for shipbuilding and river transport; (6) the Department of Social Clubs and Hotels, which manages wedding halls, restaurants, cafes, and other facilities; (7) the Department of Medical Services of the Armed Forces, which builds and manages military hospitals admitting civilians for fees; (8) Armed Forces Land Project Organization" (14).

10. "Military Expenditure (% of GDP)—Egypt, Arab Rep.," World Bank, accessed December 20, 2018, https://data.worldbank.org/indicator/MS.MIL.XPND.GD.ZS?locations=EG&view=chart.
11. Springborg, *Mubarak's Egypt*, 95.
12. Springborg, 95, 114–116.
13. Mahmoud S. Mohieldin and Peter W. Wright, "Formal and Informal Credit Markets in Egypt," *Economic Development and Cultural Change* 48, no. 3 (2000): 657–670.
14. Springborg, *Mubarak's Egypt*, 73.
15. Roberto Roccu, *The Political Economy of the Egyptian Revolution: Mubarak, Economic Reforms and Failed Hegemony* (London: Palgrave Macmillan, 2013).
16. Yezid Sayigh, *Owners of the Republic: An Anatomy of Egypt's Military Economy* (Washington, D.C.: Carnegie Endowment for International Peace, 2019), 9.
17. Barayez, "This Land Is Their Land."
18. Abul-Magd, *Militarizing the Nation*, 138, 156, 172,175.
19. Abul-Magd, 15.
20. Sayigh, *Owners of the Republic*, 6–7.
21. World Bank, *From Privilege to Competition: Unlocking Private-Led Growth in the Middle East and North Africa* (Washington, D.C.: International Bank for Reconstruction and Development/World Bank, 2009), 26.
22. David Sims, *Egypt's Desert Dreams: Development or Disaster?* (Cairo: American University in Cairo Press, 2015).
23. However, it should be noted that this situation applied until 2019, when the military embarked on an ambitious expansion in its cement production. We just do not yet have the data to show how much the share of military-held factories has risen.
24. Barayez, "This Land Is Their Land."
25. Sims, *Egypt's Desert Dreams*.
26. Galila El-Kadi, *Al-tahaddur Al-`ashwa'i* [Random urbanization], trans. Menha El-Batrawi (Cairo: Al-markaz Al-qawmi Lil-tarjama, 2009).
27. Abul-Magd, *Militarizing the Nation*, 116.
28. Siddiqa, *Military Inc.*, 156.
29. Barayez, "This Land Is Their Land."
30. For instance, Hussein Sabbour, a major real estate developer and the head of Egyptian Businessmen Association, voiced concerns about the potential crowding out

of private developers because of the rising role of military-affiliated developers in an interview with the BBC. See "Bitawqit misr: Munaqasha ma` adla` manzumat al-`aqarat fi misr" [On Egyptian time: A discussion of the real estate framework in Egypt], BBC News, August 4, 2019, YouTube video, 52:33, https://www.youtube.com/watch?v=5xvNleMarss&t=2729s.

31. Angela Joya, "The Military and the State in Egypt: Class Formation in the Post-Arab Uprisings," *British Journal of Middle Eastern Studies* 47, no. 5 (2018): 1–21.
32. Shana Marshall, *The Egyptian Armed Forces and the Remaking of an Economic Empire* (Washington, D.C.: Carnegie Endowment for International Peace, 2015).
33. Abul-Magd, *Militarizing the Nation*, 199.
34. Hicham Bou Nassif, "'Second-Class': The Grievances of Sunni Officers in the Syrian Armed Forces," *Journal of Strategic Studies* 38, no. 5 (August 2015): 626–649.
35. Siddiqa, *Military Inc.*, 54.
36. Lesley McCulloch, "*Trifungsi*: The Role of the Indonesian Military in Business," in *The Military as an Economic Actor: Soldiers in Business*, ed. Jörn Brömmelhörster and Wolf-Christian Paes (London: Palgrave Macmillan, 2003), 94–124.
37. Vedi R. Hadiz and Richard Robison, "The Political Economy of Oligarchy and the Reorganization of Power in Indonesia," *Indonesia*, no. 96 (October 2013): 35–57.
38. Marshall, *The Egyptian Armed Forces*.
39. Robert Springborg, "Egypt's Cobra and Mongoose," *Foreign Policy*, February 27, 2012, https://foreignpolicy.com/2012/02/27/egypts-cobra-and-mongoose/.
40. Tai Ming Cheung, "The Rise and Fall of the Chinese Military Business Complex," in *The Military as an Economic Actor*, ed. Jörn Brömmelhörster and Wolf-Christian Paes (London: Palgrave Macmillan, 2003), 52–73.
41. Siddiqa, *Military Inc.*, 173.

9. THE UPRISING OF 2011 AND THE NEW REGIME

1. On the surprising nature of events—and the reasons for these surprises—see Nathan J. Brown, "Constitutions and the Public Sphere," in *The Arab Uprisings Explained: New Contentious Politics in the Middle East*, ed. Marc Lynch (New York: Columbia University Press, 2014), 296–312.
2. One interesting work on the relationship between the Brotherhood and Salafis, written before the 2011 uprising, is Husam Tammam, *Tasalluf al-ikhwan* [The Salafization of the Brotherhood] (Alexandria: Maktabat al-iskandiryya, 2010).
3. Shimaa Hatab, "Abortive Regime Transition in Egypt: Prodemocracy Alliance and Demand-Making Framework," *Democratization* 25, no. 4 (2018): 579–596.
4. Dalia Othman al-Bahrawi, "Al-Jaysh ya`ud ila al-shari`" [The army returns to the street], *Al-Masry Al-Youm*, June 27, 2013, 5.
5. On the economic concerns and nonideological social conservatism of Egyptian voters, see Tarek Masoud, *Counting Islam Religion: Class and Elections in Egypt* (Cambridge: Cambridge University Press, 2014).
6. Human Rights Watch, "Egypt: Rab`a Killings Likely Crimes Against Humanity," news release, August 12, 2014, https://www.hrw.org/news/2014/08/12/egypt-rab-killings-likely-crimes-against-humanity.

7. *Eshhad Quarterly Trend Report, July–September 2017* (Washington, D.C.: Eshhad: Center for the Protection of Minorities, 2017), https://static1.squarespace.com/static/5947e4266a49635915ac0a31/t/5a3be56bec212dde8924ff28/1513874811863/Q3_2017.pdf, 5.
8. Indeed, the 2014 Constitution was technically a revision of the 2012 Constitution—even though the amendments were very extensive, the continuity in many provisions allowed the military and other bodies to maintain anything they received in the 2012 draft that they wished to keep.
9. See Yusuf Auf, "The State of Emergency in Egypt: An Exception or Rule?," Atlantic Council, February 2, 2018, https://www.atlanticcouncil.org/blogs/menasource/the-state-of-emergency-in-egypt-an-exception-or-rule/.
10. Todd Ruffner, *Under Threat: Egypt's Systematic Campaign against NGOs*, Project on Middle East Democracy, March 2015, https://pomed.org/wp-content/uploads/2015/03/Under-Threat-Egypts-Systematic-Campaign-against-NGOs.pdf.
11. Human Rights Watch, *We Do Unreasonable Things Here—Torture and National Security in al-Sisi's Egypt*, September 2017, https://www.hrw.org/sites/default/files/report_pdf/egypt0917_web.pdf.
12. Gamal Essam El-Din, "Egypt Parliament Approves First Vote on New Cyber-Crime Law," *Ahram Online*, May 14, 2018, http://english.ahram.org.eg/NewsContent/1/64/299488/Egypt/Politics-/Egypt-parliament-approves-first-vote-on-new-cyberc.aspx; "Egypt Filters 34,000 Domains in Bid to Block Opposition Campaign Platform," NetBlocks, April 15, 2019, https://netblocks.org/reports/egypt-filters-34000-domains-in-bid-to-block-opposition-campaign-platform-7eA1blBp.
13. Shimaa Hatab, "Threat Perception and Democratic Support in Post-Arab Spring Egypt," *Comparative Politics* 53, no. 1 (2020): 69–98.
14. Mona Abisourour, "The Egyptian Devaluation—One Year Later," Infomineo, January 2, 2018, https://infomineo.com/egyptian-devaluation-one-year-later/.
15. The barred candidate, Sami Anan, had been prominent in post-2011 politics. See Al-Yawm Al-Sabi', "Nanshur taqrir lijan al-barlaman hawl qanun mu`amalat kubar qadat al-quwwat al-musallaha" [We publish the report of the Parliamentary Committee on the Law of Treatment of Senior Armed Forces Judges], *Youm7*, July 10, 2018, https://www.youm7.com/story/2019/7/10/%D9%86%D9%86%D8%B4%D8%B1-%D8%AA%D9%82%D8%B1%D9%8A%D8%B1-%D9%84%D8%AC%D9%86%D8%A9-%D8%A7%D9%84%D9%82%D9%88%D9%89-%D8%A7%D9%84%D8%B9%D8%A7%D9%85%D9%84%D8%A9-%D8%A8%D8%A7%D9%84%D8%A8%D8%B1%D9%84%D9%85%D8%A7%D9%86-%D8%B9%D9%86-%D9%85%D8%B4%D8%B1%D9%88%D8%B9-%D9%82%D8%A7%D9%86%D9%88%D9%86-%D8%A7%D9%84%D8%AA%D8%A3%D9%85%D9%8A%D9%86%D8%A7%D8%AA/4327836. See also Maged Mandour, "The Military's Immunity in Egypt," Carnegie Endowment for International Peace, July 24, 2018, https://carnegieendowment.org/sada/76904.
16. "Egypt Parliament Passes Constitutional Amendments, Extends President's Term Limit," *Ahram Online*, April 16, 2019, http://english.ahram.org.eg/NewsContent/1/64/330131/Egypt/Politics-/UPDATED-Egypt-parliament-passes-constitutional-ame.aspx.

A SELECTIVE GUIDE TO SCHOLARLY WRITING ON EGYPT

In this book, we have drawn extensively from work done by our colleagues in various disciplines. We have all conducted our own research on Egyptian politics and consulted with each other on what to present here. But we have also relied on the work of many others. In the notes, we have cited works that we have relied on for particular pieces of information, but we also wish to provide a guide for readers who wish to know more about particular topics we address.

Our guide is restricted to scholarly writings, and even then it is selective; we draw attention to particular works that we find helpful or broad but pass over others that are very strong in order not to overburden the reader (and because of our own limitations in terms of how much we can read and evaluate about a country that has generated so much interest and insightful writing). *This is primarily a guide to English-language literature, but we have included a few works in Arabic.* Our guide roughly follows the structure of the book, focusing first on politics and history, then on society and economics, in that order. We close with some brief suggestions about writings that are beginning to emerge about the most recent developments in Egyptian politics.

EGYPTIAN POLITICS, THE STATE, AND THE REGIME

Modern Egyptian political history has received a great deal of scholarly attention in recent decades. Two good general works on Egyptian history are Arthur Goldschmidt's *Modern Egypt: The Formation of a Nation State* (Boulder, Colo.: Westview Press, 2004) and Bruce K. Rutherford and Jeannie Sowers, *Modern Egypt: What Everyone Needs to Know* (Oxford: Oxford University Press, 2018). Nineteenth-century social and political history is a particularly rich field; two helpful works are Khaled Fahmy, *All the Pasha's Men: Mehmed Ali, His Army and the Making of Modern Egypt* (Cambridge: Cambridge University Press, 1998), and Raouf Abbas and Assem El-Dessouky, *The Large Landowning Class and the Peasantry in Egypt, 1837–1952* (Syracuse, N.Y.: Syracuse University Press, 2011). And the short liberal and parliamentary experiment under the monarchy is the subject of Afaf Lutfi Al-Sayyid Marsot's *Egypt's Liberal Experiment, 1922–36* (Berkeley: University of California Press, 1978).

Egypt's change of regime in 1952 is the subject of Joel Gordan's *Nasser's Blessed Movement* (Cairo: American University in Cairo Press, 2016). On this subject, also see Tariq al-Bishri, *Al-dimuqratiyah wa-nizam 23 yulyu 1952–1970* [Democracy and the July 23 regime 1952–1970] (Cairo: Dar al-Hilal, 1991); 'Abd al-Rahman al-Rafi'i, *Thawrat 23 Yulyu 1952* [The July 23 revolution] (Cairo: Maktabat al-Nahda al-Misriyya, 1959); Muhammed Fawzy, *Harb al-thalath sanawat* [The war of the three years] (Cairo: Dar al-Mustaqbal al-'Arabi, 1986); Sherif Younis, *Nida' al-sha'b: Tarikh naqdi li-l-idolojiyya al-nasiriyya* [The call of the people: A critical history of the Nasserist ideology] (Cairo: Dar al-Shoruq, 2012); Sherif Younis, *Al-zahf al-muqaddas: Muzaharat al-tanahi wa tashakul 'ibadat nasir* [The holy creep: The abdication demonstrations and the formation of Nasser worship] (Cairo: Dar Mirit, 2005); Abdel Majid Farid, *Min mahadir ijtima'at 'abd al-nasir al-'arabiyya wa-duwliyya 1967–1970* [From the minutes of Abdel Nasser's Arab and international meetings, 1967–1970] (Beirut: Mu'ssasat al-abhath al-'arabiyya, 1985).

Some documents and memoirs from former officials under Nasser's regime and his close circle include *Watha'iq thawrat yulyu: Falsafit al-thawra (1953–1954), Al-mithaq 1962, bayan 30 maris 1969* [The documents of the July revolution: The philosophy of the revolution (1953–1954); the charter of 1962; the declaration of March 30, 1969] (Cairo: Dar al-Mustaqbal al-'Arabi, 1991); Salah Nasr, *Mudhakkirat Salah Nasr: Al-thawra, al-mukhabarat, al-naksa* [Memoirs of Salah Nasr: The revolution, intelligence, and setback] (Cairo: Dar al-Khayal, 1999); Khalid Muhi al-Din, *Wa-l-an atakallam* [And now I speak up] (Cairo: al-Ahram Center for Translation and Publishing, 1992); Mohamed Hassanein Heikal, *Mudhakkirat fi al-siyasa al-misriyya* [Memoirs in Egyptian politics], 3 vols. (Cairo: Dar al-Ma'arif, 1977)

An account of Egypt's politics that stresses the economic dimension is Amr Adly's *Cleft Capitalism: The Social Origins of Failed Market Making in Egypt* (Stanford, Calif.: Stanford University Press, 2020). For more information on the role of the state in reengineering social classes in the postcolonial era, see Nazih Ayubi, *Over-stating the Arab State: Politics and Society in the Middle East* (London: I. B. Tauris, 1995). Another influential comparative account is Joel S. Migdal, *The State in Society: Studying How States and Societies Transform and Constitute One Another* (Cambridge: Cambridge University Press, 2001).

There are also many works on institutions. On the Egyptian military's political role, see Steven A. Cook, *Ruling But Not Governing: The Military and Political Development in Egypt, Algeria, and Turkey* (Baltimore, Md.: Johns Hopkins University Press, 2007). For a historical perspective, Robert Springborg's *Mubarak's Egypt: Fragmentation of the Political Order* (Boulder, Colo.: Westview Press, 1989) is one key work, while another is Hazem Kandil, *Soldiers, Spies, and Statesmen: Egypt's Road to Revolt* (London: Verso, 2012). And on the Egyptian judiciary, again there are many writings. A strong compilation of essays can be found in Natalie Bernard-Maugiron, ed., *Judges and Political Reform in Egypt* (Cairo: American University of Cairo Press, 2015). Nathan J. Brown examines the historical development of the judiciary and its centrality to state-building efforts and its usefulness even to authoritarian rulers in *The Rule of Law in the Arab World: Courts in Egypt and the Gulf* (Cambridge: Cambridge University Press, 1997). Tamir Moustafa, "Law versus the State: The Judicialization of Politics in Egypt," *Law & Social Inquiry* 28, no. 4 (2003): 883–930, develops an explanation of how a strong constitutional court was established under authoritarian conditions.

SOCIAL AND IDEOLOGICAL STRUGGLES

On the origins and consequences of political-ideological struggle in Egyptian society, see Raymond William Baker, *Sadat and After: Struggles for Egypt's Political Soul* (Cambridge, Mass.: Harvard University Press, 1990), and Kirk Beattie, *Egypt During the Nasser Years: Ideology, Politics, and Civil Society* (Boulder, Colo.: Westview Press, 1994). Roger Owen, *State, Power and Politics in the Making of the Modern Middle East* (New York: Routledge, 1992), traces the emergence of the state in the Middle East broadly and shows how the "remaking" of individual states in the 1990s led to certain political and social developments, including party formation and feckless political competition and the politics of Islamic revival.

Some older works focused on how Egyptian society was organized in general and by examining specific groups before 1952. Hassan al-Banna, *Mudhakkirat al-da'wa wa-l-da'iyya* [Memoirs of preaching and the preacher] (Cairo: Islamic Da'wa Publisher, 2001), and Richard Mitchell, *The Society of the Muslim Brothers* (Oxford: Oxford University Press, 1969), focus primarily on the Muslim Brotherhood, its sociological origins, and its internal dynamics. Some core readings on the national liberation movements and sociocultural formation of class interests, contours of political struggles, and gender identity include 'Asim al-Disuqui, *Kibar mullak al-aradi al-zira'iyya wa-dawruhum fi al-mujtama' al-misri 1914–1952* [Large landowners and their role in Egyptian society, 1914–1952] (Cairo: Dar al-Shuruq, 2008); Amin 'Izz al-Din, *Tarikh al-tabaqa al-'amila al-misriyya mundh nasha'tiha hatta thawrat 1919* [The history of the Egyptian working class since its emergence until the 1919 revolution] (Cairo: Dar al-Kitab al-'Arabi, 1967); Louis 'Awad, *Tarikh al-fikr al-misri al-hadith min 'asr isma'il ila thawrat 1919* [The history of modern Egyptian thought from Ismail's era to the 1919 revolution] (Cairo: Madbouly Bookshop, 1969); Joel Beinin and Zachary Lockman, *Workers on the Nile: Nationalism, Communism, Islam, and the Egyptian Working Class, 1882–1954* (London: I. B. Tauris, 1988); 'Ali Muhammad Shalabi, *Misr al-fatah wa dawruha fi al-siyasa al-misriyya 1933–1941* [Young Egypt and its role in Egyptian politics, 1933–1941] (Cairo: Dar al-Kitab al-Jami'i, 1982); Leila Ahmed, *Women and Gender in Islam: Historical Roots of a Modern Debate* (New Haven, Conn.: Yale University Press, 1992); Margot Badran, *Feminists, Islam, and Nation: Gender and the Making of Modern Egypt* (Princeton, N.J.: Princeton University Press, 1995); and Hind Wassef and Nadia Wassef, *Daughters of the Nile: Photographs of Egyptian Women's Movements, 1900–1960* (Cairo: American University in Cairo Press, 2001).

Anouar Abdel-Malek's *Egypt: Military Society: The Army Regime, the Left, and Social Change under Nasser* (New York: Random House, 1968) examines the deep impact of Nasser's regime on Egyptian society. For a description of civil society groups under Mubarak's reign, see Mustapha Kamel Al-Sayyid, "A Civil Society in Egypt?," *Middle East Journal* 47, no. 2 (January 1993): 228–242, which questions the existence of civil society in Egypt and the factors likely to affect its evolution. Maha Abdelrahman's *Civil Society Exposed: The Politics of NGOs in Egypt* (London: I. B. Tauris, 2004) is also useful for this period.

On the changing role of professional syndicates in Egyptian politics during the Nasser era, see Robert Springborg, "Professional Syndicates in Egyptian Politics, 1952–1970," *International Journal of Middle East Studies* 9, no. 3 (October 1978): 275–295. Also of interest is Robert Bianchi, *Unruly Corporatism: Associational Life in Twentieth-Century Egypt* (Oxford: Oxford University Press, 1989).

More recent works have examined the protest movements that set the stage for the 2011 mass uprising, and the legacy of alliance formation between polarized groups within the political opposition. Maha Abdelrahman's *Egypt's Long Revolution: Protest Movements and Uprisings* (London: Routledge, 2015) builds on this trend to understand what sustains activism and movements in radically different circumstances from those in which they arose. She also challenges the conventional wisdom that portrays civil society as a force of freedom and justice.

For other invisible forms of social resistance, Asef Bayat's *Life as Politics: How Ordinary People Change the Middle East* (Stanford, Calif.: Stanford University Press, 2013) examines day-to-day political action. He shows that though not visible on the world stage as a mass protest or a full-scale revolution, millions of people across the Middle East are creating new social spaces within which to make their claims heard.

For further details on how the regime maintained its coherence in the face of mounting social resistance, Jason Brownlee's *Authoritarianism in an Age of Democratization* (New York: Cambridge University Press, 2007) offers an institutional and elite-centered approach to conclude that the softliners needed to approach moderate opposition and orchestrate democratic transitions have been "dormant" in Egypt under Mubarak's reign.

For an integrative account of the role of religion in different domains in Egypt, two good books offer further details on religion, politics, and society in Egypt: Nathan J. Brown, *Arguing Islam after the Revival of Arab Politics* (New York: Oxford University Press, 2017), and Salwa Ismail,

Rethinking Islamist Politics: Culture, the State and Islamism (London: I. B. Tauris, 2006). Carrie Wickham's *Mobilizing Islam: Religion, Activism and Political Change in Egypt* (New York: Columbia University Press, 2002) explores the Islamic revival. The Muslim Brotherhood's emergence and political role has spawned a large amount of writing. Tarek Masoud's *Counting Islam: Religion, Class, and Elections in Egypt* (Cambridge: Cambridge University Press, 2014) is a particularly strong examination of the Brotherhood in the electoral arena. Charles Tripp's *Islam and the Moral Economy* (Cambridge: Cambridge University Press, 2006) sheds lights on how Islamic thinkers drew on Islamic jurisdiction to tackle socioeconomic issues, such as property rights, economic exploitation, and Islamic finance in an effort to offer an Islamic alternative to capitalism (one that differs from anarchism, socialism, and Marxism).

POLITICAL ECONOMY

Contemporary Egyptian economic history has been the subject of a number of academic works. Mahmoud Abdel-Fadil's *The Political Economy of Nasserism: A Study in Employment and Income Distribution Policies in Urban Egypt, 1952–72* (Cambridge: Cambridge University Press, 1980) gives a comprehensive account of the state-led development phase of the 1950s and 1960s and is well supported by data that covers processes of industrialization, land reform, urbanization, and the nationalization of foreign and Egyptian private-sector firms between 1957 and 1962. Ibrahim 'Amir, *Al-ard wa-l-fallaḥ: Al-mas'ala al-zira'iyya fi misr* [The land and the peasant: The agrarian question in Egypt] (Cairo: Al-Dar al-Misriyya li-l-Nashr wa-l-Tawzi`, 1958), provides an early but comprehensive account of relations in the Egyptian countryside through the nineteenth and early twentieth centuries. 'Amer depicts how the forces of modernization through the incorporation of Egypt's agricultural sector into the European division of labor reshaped social and political relations in the country. John Waterbury's *The Egypt of Nasser and Sadat: The Political Economy of Two Regimes* (Princeton, N.J.: Princeton University Press, 1983) is another important work. Waterbury provides a rich and well-corroborated read of the public-sector-dominated model of development under Nasser and the political economy of *infitah* that the Sadat regime pursued in the mid-1970s. In a similar vein, Khaled Ikram gives a thorough, detailed, and cross-sectoral account of

A SELECTIVE GUIDE TO SCHOLARLY WRITING ON EGYPT

Egypt's economy from the 1952 military takeover through 2000 in *The Egyptian Economy, 1952–2000: Performance, Policies, Issues* (London: Routledge, 2007). Mahmud 'Abd al-Fadil also provides a panoramic view of Egypt's political economy under Nasser and Sadat in his book *Al-iqtisad al-misri bayna al-takhtit al-markazi wa-l-infitah al-iqtisadi* [The Egyptian economy between central planning and the open-door policy] (Cairo: Ma'had al-Inma' al-'Arabi, 1980).

Samia Imam's classic *Man yamluk misr? Dirasa tahliliyya li nukhbat al-infitah* [Who owns Egypt? An analytical study of the social roots of the open-door elite in the Egyptian society] (Cairo: Dar al-Mustaqbal al-'Arabi) is an empirically rich mapping and analysis of Egypt's earliest business elites in the first decade after *infitah* from a class angle. Adil Husayn also held a critical view informed by Marxism and dependency theories in *Al-iqtisad al-misri min al-istiqlal ila-l-taba'iyya* [The Egyptian economy from independence to dependency] (Cairo: Dar al-Mustaqbal al-'Arabi, 1982).

Samer Soliman's *The Autumn of Dictatorship: Fiscal Crisis and Political Change in Egypt* (Stanford, Calif.: Stanford University Press, 2011) focuses on the political economy of state finances under Mubarak and explores the links between authoritarian regime dynamics, the prospects of democratization, and the management of a structural fiscal crisis. In Soliman's tradition, Amr Adly's *State Reform and Development in the Middle East: Turkey and Egypt in the Post-liberalization Era* (London: Routledge 2012) reconstructs state policies and institutional arrangements in the fields of trade and industrialization under Mubarak. It also explores how Egypt's external economic position impacted regime dynamics and development prospects in the lead-up to the 2011 revolt. Galal Amin's *Misr w-al-misriyyun fi 'ahd mubarak (1981–2008)* [Egypt and the Egyptians under Mubarak (1981–2008)] (Cairo: Dar Mirit, 2009) is an academically informed critical read of Egypt's political economy and society under Mubarak. In this critical and at times playful account, Amin combines a thorough economic analysis of the major shifts associated with the structural adjustment program, fiscal crisis, and the mass migration to oil-rich Arab neighbors with an account of the changes in social relations, attitudes, and values experienced in Egypt during the Mubarak era. Roberto Roccu explicitly addresses the political economy of the January 2011 revolution in *The Political Economy of the Egyptian Revolution: Mubarak, Economic Reforms and Failed Hegemony* (Basingstoke, UK: Palgrave Macmillan, 2013).

Employing a Gramsci-inspired analysis, Roccu traces the revolution in Egypt back to neoliberal reforms that exacerbated the regime's crisis of hegemony. Finally, 'Adil Ghunaym followed a similar Gramscian approach in his *Azmat al-dawla al-misriyya al-muʿasira* [The crisis of the contemporary Egyptian state] (Cairo: Dar al-ʿAlam al-Thalith, 2005), which provides a complex condensed read of Egypt's modern political economy.

Arabic writings appeared in the aftermath of the 2011 uprising, of which several are worth noting here. Amr ʿAdly and Fatma Ramaḍan edited a volume titled *Suʿud wa uful al-haraka al-ʿummaliyyah fi misr (2006–2016): Al-ʿummal, wa-l-siyasa wa-l-dawla* [The rise and fall of Egypt's labor movement (2006–2016): Workers, politics, and the state] (Cairo: Dar al-Maraya, in support from Rosa Luxemburg Foundation, 2018). The anthology documented some of the major developments in the labor movement in Egypt in the years leading to the uprising and in its immediate aftermath. In a similar vein, Muhammad Jad's anthology *Mullak misr: Qissat suʿud al-raʾsmaliyya al-misriyya* [Egypt's owners: The story of the advent of Egyptian capitalism] (Cairo: Dar al-Maraya, 2018) gave an empirically rich and detailed sectoral analysis of Egypt's economy since *infitah* from a political economy perspective.

While there are many writings on Egyptian political economy generally, there is somewhat of a dearth of information and analysis on the military due to a lack of transparency in the name of national security and institutional autonomy. However, some authors have tackled the military economy in Egypt in recent years. Zeinab Abul-Magd, *Militarizing the Nation: The Army, Business, and Revolution in Egypt* (New York: Columbia University Press, 2017), is one recent and useful work. Springborg's *Mubarak's Egypt*, mentioned above, tackles in a broad fashion the transformations of the Mubarak regime in the 1980s, with Springborg's unique access to information enabling him to write one of the most comprehensive accounts of the political economy of the Egyptian army. Indeed, all subsequent works have capitalized on Springborg's analysis. Yezid Sayigh also discussed the interplay between politics and economics in the Egyptian army, with a special focus on the postrevolutionary period, in a series of policy reports and papers published by the Carnegie Endowment for International Peace. See, for instance, *Above the State: The Officers' Republic in Egypt* (Washington, D.C.: Carnegie Endowment for International Peace, 2012).

A SELECTIVE GUIDE TO SCHOLARLY WRITING ON EGYPT

2011 AND AFTER

The Egyptian uprising of 2011 and its tumultuous aftermath have generated a great deal of writing, with the period likely to remain a topic of fascination for years to come. It is not yet clear which analytical approaches and contributions will stand the test of time, but there are strong candidates in particular areas that seem likely to be helpful. For instance, on labor protest, one account that straddles the 2011 uprising is Dina Bishara's *Contesting Authoritarianism: Labor Challenges to the State in Egypt* (Cambridge: Cambridge University Press, 2018). On "authoritarian learning" and the regime's adaptive strategies to reshape existing institutional, discursive, and regulatory arrangements and mitigate popular challenges, see Steven Heydemann and Reinoud Leenders, "Authoritarian Learning and Counterrevolution," in *The Arab Uprisings Explained: New Contentious Politics in the Middle East*, edited by Marc Lynch (New York: Columbia University Press, 2013). More generally, Lynch's edited volume is comprised of a series of efforts by leading scholars to grapple with events from various angles almost as they were occurring. For more details on how perceptions of political Islam as a threat drove both masses and elites to become disillusioned with democracy between 2011 and 2013, see Shimaa Hatab, "Threat Perception and Democratic Support in Post Arab Spring Egypt," *Comparative Politics* 53, no. 1 (October 2020): 69–98. That article draws on insights from political psychology showing that in times of rapid change and fast-paced transition, citizens rely on cues interpreted through bounded rationality. Bahgat Korany, ed., *Al-rabi` al-`arabi fi misr: Al-thawra wama ba`diha* [The Arab Spring in Egypt: The revolution and its aftermath] (Beirut: Centre for Arab Unity Studies, 2012), investigates the multifaceted political dynamics that shaped the period after Mubarak's ouster. The volume focuses on institutional and grassroots politics and the intersection between these domains. For the regional dimension of Egyptian autocracy and the role of Saudi Arabia in supporting regimes in Egypt, see Oisín Tansey, Kevin Koehler, and Alexander Schmotz, "Ties to the Rest: Autocratic Linkages and Regime Survival," *Comparative Political Studies* 50, no. 9 (2017): 1221–1254.

BIBLIOGRAPHY

Abbas, Raouf, and Asem El-Dessouky. *The Large Landowning Class and the Peasantry in Egypt, 1837–1952*. Syracuse, N.Y.: Syracuse University Press, 2011.
'Abd al-Hay, Ahmad, Khayri 'Umar, 'Abd al-Hafez El-Sawi, and Wisam Fu'ad. *Al-mu'arada al-mustabaha* [Violated opposition]. Cairo: Sawasiyya Center for Human Rights, 2006.
'Abd al-Fadil, Mahmoud. *Al-iqtisad al-misri bayn al-takhtit al-markazi wa-l-infitah al-iqtisadi* [The Egyptian economy between central planning and open-door policy]. Cairo: Ma'had al-Inma' al-'Arabi, 1980.
——. *The Political Economy of Nasserism: A Study in Employment and Income Distribution Policies in Urban Egypt, 1952–72*. Cambridge: Cambridge University Press, 1980.
Abdel Majid, Farid. *Min mahadir ijtima'at 'abd al-nasir al-'arabiyya wa-l-duwawliyya 1967–1970* [From the minutes of Abdel Nasser's Arab and international meetings, 1967–1970]. Beirut: Mu'assasat al-Abhath al-'Arabiyya, 1985.
Abdel-Malek, Anouar. *Egypt: Military Society: The Army Regime, the Left, and Social Change under Nasser*. New York: Random House, 1968.
Abdelrahman, Maha. *Civil Society Exposed: The Politics of NGOs in Egypt*. London: Tauris Academic Studies, 2004.
——. *Egypt's Long Revolution: Protests Movements and Uprisings*. London: Routledge, 2015.
——. "'With the Islamists?—Sometimes. With the State?—Never!' Cooperation Between the Left and Islamists in Egypt." *British Journal of Middle Eastern Studies* 36, no. 1 (2009): 37–54.
Abdulhaq, Najat. *Jewish and Greek Communities in Egypt: Entrepreneurship and Business before Nasser*. London: I. B. Tauris, 2016.

BIBLIOGRAPHY

Abisourour, Mona. "The Egyptian Devaluation—One Year Later." Infomineo, January 2, 2018. https://infomineo.com/egyptian-devaluation-one-year-later/.

Abul-Magd, Zeinab. *Militarizing the Nation: The Army, Business, and Revolution in Egypt*. New York: Columbia University Press, 2017.

Adams, Paul S. "Corporatism in Latin America and Europe: Origins, Developments, and Challenges in Comparative Perspective." In *Authoritarianism and Corporatism in Latin America Revisited*, edited by Howard J. Wiarda, 58–87. Gainesville: University Press of Florida, 2004.

Adly, Amr. *Cleft Capitalism: The Social Origins of Failed Market Making in Egypt*. Stanford, Calif.: Stanford University Press, 2020.

——. *State Reform and Development in the Middle East: Turkey and Egypt in the Post-liberalization Era*. London: Routledge, 2012.

Adly, Amr, and Fatima. Ramadan. *Su`ud wa uful al-haraka al-`ummaliyyah fi miṣr (2006–2016): Al-`ummal, wa-l-siyasa wa-l-dawla* [The rise and fall of Egypt's labor movement (2006–2016): Workers, politics, and the state]. Cairo: Dar al-Maraya, with support from the Rosa Luxemburg Foundation, 2018.

Ahmed, Leila. *Women and Gender in Islam: Historical Roots of a Modern Debate*. New Haven, Conn.: Yale University Press, 1992.

Almond, Gabriel A., and Sidney Verba. *The Civic Culture: Political Attitudes and Democracy in Five Nations*. Princeton, N.J.: Princeton University Press, 1963.

Alves, Maria Helena. *State and Opposition in Military Brazil*. Austin: University of Texas Press, 1985.

Amin, Galal. *Misr w-al-Misriyun fi `ahd Mubarak (1981–2008)* [Egypt and the Egyptians under Mubarak (1981–2008)]. Cairo: Dar Mirit, 2009.

`Amir, Ibrahim. *Al-arḍ wa-l-fallah: Al-mas'ala al-zira`iyya al-misri* [The land and the peasant: The agrarian question in Egypt]. Cairo: Al-dar al-misriyya li-l-nashr wa-l-tawzi`, 1958.

Amsden, Alice Hoffenberg. *The Rise of "The Rest": Challenges to the West from Late-Industrializing Economies*. Oxford: Oxford University Press, 2001.

Assad, Ragui, ed. *Suq al-`amal al-misriyya fi al-alfiya al-jadid* [The Egyptian labor market in the new millennium]. Cairo: Economic Research Forum and Al-Ahram Center, 2010.

`Awad, Louis. *Tarikh al-fikr al-misri al-hadith min `asr isma`il ila thawrat 1919* [The history of modern Egyptian thought from Ismail's era to the 1919 revolution]. Cairo: Madbouly Bookshop, 1969.

Ayubi, Nazih. *Over-Stating the Arab State: Politics and Society in the Middle East*. London: I. B. Tauris, 1995.

Badi, Sulafa, Lisha Wang, and Stephen Pryke. "Relationship Marketing in Guanxi Networks: A Social Network Analysis Study of Chinese Construction Small and Medium-Sized Enterprises." *Industrial Marketing Management*, no. 60 (2017): 204–218.

Badran, Margot. *Feminists, Islam, and Nation: Gender and the Making of Modern Egypt*. Princeton, N.J.: Princeton University Press, 1995.

Bahrawi, Dalia Othman al-. "Al-jaysh ya`ud ila al-shari` " [The army returns to the street]. *Al-Masry Al-Youm*, June 27, 2013. https://to.almasryalyoum.com/article2.aspx?ArticleID=387674.

Baker, Raymond William. *Sadat and After: Struggles for Egypt's Political Soul*. Cambridge, Mass.: Harvard University Press, 1990.

BIBLIOGRAPHY

Banna, Hassan al-. *Mudhakirat al-da`wa wa al-da`iyya* [Memoirs of preaching and the preacher]. Cairo: Islamic Da`wa Publisher, 2001.
Bayat, Asef. *Life as Politics: How Ordinary People Change the Middle East*. Stanford, Calif.: Stanford University Press, 2013.
Beattie, Kirk. *Egypt During the Nasser Years: Ideology, Politics, and Civil Society*. Boulder, CO.: Westview Press, 1994.
Beinin, Joel. *The Dispersion of Egyptian Jewry: Culture, Politics, and the Formation of a Modern Diaspora*. Berkeley: University of California Press, 1998.
——. "Workers Protest in Egypt: Neoliberalism and Class Struggle in 21st Century." *Social Movement Studies* 8, no. 4 (2009): 449–454.
Beinin, Joel, and Zachary Lockman. *Workers on the Nile: Nationalism, Communism, Islam, and the Egyptian Working Class, 1882–1954*. London: I. B. Tauris, 1988.
Ben-Nfissa, Sara. *The Relationship between the Egyptian State and NGOs since the 19th Century*. Cairo: Al-Ahram Center for Political and Strategic Studies, 1994.
Bernard-Maugiron, Natalie, ed. *Judges and Political Reform in Egypt*. Cairo: American University of Cairo Press, 2015.
Bianchi, Robert. *Unruly Corporatism: Associational Life in Twentieth-Century Egypt*. New York: Oxford University Press, 1989.
Bishara, Dina. *Contesting Authoritarianism: Labor Challenges to the State in Egypt*. Cambridge: Cambridge University Press, 2018.
Bishri, Tariq al-. *Al-dawla wa-l-kanisa* [The state and the church]. Cairo: Al-Shuruq, 2011.
——. *Al-dimuqratiyya wa-nizam 23 yulyu 1952–1970* [Democracy and the 23rd July regime, 1952–1970]. Cairo: Dar al-Hilal, 1991.
Bou Nassif, Hicham. "'Second-Class': The Grievances of Sunni Officers in the Syrian Armed Forces." *Journal of Strategic Studies* 38, no. 5 (2015): 626–649.
Bourdieu, Pierre. *Pascalian Meditations*. Stanford, Calif.: Stanford University Press, 2000.
——. "The Production of Belief: Contribution to an Economy of Symbolic Goods." Translated by Richard Nice. *Media, Culture & Society* 2, no. 3 (1980): 261–293.
Brömmelhörster, Jörn, and W. Paes, eds. *The Military as an Economic Actor: Soldiers in Business*. London: Palgrave Macmillan, 2003.
Brown, Nathan J. *Arguing Islam after the Revival of Arab Politics*. New York: Oxford University Press, 2017.
——. "Constitutions and the Public Sphere." In *The Arab Uprisings Explained: New Contentious Politics in the Middle East*, edited by Marc Lynch, 296–312. New York: Columbia University Press, 2014.
——. *The Rule of Law in the Arab World: Courts in Egypt and the Gulf*. Cambridge: Cambridge University Press, 1997.
Brownlee, Jason. *Authoritarianism in an Age of Democratization*. New York: Cambridge University Press, 2007.
Bush, Ray, and David Seddon. "Editorial: North Africa in Africa." *Review of African Political Economy* 26, no. 82 (2007): 435–439.
Cole, Juan R. I. *Colonialism and Revolution in the Middle East: Social and Cultural Origins of Egypt's `Urabi Movement*. Princeton, N.J.: Princeton University Press, 1992.
Collier, Ruth Berins, and David Collier. "Inducements versus Constraints: Disaggregating "Corporatism." *American Political Science Review* 73, no. 4 (1979): 967–986.

BIBLIOGRAPHY

Cook, Steven A. *Ruling But Not Governing: The Military and Political Development in Egypt, Algeria, and Turkey.* Baltimore, Md.: Johns Hopkins University Press, 2007.
Cuno, Kenneth M. *Modernizing Marriage: Family, Ideology, and Law in Nineteenth- and Early Twentieth-Century Egypt.* Syracuse, N.Y.: Syracuse University Press, 2015.
———. *The Pasha's Peasants: Land, Society, and Economy in Lower Egypt, 1740–1858.* Cambridge: Cambridge University Press, 1992.
Disuqui, 'Asim al-. *Kibar mullak al-aradi al-zira`iyya wa-dawruhum fi al-mujtama` al-misri 1914–1952* [Major landowners and their role in the Egyptian society, 1914–1952]. Cairo: Dar al-Shuruq, 2008.
Dodson, Michael. "Nicaragua: The Struggle for the Church." In *Religion and Political Conflict in Latin America*, edited by Daniel H. Levine, 79–105. Chapel Hill: University of North Carolina Press, 1986.
Drogus, Carol Ann, and Hannah Stewart-Gambino. *Activist Faith: Grassroots Women in Democratic Brazil and Chile.* University Park: Pennsylvania State University Press, 2005.
Elyachar, Julia. *Markets of Dispossession: NGOs, Economic Development, and the State in Cairo.* Durham, N.C.: Duke University Press, 2005.
Evans, Peter B. *Embedded Autonomy: States and Industrial Transformation.* Princeton, N.J.: Princeton University Press, 2012.
Fahmy, Khaled. *All the Pasha's Men: Mehmed Ali, His Army and the Making of Modern Egypt.* Cairo: American University in Cairo Press, 1997.
Fawzy, Muhammed. *Harb al-thalath sanawat* [The war of three years]. Cairo: Dar al-Mustaqbal al-`arabī, 1986.
Fogel, Ramón. *Movimientos Campesinos en el Paraguay.* Asunción: Centro Paraguayo de Estudios Sociológicos, 1986.
Foucault, Michel, Arnold I. Davidson, and Graham Burchell. *The Birth of Biopolitics: Lectures at the Collège de France, 1978–1979.* New York: Palgrave Macmillan, 2008.
Gerges, Fawaz A. *Making the Arab World: Nasser, Qutb, and the Clash That Shaped the Middle East.* Princeton, N.J.: Princeton University Press, 2018.
Goldschmidt, Arthur. *Modern Egypt: The Formation of a Nation State.* Boulder, Colo.: Westview Press, 2004.
Gordon, Joel. *Nasser's Blessed Movement: Egypt's Free Officers and the July Revolution.* Oxford: Oxford University Press, 1992.
Greif, Avner. "History Lessons: The Birth of Impersonal Exchange: The Community Responsibility System and Impartial Justice." *Journal of Economic Perspectives* 20, no. 2 (2006): 221–236.
Gunaym, Adil. *Azmat al-dawla al-Misriyya al-mu`asira* [The crisis of the contemporary Egyptian state]. Cairo: Dar al-`Alam al-Thalith, 2005.
Hadiz, Vedi R., and Richard Robison. "The Political Economy of Oligarchy and the Reorganization of Power in Indonesia." *Indonesia*, no. 96 (2013): 35–57.
Haenni, Patrick. *L'islam de marché.* Paris: Editions du Seuil, 2005.
Hall, Peter, and David Soskice, eds. *Varieties of Capitalism: The Institutional Foundations of Comparative Advantage.* Oxford: Oxford University Press, 2001.
Hanafy, Shima. "Sectoral FDI and Economic Growth: Evidence from Egyptian Governorates." MAGKS Joint Discussion Paper Series in Economics, no. 37. School of Business and Economics, Philipps-Universität Marburg, 2015.

BIBLIOGRAPHY

Hanley, Will. *Identifying with Nationality: Europeans, Ottomans, and Egyptians in Alexandria*. New York: Columbia University Press, 2017.

Hansen, Bent. *The Political Economy of Poverty, Equity, and Growth: Egypt and Turkey*. Oxford: Oxford University Press, 1991.

Hassan, Mai, and Friedrich Schneider. "Modelling the Egyptian Shadow Economy: A Currency Demand and a MIMIC Model Approach." CESifo Working Paper Series no. 5727, 2016.

Hatab, Shimaa. "Abortive Regime Transition in Egypt: Prodemocracy Alliance and Demand-Making Framework." *Democratization* 25, no. 4 (2018): 579–596.

———. "Threat Perception and Democratic Support in Post Arab Spring Egypt." *Comparative Politics* 53, no. 1 (2020): 69–98.

Heydemann, Steven, and Reinoud Leenders. "Authoritarian Learning and Counterrevolution." in *The Arab Uprisings Explained: New Contentious Politics in the Middle East*, edited by Marc Lynch, 75–92. New York: Columbia University Press, 2013.

Human Rights Watch. "Egypt: Rab`a Killings Likely Crimes Against Humanity." News release, August 12, 2014. https://www.hrw.org/news/2014/08/12/egypt-rab-killings-likely-crimes-against-humanity.

———. *We Do Unreasonable Things Here: Torture and National Security in al-Sisi's Egypt*. September 2017. https://www.hrw.org/sites/default/files/report_pdf/egypt0917_web.pdf.

Ḥussein, Adil. *Al-iqtiṣad al-miṣri min al-istiqlal ila al-taba`iyya* [The Egyptian economy from independence to dependency]. Cairo: Dar al-Mustaqbal al-`arabī, 1982.

Ibn Khaldon Center. *Al-mujtama` al-madani wal-tahawwul al-dimuqrati fi al-watan al-`arabi: Al-taqrir al-sanawi* [Civil society and democratic transition in the Arab region: The annual report]. Cairo: Ibn Khaldon Center, 1996.

Ikram, Khalid. *The Egyptian Economy, 1952–2000: Performance Policies and Issues*. London: Routledge, 2007.

Imam, Samiya Sa`id. *Man yamluk misr? Dirasa taḥliliyya li-nukhbat al-infitaḥ al-iqtisadi fi al-mujtama` al-misr, 1974–1980* [Who owns Egypt? An analytical study of the social roots of the open-door elite in Egyptian society, 1974–1980]. Cairo: Dar al-Mustaqbal al-`arabī, 1986.

Ismail, Salwa. *Rethinking Islamist Politics: Culture, the State and Islamism*. London: I. B. Tauris, 2006.

Issawi, Charles. *Egypt: An Economic and Social Analysis*. New York: Oxford University Press, 1947.

`Izz al-Din, Nahid. *Al-`ummal wa-rijal al-`amal: Tahawwulat al-furaṣ al-siyasiyya fi misr* [Labor and businessmen: The changing political opportunities in Egypt]. Cairo: Markaz al-Ahram li-l-dirasat al-siyasiyya wa-l-istiratijiyya, 2003.

`Izz el-Din, Amin. *Tarikh al-tabaqa al-`amilah al-misriyya mundh nash'atiha hatta thawrat 1919* [The history of the Egyptian working class since its emergence until the 1919 revolution]. Cairo: Dar al-Katib al-`Arabi, 1967.

Jad, Muhammad. *Mullak miṣr: Qissat su`ud al-ra'smaliyya al-misriyya* [Egypt's owners: The story of the advent of Egyptian capitalism]. Cairo: Dar al-Maraya, 2018.

Joya, Angela. "The Military and the State in Egypt: Class Formation in the Post-Arab Uprisings." *British Journal of Middle Eastern Studies* 47, no. 5 (2018): 1–21.

BIBLIOGRAPHY

Kadi, Galila El-. *Al-tahaddur al-'ashwa'i* [Random urbanization]. Translated by Menha El-Batrawi. Cairo: Al-Markaz al-Qawmī li-l-Tarjama, 2009.

Kandil, Hazem. *Soldiers, Spies, and Statesmen: Egypt's Road to Revolt*. London: Verso, 2012).

Kassem, May. *Egyptian Politics: The Dynamics of Authoritarian Rule*. Boulder, Colo.: Lynne Rienner Publishers, 2004.

Khan, Mushtaq H., and Kwame Sundaram Jomo, eds. *Rents, Rent-Seeking and Economic Development: Theory and Evidence in Asia*. Cambridge: Cambridge University Press, 2000.

Korany, Bahgat, ed. *Al-rabi' al-'arabi fi misr: Al-thawra wama ba'daha* [The Arab Spring in Egypt: The revolution and its aftermath]. Beirut: Centre for Arab Unity Studies, 2012.

Krämer, Gudrun. *The Jews in Modern Egypt, 1914–1952*. London: I. B. Tauris, 1989.

Laskier. Michael M. "Egyptian Jewry under the Nasser Regime, 1956–70." *Middle Eastern Studies* 31, no. 3 (1995): 573–619.

Lauzière, Henri. *The Making of Salafism: Islamic Reform in the Twentieth Century*. New York: Columbia University Press, 2015.

Linz, Juan. "An Authoritarian Regime: Spain." In *Cleavages, Ideologies and Party Systems: Contributions to Comparative Political Sociology*, vol. 10, edited by Erik Allardt and Yrjo Littunen, 1467–1531. Helsinki: Academic Bookstore, 1964.

Lynch, Marc. *The Arab Uprising: The Unfinished Revolutions of the New Middle East*. New York: Public Affairs, 2013.

Mabro, Robert. *The Egyptian Economy, 1952–1972*. Oxford: Oxford University Press, 1974.

Mahdi, 'Aliya' al-, and Ahmad Rashid. "Al-munakh al-mutaghayyir wa-tanmiyat al-mashru'at al-saghira wa-l-mutanahiyat al-sighar fi misr 2006" [The changing environment and the development of small and micro projects in Egypt 2006]. In *Suq al-'amal al-misriyya fi-l-alfiyya al-jadida* [The Egyptian labor market in the new millennium], edited by Ragui Assaad, 87–116. Cairo: Economic Research Forum and Al-Ahram Center, 2010.

Mahdi, Rabab El-. "The Democracy Movement: Cycles of Protest." In *Egypt: The Moment of Change*, edited by Rabab El-Mahdi and Philip Marfleet, 87–102. London: Zed Books, 2009.

———. "Labor Protests in Egypt: Causes and Meanings." *Review of African Political Economy* 38, no. 129 (2011): 387–402.

Mahmood, Saba. *Politics of Piety: The Islamic Revival and the Feminist Subject*. Princeton, N.J.: Princeton University Press, 2005.

Malloy, James. "Authoritarianism and Corporatism in Latin America: The Modal Pattern." In *Authoritarianism and Corporatism in Latin America*, edited by James M. Malloy, 3–19. Pittsburgh, Penn.: University of Pittsburgh Press, 1977.

Mandour, Maged. "The Military's Immunity in Egypt." Carnegie Endowment for International Peace, July 24, 2018. https://carnegieendowment.org/sada/76904.

Mani, Kristina. "Militaries in Business: State-Making and Entrepreneurship in the Developing World." *Armed Forces & Society* 33, no. 4 (2007): 591–611.

Marshall, Shana. *The Egyptian Armed Forces and the Remaking of an Economic Empire*. Washington, D.C.: Carnegie Endowment for International Peace, 2015.

BIBLIOGRAPHY

Masoud, Tarek. *Counting Islam Religion, Class and Elections in Egypt*. Cambridge: Cambridge University Press, 2014.

McCulloch, Lesley. "*Trifungsi*: The Role of the Indonesian Military in Business." In *The Military as an Economic Actor: Soldiers in Business*, edited by Jörn Brömmelhörster and Wolf-Christian Paes, 94–123. London: Palgrave Macmillan, 2003.

Menza, Mohamed Fahmy. *Patronage Politics in Egypt: The National Democratic Party and Muslim Brotherhood in Cairo*. London: Routledge, 2012.

Migdal, Joel S. *The State in Society: Studying How States and Societies Transform and Constitute One Another*. Cambridge: Cambridge University Press, 2001.

Mitchell, Richard. *The Society of the Muslim Brothers*. Oxford: Oxford University Press, 1969.

Mohieldin, Mahmoud S., and Peter W. Wright. "Formal and Informal Credit Markets in Egypt." *Economic Development and Cultural Change* 48, no. 3 (2000): 657–670.

Moore, Clement Henry. *Images of Development: Egyptian Engineers in Search of Industry*. Cambridge, Mass.: MIT Press, 1980.

Moustafa, Tamir. "Law versus the State: The Judicialization of Politics in Egypt." *Law & Social Inquiry* 28, no. 4 (2003): 883–930.

Naggar, Ahmad El-. *Al-inhiyar al-iqtisadi fi ʿasr mubarak* [Economic collapse in Mubarak's time]. Cairo: Dar Mirit, 2009.

Oraby, Mona. "Authorizing Religious Conversion in Administrative Courts: Law, Rights, and Secular Indeterminacy." *New Diversities* 17, no. 1 (2015): 64–75.

Owen, Roger. *State, Power and Politics in the Making of the Modern Middle East*. New York: Routledge, 1992.

Pion-Berlin, David, and Craig Arceneaux. "Decision-Makers or Decision-Takers? Military Missions and Civilian Control in Democratic South America." *Armed Forces & Society* 26, no. 3 (2000): 413–436.

Polanyi, Karl. *The Great Transformation*. Boston: Beacon Press, 1957.

Rafi'i, Abd al-Rahman al-. *Thawrat 23 Yulyu 1952* [The July 23 revolution]. Cairo: Maktabat al-Nahda al-Misriyya, 1959.

Ramadan, Fatima, and Amr Adly. *Low-Cost Authoritarianism: The Egyptian Regime and Labor Movement since 2013*. Washington, D.C.: Carnegie Endowment for International Peace, 2015.

Richards, Alan. *Egypt's Agricultural Development, 1800–1980: Technical and Social Change*. Boulder, Colo.: Westview Press, 1982.

Roccu, Roberto. *The Political Economy of the Egyptian Revolution: Mubarak, Economic Reforms and Failed Hegemony*. London: Palgrave Macmillan, 2013.

Rock-Singer, Aaron. *Practicing Islam in Egypt: Print Media and Islamic Revival*. Cambridge: Cambridge University Press, 2019.

Ruffner, Todd. *Under Threat: Egypt's Systematic Campaign Against NGOs*. Project on Middle East Democracy, March 2015. https://pomed.org/wp-content/uploads/2015/03/Under-Threat-Egypts-Systematic-Campaign-against-NGOs.pdf.

Rutherford, Bruce K., and Jeannie Sowers. *Modern Egypt: What Everyone Needs to Know*. Oxford: Oxford University Press, 2018.

Ryand, Gingeras. "Last Rites for a 'Pure Bandit': Clandestine Service, Historiography, and the Origins of the Turkish 'Deep State.'" *Past and Present* 206, no. 1 (2010): 151–174.

Sayigh, Yezid. *Above the State: The Officers' Republic in Egypt*. Washington, D.C.: Carnegie Endowment for International Peace, 2012.
——. *Owners of the Republic: An Anatomy of Egypt's Military Economy*. Washington, D.C.: Carnegie Endowment for International Peace, 2019.
Sayyid, Mustapha Kamel al-. "A Civil Society in Egypt?" *Middle East Journal* 47, no. 2 (1993): 228–242.
Sayyid Marsot, Afaf Lutfi. *Egypt's Liberal Experiment, 1922–36*. Berkeley: University of California Press, 1978.
Schmitter, Philippe C. "Still the Century of Corporatism." *Review of Politics* 36, no. 1 (1974): 85–131.
Schneider, Ben Ross. "Hierarchical Market Economies and Varieties of Capitalism in Latin America." *Journal of Latin American Studies* 41, no. 3 (2009): 553–575.
Sedra, Paul. "Class Cleavages and Ethnic Conflict: Coptic Christian Communities in Modern Egyptian Politics." *Islam and Christian-Muslim Relations* 10, no. 2 (1999): 219–235.
Shalabi, ʿAli Muhammad. *Misr al-fatah wa dawruha fi al-siyasa al-misriyya 1933–1941* [Young Egypt and its role in Egyptian politics, 1933–1941]. Cairo: Dar al-Kitab al-Jamiʿi, 1982.
Shenhav, Yehouda. *The Arab Jews: A Postcolonial Reading of Nationalism, Religion, and Ethnicity*. Stanford, Calif.: Stanford University Press, 2006.
Shukri, Ghali. *Al-thawra al-mudadda fi misr* [The counterrevolution in Egypt]. Cairo: Al-Ahali, 1987.
Siddiqa, Ayesha. *Military Inc.: Inside Pakistan's Military Economy*. London: Pluto Press, 2007.
Sims, David. *Egypt's Desert Dreams: Development or Disaster?* Cairo: American University in Cairo Press, 2015.
Soliman, Samer. *The Autumn of Dictatorship: Fiscal Crisis and Political Change in Egypt*. Stanford, Calif.: Stanford University Press, 2011.
——. *Al-nizam al-qawi wa-l-dawla al-daʿifa: Idarat al-azma al-maliyya wa-l-taghyir al-siyasi fi ʿahd mubarak* [The strong regime and the weak state: The management of financial crisis and political change in the time of Mubarak]. Cairo: General Organization of Culture Palaces, 2005.
——. "State and Industrial Capitalism in Egypt." *Cairo Papers in Social Science* 21, no. 2 (1998): 72–82.
Springborg, Robert. *Mubarak's Egypt: Fragmentation of the Political Order*. Boulder, Colo.: Westview Press, 1989.
——. "Professional Syndicates in Egyptian Politics, 1952–1970." *International Journal of Middle East Studies* 9, no. 3 (1978): 275–295.
Stark, David. "Recombinant Property in East European Capitalism." *American Journal of Sociology* 101, no. 4 (1996): 993–1027.
Starrett, Gregory. *Putting Islam to Work: Education, Politics, and Religious Transformation in Egypt*. Berkeley: University of California Press, 1998.
Stepan, Alfred. *The State and Society: Peru in Comparative Perspective*. Princeton, N.J.: Princeton University Press, 1978.
Stevens, Evelyn. "Mexico's PRI: The Institutionalization of Corporatism?" In *Authoritarianism and Corporatism in Latin America*, edited by James M. Malloy, 227–257. Pittsburgh, Penn.: University of Pittsburgh Press, 1977.

BIBLIOGRAPHY

Stevenson, Lois. *Private Sector and Enterprise Development: Fostering Growth in the Middle East and North Africa*. Ottawa: International Development Research Center, 2010.

Stiglitz, Joseph E. *Wither Socialism?* Cambridge, Mass.: MIT Press, 1994.

Tadros, Mariz. *Copts at the Crossroads: The Challenges of Building Inclusive Democracy in Egypt*. Cairo: American University in Cairo Press, 2013.

Tammam, Husam. *Tasalluf al-ikhwan* [The Salafization of the Brotherhood]. Alexandria: Maktabat al-Iskandiryya, 2010.

Tansey, Oisín, Kevin Koehler, and Alexander Schmotz. "Ties to the Rest: Autocratic Linkages and Regime Survival." *Comparative Political Studies* 50, no. 9 (2017): 1221–1254.

Tawila, 'Abd al-Satar al-. *Sharikat tawzif al-amwal wa-l-mustaqbal al-ghamid* [Capital investment companies and the uncertain future]. Cairo: Al-Sawi, 1988.

Tilly, Charles. "War Making and State Making as Organized Crime." In *Bringing the State Back In*, edited by Peter Evans, Dietrich Rueschemeyer, and Theda Skocpol, 169–191. Cambridge: Cambridge University Press, 1985.

Trinkunas, Harold. "Crafting Civilian Control in Argentina and Venezuela." In *Civil-Military Relations in Latin America: New Analytical Perspectives*, edited by David Pion-Berlin, 161–193. Chapel Hill: University of North Carolina Press, 2001.

Tripp, Charles. *Islam and the Moral Economy*. Cambridge: Cambridge University Press, 2006.

Wassef, Hind, and Nadia Wassef. *Daughters of the Nile: Photographs of Egyptian Women's Movements, 1900–1960*. Cairo: American University in Cairo Press, 2001.

Waterbury, John. *The Egypt of Nasser and Sadat: The Political Economy of Two Regimes*. Princeton, N.J.: Princeton University Press, 1983.

Wickham, Carrie. *Mobilizing Islam: Religion, Activism and Political Change in Egypt*. New York: Columbia University Press, 2002.

Williamson, Oliver E. "Vertical Integration and Related Variations on a Transaction-Cost Economics Theme." In *New Developments in the Analysis of Market Structure*, edited by G. Frank Mathewson and Joseph Stiglitz, 149–176. London: Palgrave Macmillan, 1986.

Yom, Sean L. *From Resilience to Revolution: How Foreign Interventions Destabilize the Middle East*. New York: Columbia University Press, 2016.

Yunis, Sherif. *Nida' al-sha'b: Tarikh Naqdi li-l-idolojiyya al-nasiriyya* [The call of the people: A critical history of the Nasserist ideology]. Cairo: Dar al-Shuruq, 2012.

——. *Al-zahf al-muqaddas: Muzaharat al-tanahi wa tashakkul 'ibadat nasir* [Holy creep: The abdication demonstrations and the formation of Nasser worship]. Cairo: Dar Mirit, 2005.

INDEX

Abdel Nasser, Gamal. *See* Nasser, Gamal 'Abd al-
Abu al-Enein, Mohamed, 166
Abu Ghazala, 'Abd al- Halim, 185–186, 188
Adly, Amr, x
advocacy groups, 97
agricultural cooperatives, 79
Agriculture, Ministry of, 87
Albania, 5
Algeria, 47
'Amr, 'Abd al-Hakim, 50, 60
Amsden, Alice, 170
Anti-Cyber and Information Technology Crimes Law (2018), 229
April 6 Youth Movement, 109
Arab socialism, 28, 37–38, 72
Arab Socialist Union, 8, 36–37, 50–51, 52–67, 75–78, 80–83, 90, 183; creation, 75; disestablishment, 40
Argentina, xi, 67, 84, 186
army. *See* military, Egyptian
Assad, Ragui, 158
associations. *See* advocacy groups; April 6 Youth Movement; Bar Association; business associations; Kifaya; labor movement; nongovernmental organizations
authoritarianism, 3, 13, 44–62, 65–91, 107, 109, 110, 114, 131, 205, 207, 209, 210, 219, 233, 234; corporatism, 63; definition, 10; democratization, 93; Latin America, 104; Nasserism, 23; regimes, 11, 21, 22, 44–45; scholarship on, 46; socialism and corporatism, 14; state-regime distinction, 44–47; uprising of 2011, 18. *See also* deep state; *regime types*
Azhar, al-, 51, 103, 124–126; institutional independence of, 13, 45; and Islamic religious establishment, 134, 136, 144, 210, 223, 239n5; monarchy, 50; as strong institution, 10, 28

Bar Association, 72, 73, 82, 88, 89
Bonaparte, Napoleon, 30
Bourdieu, Pierre, 149
Brazil, xi, 67, 104, 220
Britain, 54, 59, 117; occupation of Egypt, 5, 6, 27, 29, 31–35; and revolt of 1919, 9, 33; rivalry with France, 4, 30;

INDEX

Britain (*continued*)
  treaty with Egypt in 1936, 6, 34;
  war with Ottoman Empire, 6, 33;
  withdrawal from Egypt, 35; in
  World War II, 35. *See also* Egyptian
  independence; khedival state;
  Suez Canal
Brown, Nathan J., x
business associations, 100

Cairo, 4, 5, 30, 31, 33, 53, 77, 78, 107, 167, 187, 188, 197, 198, 209, 210, 226
capitulations, 30, 31, 34, 37, 71, 121, 122, 124, 140, 153, 154; and Britain, 32, 33; international conference (1937), 35; policing, 35; treaty of 1936, 6. *See also* Europe
Catholic Church, 103, 126, 134; and authoritarianism, 49, 104
Central Agency for Public Mobilization and Statistics, 174
China, 152, 162, 172, 173, 177, 180, 181, 198, 199, 202, 203, 242–243n29; military, 17; personalized regime, 46
Civic Forum (Czechoslovakia), 211
command economy, 148, 154, 155, 159
constitution, Egyptian, 41, 42, 47, 54, 77, 184, 218, 232, 248n8; Copts and, 128; monarchy, 50; of 1923, 6, 34; of 1971, 126, 197; post-1952, 55; post-2011, 61, 200, 212, 214, 219, 220, 223; post-2013, 225, 227
Consultative Assembly, 31, 32
corporatism, ix, xii, 18, 38, 63–75, 83–91, 109–110, 205, 236n1; authoritarianism and socialism, 3; definition of, 2, 11; end of, 15; and interest representation, 69; society under, 14; state corporatism, 66. *See also* authoritarianism; socialism
cotton, 5, 7, 29, 30, 31, 153; different economic policies, 35–36
coup of 2013, 1, 18, 42, 54, 57, 61–62, 129, 164, 178, 184, 190, 196, 197, 201–202, 204, 207, 215, 223, 224, 226, 227–234; terminological controversy, 10. *See also* uprising of 2011

crony capitalism, xii, 148, 151, 152, 162, 164, 165, 166, 168–172, 181, 199; definition of, 146
Czechoslovakia, 211

Day of Rage, 209
deep state, 47–48; authoritarianism, 13; Turkish origin of term, 47; uprising of 2011, 1, 223, 233. *See also* uprising of 2011
Defense, Ministry of, 185, 193, 194, 245–246n9
developmental state, 152, 153, 163, 170–172, 178

East Asia, 3–4, 145, 150, 152–153, 172, 173, 178
Education, Ministry of, 48, 239n5
Egyptian Citizenship Law of 1929, 122
Egyptian Federation of Independent Trade Unions, 216
Egyptian independence (1922), 6, 121, 140, 144, 153–155, 184; aftermath of, 33–35; British declaration of, 33
Egyptian Nationality Law, 123
Egyptian Trade Union Federation, 77, 108, 215
El Kadi, Galila, 167
Elaraby family, 165
Elsewedy family, 165
Europe, 54, 59, 87, 93, 95, 103, 116, 118, 121, 123, 133, 140, 145, 153, 230; authoritarianism in southern Europe, 49; and capitulations, 30; and Egyptian state-formation, 3, 12, 21–22, 26–27, 29–30; importation from Egypt, 5, 30–31; influence in Egypt, 30, 31; liberalizing policies in Eastern Europe, 3–4; traffic with India, 4. *See also* state formation
Evans, Peter, 170

Federation of Chambers of Commerce, 101
Federation of Chambers of Industry, 101, 166
feminist organizations, 7, 10
Finance, Ministry of, 109
foreign direct investment (FDI), 158

INDEX

Foucault, Michel, 150
France, 45; citizens and firms in Egypt, 121, 154; 1798 occupation of Egypt, 4, 5, 27, 29, 30, 117; and Suez Canal, 35, 37, 124. *See also* judiciary, Egyptian
Free Officers, 36–37, 40, 50, 51, 59, 65, 67, 68, 69, 72, 73, 74, 76, 79, 80, 82, 114, 120, 129, 210, 231, 237n10. *See also* military, Egyptian; Nasser, Gamal ʿAbd al-; Sadat, Anwar al-
Friday of Anger, 209
Fuad (king of Egypt), 6

Germany: compared to Egypt, 47; coordinated market economy of, 167; religion and politics of, 112
Ghabbour family, 165, 243n32
global South, 21–22, 152, 160–162, 169, 170, 195
gross domestic product (GDP), 157, 158, 163, 169, 173, 174, 186, 191, 242n20
Gulf countries, 132, 137, 138, 141, 157, 199

habitus, ix, 139–140, 191, 196; defined, 149; economy, 146, 151, 152–153, 159–163, 164, 166, 167, 175, 208
Hassan, Mai, 169
Hatab, Shimaa, x
Housing, Ministry of, 190
Hussein, Saddam, 46

Imam, Samiya Saʾid, 165
import substitution industrialization, 70, 155; definition, 37–38
Independent General Union of Real Estate Tax Authority Workers, 109
India, 4, 112, 162
Indonesia, 17, 180, 181, 199–201
Industry, Ministry of, 101, 171
infitah, 16, 39, 78, 81, 101, 133, 140, 142, 147, 149, 156–159, 162, 164, 165, 169, 171, 195
Interior, Ministry of the, 183, 210, 225
International Monetary Fund (IMF), 156, 157, 164
Islamic Revival, 129, 130, 132, 133, 134, 135, 144

Islamists, 41, 42, 54, 62, 68, 84–85, 88–89, 94, 97, 99, 103, 105, 107, 121, 123, 125, 129, 132–134, 207, 211–234
Ismaʾil (khedive), 31
Israel, 124; peace treaty, 9, 88, 156, 182, 185, 186, 188, 199; Suez Canal war, 37, 39, 124, 140, 154; war of 1948, 7, 36, 59, 120, 123; war of 1967, 8, 39, 56, 60, 78, 156; war of 1973, 130, 156. *See also* military, Egyptian; Muslim Brotherhood
Istanbul, 4
Italy, 67, 117

Jews, in Egypt, 37, 54, 114–116, 120, 121–124, 140, 153, 154, 239n7
Jomo, Kwame Sundaram, 166
Judges Club, 40, 56–57
judiciary, Egyptian: 22, 49, 54–57, 58, 59, 62, 201, 210, 221, 222, 223, 227, 228, 232, 233; French influence on, 32, 54; independence of, 41, 45, 48; and monarchy, 50; as strong institution, 10; unification of, 35. *See also* Judges Club; Mixed Courts
July 1952, events of, 7, 9–10, 50, 55, 57, 59–60, 65, 73, 77, 82, 88, 91, 101, 114, 120, 127, 154, 182–183, 205, 210, 231; increased state-building, 36. *See also* military, Egyptian; Nasser, Gamal ʿAbd al-
June 1967, war of, 8, 39, 56, 60, 78, 128, 129, 156, 183, 185, 188, 196
Justice, Ministry of, 57

Khamis, Mohamed Fareed, 166
Khan, Mushtaq, 166
khedival state, 29–32
Kifaya, 106–108, 110, 209
Kuwait, 157

labor movement and unions, 76, 86; activism, 78; code of 1959, 77; confederation, 86; law, 86, 108; opposition, 87; organizations, 79, 86, 109; protests and, 108; unions, 84, 86, 85; and unrest, 108. *See also* Independent General Union of Real Estate Tax Authority Workers; syndicates

INDEX

landowners, large, 6, 32, 37, 72, 127, 153, 154
land reform, 37, 71, 76, 79, 80, 87, 154, 155
Latin America, 63, 65–75, 76, 83, 84, 87, 91, 95, 103, 104, 109, 110, 112, 133, 134, 219, 220, 230; authoritarianism in, 49; and Egyptian society, 3, 14; and liberalizing policies, 3
Law 12 of 1995 (unions), 86
Law 14 of 2012 (Sinai development), 189
Law 22 of 1964 (associations), 96
Law 32 of 1964 (associations), 76
Law 35 of 1976 (unions), 79
Law 35 of 1981 (unions), 237n13
Law 40 of 1977 (parties), 90
Law 43 of 1974 (investment), 155
Law 43 of 1974 (joint ventures), 78
Law 84 of 2002 (NGOs), 100
Law 100 of 1993, 89
Law 146 of 1988 (banking), 141
Law 203 of 1991 (adjustment program), 161
laws. *See specific laws*
Liberation Rally, 75
liberation theology, 104, 133
Libya, 157

Mahalla al-Kubra, 78, 108
Malaysia, 177
Manpower and Vocational Training, Ministry of, 79
Mansour family, 165
Mao Zedong, 46
Marxism, 118; Marxist-Leninist economies, 155; Marxists, 88; tradition, 151, 173
media, 114, 190, 198; nationalization of, 72; new and old, 1, 25, 236n6; opposition and independent, 40, 134, 229; religious, 135, 143; state-owned, 41, 49, 54, 57–58, 62, 134, 210, 215, 218, 224, 227
Mexico, 67, 76, 84
military, Egyptian, 42; and Britain, 30, 32, 33; courts, 55, 57, 72; as economic actor, 11, 17, 146, 178, 179–203; expansion of, 5, 30, 35; and Nasser, 37, 40, 41, 50, 65; and the overthrow of the monarchy, 7, 36, 50, 65, 77; participation in 1948 war, 36; post-Nasser, 41; role in 2011 uprising, 42, 125, 210–234; and state-formation, 12, 27, 30; as strong institution, 10, 13, 22, 49, 54, 58–61, 62. *See also* Britain; Nasser, Gamal 'Abd al-; Supreme Council of the Armed Forces (SCAF); Urabi, Ahmad
Military Decree no. 34, 217
Military Production, Ministry of, 186, 197, 245–246n9
ministries, Egyptian government. *See specific ministries*
Mixed Courts, 32–35, 54, 140
monarchy, Egyptian, 6, 7, 49, 59, 182; abolishment of, 36, 50
Montreux Convention (1937), 154. *See also* capitulations
Morsi, Muhammad, 220–233; election as a president, 42, 201, 220–224; overthrow of, 42, 61, 125, 207; tenure of, 128, 197, 199
Mubarak, Gamal, 52, 106, 209
Mubarak, Hosni, 45, 52, 60, 128, 139, 142, 166, 176, 177, 183, 186, 188, 189, 194, 195, 196, 198, 204–221; ouster of, 18, 42, 53, 61, 183, 196, 197, 204, 206, 207; political liberalization and, 41, 157; and post-Nasser system, 8
Muhammed Ali: confrontation with Ottomans, 5, 30; descendants of, 5, 6, 31, 32, 34; military of, 5, 30; rise of dynasty, 4, 5, 29, 30; taxation under, 5, 30
Muslim Brotherhood, 7, 8, 10, 36, 41, 42, 55, 69, 72, 74, 97, 107, 114, 115, 118, 119–121, 131, 133, 138, 141, 142, 144, 164, 165, 176, 184, 199, 210, 213, 231, 243n32; rise of, 6, 34, 88–89. *See also* Nasser, Gamal 'Abd al-
mutiny, Central Security Forces (1986), 157, 183

Nasser, Gamal 'Abd al-, 7, 58, 60, 65, 72, 75, 76, 82, 86, 88, 107, 127, 128, 156, 164, 182, 183, 192, 197, 230, 231, 237n15, 237n18, 239n7; assassination attempt, 72; death and after, 8, 40, 51; foreign policy, 38–39; July 1952, 7, 36; military,

17, 40; Naguib-Nasser power struggle, 82. regime, 1, 22, 36, 50–51; relations with Muslim Brotherhood, 8. *See also* authoritarianism: state-regime distinction; Israel; July 1952, events of
Nasserism, 8, 17, 23, 40, 45, 58, 164; post-1967, 39–40, 86, 88, 107, 156, 182; regime, 1, 22, 36, 50–51; relations with Muslim Brotherhood, 8. *See also* authoritarianism: state-regime distinction; Israel; July 1952, events of
Nasr, Salah, 50
National Charter, 72
National Democratic Party, 40, 51–53, 90, 101, 165, 166, 183, 194, 196, 228
National Union, 75
Nazif, Ahmed, 161, 171, 194
neoliberalism, 145, 150, 151, 195, 230
non-aligned movement, 39
nongovernmental organizations (NGOs), 91, 95, 99, 100, 138
non-Islamist actors, 68, 89, 94, 103, 201, 211, 212–234

Ottoman Empire, 121; dissolution of, 117; Egypt as a province of, 4, 5, 29, 30, 31, 32, 59, 235n2; and formation of Egyptian state, 28; rivalry with European powers, 4, 6, 33. *See also* Britain; Muhammad Ali

parliament, 7, 28, 31, 32, 52, 53, 54, 57, 58, 59, 69, 80, 109, 117, 125, 133, 142, 166, 196, 200, 211, 212, 213, 214, 216, 217, 219, 220, 221, 223, 225, 228, 229, 231, 232, 239n5; constitution of 1923, 34; during 2011 uprising, 42; pre-1952, 49; under Nasser, 37, 50, 51; upper house, 40
party politics, 89. *See also* Arab Socialist Union; Liberation Rally; National Union; platforms; Wafd
peace treaty with Israel. *See* Israel
Peronist regime (Argentina), 67
Peru, 67, 76
piety groups, 135
platforms (within Arab Socialist Union), 90

Poland, xi, 216
Polanyi, Karl, 160
polarization, 71, 84, 94,102, 103, 104
populism, 67
Portugal, 49, 239n7
presidency, 10, 12, 27, 50, 53, 54, 60, 61, 62, 125, 129, 139, 183, 197, 211, 218, 222, 224, 225, 227, 228, 231, 232; dominance in Egyptian state, 13, 28, 41, 45, 48–49; relation with judicial structure, 48; uprising of 2011, 42
protests: food riots (1977), 36, 74, 78, 88, 156, 183; labor protests (since 2006), 108; Mahalla al-Kubra (1975), 78. *See also* uprising of 2011

Rachid, Rachid Mohamed, 171
Red Sea, 170, 189
religion, x, 1, 2, 3, 14, 15, 64, 94, 95, 105, 111–144, 206, 214, 231; after 1952, 124; and emergence of the modern Egyptian state pre-1952, 116; and market exchange and investment, 139; religionized consumption, 143. *See also* al-Azhar; Islamic revival; Islamists; piety groups; Salafism/Salafis
Religious Affairs, Ministry of, 48, 112, 126, 136
religious establishment, 51. *See* al-Azhar
regime state relations. *See* authoritarianism
revolt of 1919, 9, 33, 36, 122, 153
riots. *See* protests

Sabri, ʿAli, 51
al-Sadat, Anwar, 9, 128, 131, 228; assassination of, 132; and corrective revolution, 40; early period as president, 40; *infitah*, 147, 155, 156–159, 164; and Islamism, 131; military under, 183, 188, 196; and Nasserism, 40; and political liberalization, 41; post-Nasser system, 8, 51, 60, 82, 90
Salafism/Salafis, 114, 115, 119, 125, 214; concept, 119; early roots of, 118
al-Sanhuri, ʿAbd al-Razzaq, 50
Saudi Arabia, 119, 132, 137, 199, 202

INDEX

Sawiri family, 165
Scandinavia, 167
Schneider, Fredrich, 169
Sims, David, 170
Sinai Peninsula, 39, 170, 187, 189, 202, 227
al-Sisi, 'Abd al-Fattah, 9, 61, 126, 129, 197, 223, 225–234
Social Affairs, Ministry of, 76, 97–99
socialism, 3, 11, 42, 155; after 1950, 1, 14, 23, 28, 75, 164, 165; after Nasser, 8, 16, 88, 100, 126, 137, 156; Arab socialism, 28, 37–38, 72; and social contract, 38. See also authoritarianism; Nasser, Gamal 'Abd al-
social movements, x, xi, xii, 1, 2, 6, 8, 34, 92, 115, 117, 219
Social Solidarity, Ministry of, 229
South America. See Latin America
Soviet Union, 39, 93, 102, 110, 154, 165, 211
Spain, 49, 239n5
state formation, 2, 12, 21–22, 23, 25–43. See also Europe; military, Egyptian; regime type
state-owned enterprises (SOEs), 157, 161, 168, 175, 176
Stevenson, Lois, 174
Sudan, 33
Suez Canal, 157; and Britain, 7, 33, 35; digging of, 5,30; nationalization of, 35, 37; New Suez Canal, 197, 198; and war of 1956, 35, 124, 140, 154, 183; and war of 1967, 39
Supply, Ministry of, 48
Supreme Constitutional Court, 41, 42, 56, 61, 221, 222
Supreme Council of the Armed Forces (SCAF), 61, 212–223
syndicates (professional associations), 72, 81; as bourgeois strongholds, 82; Doctors Syndicate, 89; elections, 83; Engineers Syndicate, 89; Journalists Syndicate, 82; and Muslim Brotherhood, 88. See also Bar Association
Syria, 39, 119, 239n7

Tahrir Square, 53, 209, 226
Taiwan, 177
Tilly, Charles, 26, 29, 30
Trade Union Law 62 of 1964, 78
trade unions, 77, 79, 82, 84 85, 106
Tripartite Aggression. See Suez Canal
Trump, Donald J., 47
Tunisia, 209, 216, 239n7, 242–243n29
Turkey, 4, 172, 173, 177, 180, 181, 195, 199, 201, military of, 17. See also deep state

Ultras, 210
unified labor law of 2003, 86, 108
United Arab Emirates, 199, 202
United States of America, 39, 45, 47, 60, 107, 112, 165, 180, 186
Uprising of 2011, x, 1, 2, 8, 13, 15, 17, 18, 42–43, 48, 53, 54, 57–62, 69, 93, 95, 110, 125, 128–129, 174, 177, 180–181, 184, 196–203, 204–234
'Urabi, Ahmad, 31, 59

Velvet Revolution, 211
Vietnam, 162, 199

Wafd (political party), 6, 77, 88, 118, 121, 123, 237n10, 239n5, 243n32; abolition of, 50; decline of, 34; during monarchy, 34, 35, 49; and land reform, 37; meaning of name, 33; and 1923 constitution, 34; reemergence of, 40, 81. See also Britain
Waterbury, John, 155
Weber, Max, 151
wide state, 13
World Bank, 157, 158, 164, 173, 186, 187, 242n20, 242n28, 242–243n29
World War I, 6, 27, 29, 33, 47, 54, 117, 122, 153, 230; and martial law, 54; and riots, 36
World War II, 6, 28, 35, 38, 122, 172, 180, 230

Young Egypt, 6